Giving the Game Away

Sport, Politics and Culture
A series of books from Leicester University Press

Series editors: Stephen Wagg
Department of Sociology, University of Leicester
John Williams
Sir Norman Chester Centre for Football Research,
University of Leicester

Other titles:

Rogan Taylor	*Football and its fans*
John Bale	*Landscape of modern sport*
Neil Blain, Raymond Boyle & Hugh O'Donnell	*Sport and national identity in the European media*
Grant Jarvie & Graham Walker	*Scottish sport in the making of a nation*
John Sugden & Alan Bairner	*Sport, sectarianism and society in a divided Ireland*

Giving the Game Away

Football, Politics and Culture on Five Continents

EDITED BY STEPHEN WAGG

LEICESTER UNIVERSITY PRESS
LONDON AND NEW YORK

DISTRIBUTED IN THE UNITED STATES BY ST. MARTIN'S PRESS

LEICESTER UNIVERSITY PRESS
An imprint of Cassell Publishers Limited
Wellington House, 125 Strand, London WC2R 0BB

First published in 1995

Distributed exclusively in the USA and Canada by St. Martin's Press, Inc., Room 400, 175 Fifth Avenue, New York, NY10010, USA

British Library Cataloguing in Publication Data
A CIP catalogue record for this book is available from the British Library

ISBN 0 7185 1677 X (hb)
    0 7185 1887 X (pb)

Library of Congress Cataloging-in-Publication Data

Giving the game away : football, politics, and culture on five
  continents / edited by Stephen Wagg.
     p.   cm. – (Sport, politics, and culture)
  Includes bibliographical references and index.
  ISBN 0–7185–1677–X (hb). – ISBN 0–7185–1887–X (pb)
  1. Soccer – Political aspects – Cross-cultural studies. 2. Soccer – Social aspects
– Cross cultural studies. I. Wagg, Stephen. II. Series.
  G943.9.S64G58 1995
  796.334–dc20
                                             95-3880
                                               CIP

Typeset by Mayhew Typesetting, Rhayader, Powys
Printed and bound in Great Britain by Biddles Ltd of Guildford and King's Lynn

'The imagined community of millions seems
more real as a team of eleven named people'

Eric Hobsbawm

CONTENTS

NOTES ON CONTRIBUTORS

Maurice Biriotti Del Burgo teaches in the Department of Hispanic Studies at Birmingham University, England. He is co-editor, with Nicola Miller, of *What is an Author?* (Manchester University Press 1993).

Vic Duke lectures in the Sociology Department at Salford University, England. He is co-author of *A Measure of Thatcherism* (HarperCollins 1991) and has written a number of articles on football. An avid football spectator, he has watched games at all the English and Scottish league grounds.

Pierre Lanfranchi is a French academic based at the European University Institute in Florence, but is currently a Visiting Professor at De Montfort University in Leicester, England. He has written widely on sport.

Bill Murray is a historian teaching at La Trobe University in Australia. *The Old Firm*, his study of the historic rivalry between Glasgow Rangers and Glasgow Celtic, was published in 1984 by John Donald and he has just completed his own history of world football, published by Scolar Press in 1994.

Ossie Stuart has a doctorate from the School of Oriental and African Studies, University of London and worked subsequently at St. Antony's College, Oxford. He is now a Research Fellow in the Social Policy Research Unit at York University, England.

Stephen Wagg is Honorary Fellow in the Department of Sociology at Leicester University, England and an Associate Member of the Sir Norman Chester Centre for Football Research there. He is the author of *The Football World* (Harvester Press 1984) and, with John Williams, editor of *British Football and Social Change* (Leicester University Press 1991). He also writes on childhood and comedy, and edited *Come On Down?* (Routledge 1992) with Dominic Strinati.

David Waldstein is a journalist based in New York. He works on the *New York Post*, for whom he reports on association football. Loyally, and from a considerable distance, he supports Tottenham Hotspur.

INTRODUCTION AND ACKNOWLEDGEMENTS

Its historian wrote of *Foul*, the British satirical football magazine of the 1970s, that it 'always had its roots in a mountain of disgust' (Stewart 1975, 7). This book has similar origins. It grew out of my research on the British popular press and its coverage since the Second World War of the England football team (Wagg 1986, 1991). This research proved to be a grim and demoralizing task. The tenor of popular press journalism in this area has increasingly in the last 20 years approached a kind of patriotic derangement. The writing, as I have argued before, is substantially divorced from events. In it, there is no history and no context; there is, ultimately, only England and the culpability of her manager at any given moment. Names and faces change, but the essential story does not: if England, who devised and exported the game, are beaten, then the man in charge of the England team is not doing his job properly and he must be replaced. Other countries, in this bizarre and ultimately racist conception of the international football world, play only walk-on parts.

This book aims, in its own small way, to present another view, which is that the globe is covered with viable football nations and cultures. The hope of the contributors is that at least some sense of these cultures is conveyed in the pages that follow. Some countries are not mentioned and others are referred to maybe only in passing, but there is nevertheless a political, historical and sociological account of football on every continent. It may, therefore, provide starting points for other writers and researchers and doubtless, in the years to come, more detailed and thoroughgoing accounts of particular football cultures will be written.

Through this book I ran up a huge number of emotional and intellectual debts – debts made greater by the personal difficulty and deep sadness that I experienced during its preparation. For the help, kindness and friendship that sustained me and/or the book during that period I'd like to thank Bill Hilbourne; Deryk Clarke; Tom Sullivan; Jenny Hankey; Simon Hankey; Shirley Wagg; Sue Minton; Mary Watts; David Clayton; Rob Colls; Tony and Suzanne Russell; Julia O'Connell-Davidson; Kathleen Mannering; Keith Faulks; Stephen Hopkins; John Williams, Rogan Taylor and Janet Tiernan at the Sir Norman Chester Centre; Richard Holt; Jenny Hargreaves; Pierre Lanfranchi; my daughter, Cassie; my brother, Jeremy; and Alec McAulay. Alec believed in the book, supported it and helped significantly to shape it.

The quote from Eric Hobsbawm at the beginning of the book is taken from his book *Nations and Nationalism Since 1780: Programme, Myth, Reality* (Cambridge University Press, 1990, page 143). The book is based on a series of lectures delivered by Hobsbawm in Belfast in 1985 and I'm grateful to the *Guardian* writer Philip McCann for bringing it to my attention.

The book is dedicated to the memory of my father, who died suddenly while it was in preparation. My father played inside left in the talented Loughborough Grammar School team of 1930, the year of the first World Cup in Uruguay; he took me, as an enthralled nine year old, to my first match in 1958; he and I always talked football thereafter.

REFERENCES

Stewart, Alan (1975) 'The *Foul* years 1972–5', *Foul*, no. 30, June

Wagg, Stephen (1986) 'Naming the guilty men', in Alan Tomlinson and Garry Whannel (eds) *Off The Ball*, London, Pluto Press

Wagg, Stephen (1991) 'Playing the past', in John Williams and Stephen Wagg (eds) *British Football and Social Change*, Leicester, Leicester University Press

Stephen Wagg
Leicester
February 1994

1

THE MISSIONARY POSITION: FOOTBALL IN THE SOCIETIES OF BRITAIN AND IRELAND

Stephen Wagg

Britain was the world's first industrial nation and it was on the British mainland that the game of association football, in its modern form, was first developed. Also, as other sections of this book make clear, it was Britons, specifically English and Scots, who took the game to many of the countries and regions in which it is now played. This fact still strongly reverberates in English football culture. Indeed it now approaches the status of national myth: as I have chronicled elsewhere (Wagg 1991), the British popular media have in recent years developed a kind of national melodrama wherein the England team has the role of the missionary, on whom a host of former tutees and subject peoples has now turned. In this chapter I chart the social progress of association football in England, Scotland, Wales and Ireland and, in the course of this account, I examine some of the myths which the game in these various societies has engendered.

KICKING OFF: THE EMERGENCE OF ASSOCIATION FOOTBALL

Some of the deepest social roots of the game widely known today simply as 'football' lie in the folk games played during the Middle Ages on what are now the British Isles and Ireland. Little is known for certain of these medieval folk games. Subsequent records, however, show that a popular pastime called 'football' was prohibited, usually by the monarch, on over 30 occasions between the fourteenth and the seventeenth centuries; the unruliness of this essentially unscripted activity was perceived (by all accounts, quite correctly) to threaten life, property and public order (Dunning and Sheard 1979, 21–7).

Folk forms of football declined among the working classes after 1800 but the game survived in the English public schools, where, during the early decades of the nineteenth century, relatively well-to-do young men practised a version of football particular to their own seat of learning. Since the young aristocrats and gentry, who had recently grown in number in the public schools, had no interest in formal education and regarded their teachers as socially inferior, the pupil cultures of these schools was relatively autonomous and aggressively inegalitarian. Football was usually, in effect, a form of organized bullying wherein the stronger and older boys tyrannized the younger, weaker ones: at the highly prestigious Shrewsbury school, for instance, football was called 'douling' – a name which derives from the Greek word for 'slave' (Dunning and Sheard 1979, 48–55).

The first vestiges of the modern football code – written rules and equal numbers of players per team, for example – began to develop in the 1840s, as the culture of Britain's public schools became permeated by the recognizably more *bourgeois* values of competition, fair play and universalism. Gradual standardization of the hitherto large assortment of school-specific football games led to the emergence of two codes: the handling and the non-handling. Several of the socially most exclusive schools in England – including Eton, Harrow, Winchester, Charterhouse and Shrewsbury – played non-handling football. Former pupils of theirs, who went on to Cambridge University, became associated with a dribbling game and it was at Cambridge that the first attempts were made, in the 1840s and 50s (Dunning and Sheard 1979, 104), to produce a unified set of rules for football. These 'Cambridge rules' formed the basis for the founding in 1863 of the Football Association, the presiding organization from which 'association football' takes its name: the popular term 'soccer' is a corruption of 'association'. Other ex-public schoolboys, wedded to a more aggressive and, as they saw it, more manly code permitting the handling of both ball and opponents, formed the Rugby Football Union in 1871.

Adherents of these two codes took them into the wider society. In the case of association football the game was evangelized principally by employers and priests: many of the biggest and best known English clubs began life in the last century either as works teams or as church sides (Mason 1979, ch.2). Arsenal, for instance, took their name from the munitions factory in the London district of Woolwich, where their first players were employed; Sheffield United were founded at a cutlery firm – hence their nickname 'The Blades'; West Ham United originally represented the Thames Ironworks, and so on. Likewise, Aston Villa, Bolton Wanderers, Everton and Southampton (still known as 'The Saints') all began as church teams.

Both association and rugby football attained widespread popularity and in the latter third of the last century either code was being played all over the British Isles. There were, however, cultural differences within the two emergent football worlds which were linked to social class and region. In the Midlands and the North of England, teams, especially for association football, were overwhelmingly working class and the clubs that put out these teams were in the main administered by local businessmen – mill owners, drapers and the like. By the 1870s both association and rugby football clubs in this region were known to be paying their players, club proprietors having concluded that the amateur ideals, devoutly upheld by the higher status players and administrators in the South, were not viable elsewhere. The first professional footballers were mostly Scots who came to play for clubs in the prosperous Lancashire cotton belt (Mason 1979, 85). One such club, Preston North End, was disqualified from the FA Cup competition in 1884 on the ground that its players were professional. However, 36 of the leading clubs in the North threatened to secede from the FA; the latter relented and professionalism was legitimated the following year (Mason 1979, 95). This led, in the world of association football, to the founding of the Football League in 1888; within rugby football there was a split wherein the Northern, gate-taking clubs departed from the (resolutely amateur) Rugby Football Union to set up the Northern RFU in 1895.

As in other English sports, these divisions in class and status have inscribed much of the social history of association football in Britain. The Football League, based in Lancashire, was dominated for much of its first hundred years by provincial, small business values. Club directors tended to be Liberals (the free trade party) and Nonconformist (low church) in their religion (Fishwick 1989, 27–8). They stood essentially for temperance and local patriotism, placing club before country: 'I have a feeling', wrote Football League secretary Alan Hardaker in 1977 '. . . that if there was a referendum on the "club v. country" issue, League football would get the popular vote' (Hardaker 1977, 161). The Football Association, with its headquarters in London, strove to maintain the values of an amateur, ex-public school elite. However, no amateur team won the FA Cup after 1882 (when Old Etonians won it) and amateur football in England became increasingly its own social world. For instance, a cup competition specifically for amateurs – the FA Amateur Cup – began in 1893, and in 1907 the Amateur Football Association tried to affiliate separately to FIFA – a move successfully opposed by the FA. In keeping with this emergent pattern of separate development, professionalism also became recognized in the South in 1894, when working-class teams in the southern region formed the Southern League, to which now-eminent clubs such as Tottenham Hotspur belonged before its absorption into the Football League. (Tottenham were the only southern team to win the FA Cup before 1921: they won it in 1901, while still a Southern League side.)

The first **England** team took the field in 1872, against Scotland. This was the first international football match. All the players in that match were amateurs and when, in 1886, James Forest of Blackburn Rovers became the first professional to be selected for England – again against Scotland – the Scots objected and Forrest was obliged to wear a different shirt. England fielded her first professional captain in 1890, although amateurs continued to get into the England side quite easily until the turn of the century (Mason 1979, 100).

The old boys teams of the mid- to late nineteenth century had taken pride in their carelessness of results; indeed, many of them cared little for club affiliation either and, as in other countries such as Germany, scratch sides were popular until the turn of the century. In the 1870s, these amateur teams pioneered and practised the 'dribbling' style of play, wherein a player usually ran with the ball until he lost it. The ball should always move forwards; anything else was deemed ungentlemanly (Wagg 1984, 10). Similarly, the penalty kick, introduced in the season 1902–3 (Mason 1979, 285), was rejected by many amateur teams on the ground that a deliberate foul – for which the kick was awarded – could never be committed by gentlemen.

By contrast, the professional teams, which predominated in the North, were associated – not always by their detractors – with defensiveness, sharp practice and an unhealthy desire to win. The successful clubs in the early decades were all drawn from cities and large towns in the North and Midlands, where smokestack industries had provided much prosperity in the Victorian era. Both professional and amateur clubs continued to grow in number during the first half of the twentieth century. Pro' clubs increased from around 150 in 1914 to over 450 in 1950; amateurs at a similar rate – roughly 350 between the wars to over 400 in 1950 (Fishwick 1989, 26).

The premier club side of the 1880s was Preston North End, based in a Northern cotton town, who developed the 2–3–5 formation, which was also adopted in Scotland. Other leading sides before the First World War were Blackburn, another Lancashire mill town, Newcastle United and Sunderland, both located in the then thriving shipbuilding and mining area of the North East, and Aston Villa, situated in a district of Britain's engineering heartland, Birmingham. During this period then, as Tony Mason observes, big city clubs came to predominate (Mason 1979, 294); however, the League's maximum wage restriction, introduced for the season 1901–2, promoted a closer competition in League football than the open play of market forces would have permitted. Thus, Huddersfield Town, a team from a comparatively small Northern town, was the premier English club for a period in the 1920s; but Huddersfield's brief eminence was followed by the ascent of Arsenal – the first major club to become established in the South of the country and the first of the five big city clubs that now dominate English football (the others being Manchester United, Liverpool, Everton and Tottenham).

The achievements of Huddersfield Town and Arsenal brought to public prominence the man who managed each team successively: Herbert Chapman. Chapman enjoyed more autonomy in running his sides than was the case at most other clubs and he is widely regarded in English football culture as the first great football manager (Studd 1981).

Games in the First Division of the English Football League were increasingly popular in the first half of the twentieth century and crowds grew steadily in numbers. From an average of 25,000 in the late 1920s, crowds rose to 30,000 in 1939 and to 40,000 in 1949–50 – the 'Austerity Years' of post-war reconstruction (Fishwick 1989, 49).

FOOTBALL AND THE SUBMERGED BRITISH NATIONS: SCOTLAND, WALES AND IRELAND

For its first 30 years, 1872–1902, international football was exclusive to Britain; all the international football matches during that initial period were between constituent British nations. These nations either are or, as in the case of the Irish Republic, were at some stage assimilated into the English state;

politically, therefore, they are, borrowing Bert Moorhouse's apt phrase, 'submerged nations' (Moorhouse 1991, 201). Their football culture, particularly in the international context, reflects this – although, historically, in Wales rugby has hitherto been the dominant code.

The oldest League club in **Scotland** is Queens Park, formed in 1867. They provided all the Scotland players for the country's first international match, in 1872, and their Glasgow ground Hampden Park has staged most of Scotland's subsequent home internationals. The Scottish FA was founded in 1873 and, significantly, is based not in the capital city of Edinburgh, home of Scotland's Anglophile elite and the headquarters of the Scottish Rugby Football Union, but in the Western port of Glasgow. Glasgow, a large conurbation on the River Clyde has, historically, had a larger industrial working class and a high density of population (Patrick 1973). Many leading Scottish clubs were set up in the 1870s and early 80s; indeed, 19 clubs that were members of the Scottish FA when it celebrated its first 10 years in 1883, were still active in the Scottish League at the SFA Centenary (Rafferty 1973, 7–8); most of them remain so. Several of these clubs were situated in the Clydeside area and others in Edinburgh and Aberdeen; many of them, indeed, were to be found in Scotland's central belt (including Edinburgh and the Clydeside conurbation) where 70 per cent of Scotland's population live. But Scotland, like the Nordic countries, is a nation made up principally of small towns and much of the history, both of the SFA and the Scottish League (formed in 1890), has been of rivalry between city and countryside (Crampsey 1990, 86–92). Three clubs, for example, were to be found in the Vale of Leven, a rural area west of Glasgow. Rugby football is played mostly in the Borders area and the East of Scotland, where English culture and influence are strongest. Many Scottish rugby internationals have had English surnames; the names of those who played association football for Scotland, however, have often born the prefix Mac-, indicating descent from Scottish Highlanders. (Lou Macari, who played for Scotland in the 1970s, is one of the only members of the sizeable Scottish-Italian community to play football for Scotland; his forename is an abbreviation of 'Luigi'.)

The history of football in Scotland is dominated by the two Glasgow clubs: Rangers and Celtic. Glasgow Rangers were founded in 1872 and Glasgow Celtic in 1887. Like the Edinburgh club Hibernian, Celtic was originally exclusively for those of the Catholic religion. It was set up by Catholic priests as part of a campaign both to raise poor relief for recent Irish migrants (Murray 1984, 18) and to keep them of the faith. For much of the last hundred years, Glasgow has been associated with social conflict between Protestants and Catholics and, in that context, Rangers – its club management and supporters – became an emblem of the Protestant faction, which also dominated Glasgow's civic hierarchy.

Professionalism was legalized in Scotland in 1893. The amateur side Queens Park last won the Scottish Cup in that year; since the 1890s club football in Scotland has been dominated by the rivalry between Rangers and Celtic. This domination has few parallels anywhere in the world: Celtic have taken 35 League titles in their history and Rangers 42. Between 1905 and 1931 no other side won this title; Celtic took six consecutive League titles in the period 1905 to 1910 and a further nine consecutively from 1966 to 1974. They also have over 50 Scottish FA Cup victories between them.

The pioneering Scottish footballers of the 1880s and 90s played a passing game, which, it is widely accepted, was their invention. However, many Scottish players, throughout the history of the game in Scotland, have played in other countries – principally in England. The migration to England is as old as professional football itself in that country: a number of Scottish players signed for Lancashire clubs in the 1870s, including the famous Fergie Suter at Darwen (Mason 1979, 85–6). Those Scots who played in England were generally known as 'Anglos' and, for much of this century, their chances of playing for their country were lessened by their expatriate status: for example, one of the leading Scottish players of the 1920s, Alex James, who played in England for Preston and Arsenal, only received eight caps – a low figure even allowing for the paucity of international games in those days. Scotland was regarded as the premier football nation in the late nineteenth century. They first beat England as early as 1877 and Scottish clubs often toured abroad, but Scotland did not play her first non-British international match until 1929, beating Norway 7–3 in Oslo.

In the lifetime of the two football codes, rugby is the one to have had the greatest influence on the culture of **Wales**. In contrast to England, Scotland and Ireland, association football never gained the widespread support of the industrial working class in Wales. Rugby football was especially popular in the communities of the South Wales coalfields and, despite a perceptible decline in the late 1980s and early 90s, it is regarded by the Welsh as their national sport. Rugby is especially predominant in South Wales. There are several factors which account for this: folk football, in this case *cnappen*, which in many ways resembled modern rugby, probably survived longer in the remote Welsh valleys than elsewhere; Llandovery College, a public school set up in the 1860s for the sons of Welsh gentry, played rugby; subsequently, a number of ex-public schoolboys of the handling persuasion formed clubs in the Southern towns of Neath and Llanelli. Also, South Wales borders the South West of England where rugby became the main code. It was from this area, along with Ireland, that most of the migrant labour that supplied the Welsh coal-pits was drawn, rather than from Lancashire or west-central Scotland where association football was the favoured game (Holt 1989, 247; Smith and Williams 1980, 30–1). North Wales, with its proximity to British association football's original stronghold, the North West of England, took more readily to the non-handling game. The first Welsh association football clubs were formed in North Wales in the early 1870s, at Ruabon and nearby Wrexham, and Wales played their international matches there until 1894. (Thereafter they played usually in Swansea or Cardiff, the two largest towns in the South.) Similarly, the Welsh FA Cup was won by a Northern club – e.g. Druids, Bangor, Wrexham, Chirk – every year from its inception in 1878 to 1912.

The period after the First World War saw the growth of clubs in the more industrialized South. The principal ones – Cardiff City, Swansea Town and Newport County – all joined the English League in the 1920s: Wales has never been able to support a fully fledged association football league of its own. Cardiff took the FA Cup out of England for the only time in its history when they beat Arsenal at Wembley in 1927.

Wales first beat England in 1881 (Jeffery 1965). Their most noted player in the time before the Second World War was Billy Meredith. Meredith is one of the legends of the early British football world, who played a lot of his football for Manchester United and was an activist in the British players' union. He received his first cap for Wales in 1893 and his last in 1920, at the age of 46. All Meredith's international matches were played against England, Scotland or Ireland. Wales' first non-British international was away to France in Paris in 1933, which they drew 1–1, and their only other game abroad in the pre-Second World War period was again in Paris where this time France beat them 2–1 (Oliver 1992).

In **Ireland**, as on the British mainland, pre-industrial ball games had been popular for centuries. The historians of Irish sport, John Sugden and Alan Bairner, write: 'The oldest of these, the game of Cad, which was popular among all Celtic people, is thought to have originated at least 1,000 years ago. It involved carrying and kicking a ball across open country and resembled closely the form of football which was banned in England in 1365' (Sugden and Bairner 1993, 71). Cad became extinct in Ireland in the 1880s – the same decade in which association football began to be played there. The game of football has always been most popular in the North East of Ireland, especially in the six counties that were absorbed into the United Kingdom in 1921. The game prospered here apparently because of its strong Protestant settler culture, deriving from English and Scottish migration, which was receptive to non-Irish influences. Moreover, this region was the most industrialized part of the island, with continuing links to Scotland where the game thrived (Sugden and Bairner 1993, 72). Elsewhere in Ireland, particularly in the South, there was hostility to any game which, like cricket or 'soccer', could be seen as a cultural importation by Britain, the colonial power. The Gaelic Athletic Association (founded in 1884) promoted other sports, such as hurling, which were deemed more ethnically Irish (Sugden and Bairner 1993, 27–46). Nevertheless, there was significant competition between the two football codes and a number of Irish football clubs – Ulster FC, for instance, which was founded in 1878 – began as rugby teams and started 'soccer' sections later. The first Irish club devoted entirely to association football was Cliftonville, which was formed in 1879 (Oliver 1992).

The Irish FA was established in 1880 and the Irish Cup competition began the following year. Early participants included teams from British army regiments garrisoned in Ireland. Winners of the cup came exclusively from the North of Ireland until the early 1900s when two Dublin sides, Shelbourne in 1906 and Bohemians in 1908, took the trophy south. Likewise, the Irish League, which began in 1890, was dominated throughout its early history by teams from the North. Indeed, the League title did not even go out of the city of Belfast until 1952 when Glenavon, situated in Lurgan, County Armagh, won it (Sugden and Bairner 1993, 73). But by then the League was confined to Northern clubs in any event, clubs from the South of Ireland having seceded during the political disputes that led to the founding of the Irish Free State.

Following this partition in 1921, the southern Irish football community set up its own administrative body, the Football Association of Ireland, and its own league. Club football in the South has never been strong. Up to the political separation only Shamrock Rovers and the two Dublin clubs, Shelbourne and Bohemians, had participated regularly in the national football competitions and a number of Northern clubs who had defected to the South during the civil war were obliged, after partition, to return to Irish FA jurisdiction. There have been numerous closures, and reformations, of clubs in the South: for example, in Cork, the second largest city in the Irish Republic, there have been five different clubs, called by 14 separate names (Oliver 1992). Most of the best Irish players, whether from the North or the South, play outside the island – mostly in England and Scotland: Glasgow Celtic, Manchester United and Arsenal are all clubs which, historically, have had both Irish players and an expatriate Irish following.

Ireland played their first international match in 1882, when they were heavily defeated (13–0) by England. They didn't win a game until 1887 when they beat Wales; their first victory over Scotland came in Glasgow in 1903 and they didn't beat England until the latter came to Belfast in 1913. The following year they won the Home International Championship (involving the four British nations) outright, for the only time in their history. They didn't play a non-British international until 1951, when they took on France, again in Belfast.

The Republic, perhaps out of a sharper sense of national identity, were more active on the international stage, entering the Paris Olympics of 1924 and participating in every World Cup since 1934.

THE BRITISH NATIONS SINCE 1945: FOOTBALL, NATIONAL IDENTITIES AND MARKETS

In this section, I want to examine in tandem the processes of national myth making and commercial development that have marked the post-war progress of football in the British Isles. I will begin with what must be the central myth in this context: the myth of an England, former Football Missionary to the World, grown complacent and now receiving her come-uppance from even the most modest among her former pupils.

England expects: the FA and the people's game

During its early and formative decades, the Football Association remained wedded to the conviction that the game should, where possible, be 'uncontaminated by politics, planning or commercialism' (Wagg 1984, 24). In this, of course, they were not alone, as other chapters in this book make clear, but it's fair to say that the FA sought to maintain these ideals for some time after most other countries had found them unviable.

When football's international governing body, FIFA, was first established in 1904, the FA were invited to join. They declined. FA Secretary Sir

Frederick Wall wrote: 'The Council of the Football Association cannot see the advantages of such a Federation, but on all such matters upon which joint action was desirable they would be prepared to confer' (quoted in Tomlinson 1986, 85).

The FA nevertheless agreed to affiliate to FIFA the following year. They had apparently been assured by the FIFA nations that their expertise in these matters was indispensable and they were, in any case, mindful of the growing number of English football teams touring abroad for whom they were responsible (Rous 1978, 91). In 1908 the England team themselves undertook their first tour. The opening match of this tour was the first non-British international match to be played by England; it took place in Vienna against Austria and England won it 6–1. But, despite the growing involvement of the England side in international competition, relations between the administrative bodies continued to be fractious. In 1919, in the wake of the First World War, the FA insisted that Germany, Austria and Hungary be excluded from international football. They were backed in this by France, Belgium and Luxembourg who, when the Scandinavian nations demurred, joined the FA in seceding from FIFA and setting up the short-lived Federation of National Football Associations. This disbanded after four years and the FA re-affiliated to FIFA, but they withdrew once again in 1928, this time on the issue of how an amateur was to be defined. 'Broken time' payments, accepted on the continent of Europe and approved by the organizers of the Olympic Games, were viewed by the FA as professionalism by other means. 'Players are either amateur or professional', they asserted sternly, and continued: 'Any player registered with this Association as a professional or receiving remuneration or consideration of any sort above his necessary hotel and travelling expenses actually paid, shall be a professional. Training expenses of amateurs other than the wages paid to a trainer or coach must be paid by the players themselves' (quoted in Tomlinson 1986, 92).

This second secession by the FA lasted until 1947 and it helped to lay the foundation for a powerful post-war myth of England and her football team. The core of this myth is that England, arguably the world's first football nation, began the second half of the twentieth century as the game's unofficial world champions, unbeaten, at least by 'foreign' opposition, on her own soil. However, several factors undermine this view. First, England were beaten on their own ground as early as 1877, when Scotland defeated them 3–1 at London's Kennington Oval. They had also been beaten at home, this time at Goodison Park in Liverpool, by the Republic of Ireland in September 1949. Second, in between times, they had lost games in a number of European countries: in Spain in 1929; in Hungary and Czechoslovakia in 1934; in Belgium in 1936; in Switzerland in 1938; and in Yugoslavia in 1939. Their performance, moreover, in their first World Cup Finals, in Brazil in 1950, was not that of world champions, official or otherwise: they lost to Spain and, most notably, to the United States in the opening round. Third, on whatever pretext, England had held the international football world at a distance during a time – the 1920s and 30s – when it was expanding fast and opening up new possibilities of competition outside Europe. The FA did not enter the World Cup tournaments of 1930 (the first, held in Uruguay), 1934 or 1938, but reliable authorities such as Vittorio Pozzo, manager of Italy, judged that England were unlikely to have reached the Quarter Finals either in '34 or '38 (Oliver 1992). Nonetheless, when Hungary visited Wembley in 1953 and inflicted a heavy defeat (6–3) on their hosts, following up with an even heavier one (7–1) in Budapest six months later, the British popular press employed the vocabulary of national outrage. Which incompetents and bunglers, they asked, could have allowed this humiliation to come about? (Wagg 1984, 85–9). From that point onward, with a brief relenting in the late 1960s when England had won the World Cup, the writing of the English popular press on the England football team has been inscribed with the same sense of patriotic indignation (see Wagg 1986 and 1991).

Although this perspective had, and still has, its adherents in the English football world, others had seen the decline in the competitiveness of English football growing over a period of decades. Principal among these more far-sighted critics was Stanley Rous, who succeeded Wall as Secretary of the FA in 1934. Rous took over an organization that he later described as a 'quiet backwater' whose demeanour was 'autocratic and unhelpful' (Rous 1978, 54, 57). This organization, he judged, faced two, interrelated problems. One was the growing perception among football people, especially in European countries, that English players lacked strategy and technique; the other was that association football, having originated in England's most prestigious schools, had been abandoned by most of them and was now accorded a very low social status. By the late 1930s most private and selective schools for boys in England played rugby as their winter sport and association football was being seen widely as a game for 'men in cloth caps'.

To address these two problems Rous instituted coaching courses in 1935; the trained coaches to emerge from these courses would move, he hoped, into Football League clubs, enhancing the skills of professionals, and into the schools, winning back adherents from the handling code. A year later, in a further attempt to increase football's respectability, he set up the FA Disciplinary Committee, which began meting out severe punishments for violent conduct among the working-class professionals of the Football League (Fishwick 1989, 84–5).

This latter issue pointed up the difficulties faced by Rous in pursuing this new, essentially *technocratic* approach: the game by the 1940s and 50s had long been bound up with myths of Northern male working-class culture (Fishwick 1989; Williams and Taylor 1995). English football folklore, by this time, was peopled by 'hard men' defenders, like Wolverhampton's Stanley Cullis, who stood no nonsense – and 'skilled artisans' – midfield players (then known as inside forwards and wing halves) such as Raich Carter and Joe Mercer and wingers like Stanley Matthews and Tom Finney, known for their passing and dribbling. An important element in the mythology surrounding such players was that their gifts were untutored: they learned to play, according to popular belief, on some cobbled Northern street, often with a makeshift ball. Recently, the ex-England player Jack Charlton (a famed hard man) recalled that he and his brother Bobby (a naturally skilled forward), both members of the England side that won the World Cup in 1966, learned to play football with a rolled-up pair of socks that their father, a miner, used for work (Leith 1993). Rous' campaign to modernize English football and to raise its social standing ran counter to such myths. He knew, therefore, that Walter Winterbottom, an ex-amateur player who was appointed FA Director of Coaching and the England team's first manager in 1946, would face much opposition – although the evidence is that this opposition came mostly from the popular press (Wagg 1984, ch.7).

Coaching was established as a legitimate and desirable activity in English League clubs by the late 1950s. Winterbottom remained manager of the England team until 1963. He was described by Rous, his patron, as having 'the analytical mind of a detached scientific observer' who could disconcert football people with his 'businesslike' approach to the game. Ironically, though, it was his successor, Alf Ramsey, an ex-professional and England international, who made the most drastic departures from traditional English football culture, abandoning wingers and dropping popular players like Jimmy Greaves for their low 'work rate'.

Ramsey's team nevertheless won the World Cup in 1966 and all subsequent England managers have laboured in the shadow of that achievement. The last two – Bobby Robson (1982–90) and Graham Taylor (1990–3) – have, via the English popular press, achieved national vilification. One paper, the *Sun* (owned by Rupert Murdoch's News International), called Robson a 'Plonker' (a colloquialism for 'penis') in 1988; the same paper called Taylor a 'Turnip' following England's defeat by Sweden (i.e. 'The Swedes') in the European Nations Championship of 1992.

Rous made other important moves. One was admitting broadcasters to British football in the late 1930s. 'My own feeling', he wrote later, 'was that if football was to remain a sport of the people we should accept all the current means of keeping the sport in the public eye' (Rous 1978, 88). He also attempted in late 1940s to establish a national pools organization that would raise funds for British sport. Feeling against such an idea ran high, however, both at the FA and the Football League, and it was thrown out. There was strong opposition to commercialism, especially when it appeared to involve gambling, one of the great evils in the Nonconformist morality of the British lower middle classes. In 1936 a farcical situation had arisen when the Football League, in an effort to obstruct the prosperous pools companies (set up in the previous decade), had tried secretly to change their fixture list for one Saturday in February (see Inglis, ch.14; Murray 1994, ch.6). The League and the pools companies finally came to an arrangement in 1959 whereby the companies paid a fee for the copyright of the Football League's fixture list, the League having at last abandoned the view that such a fee would be tainted money.

Thus, Rous sought to decontaminate planning and commercialism in relation to British football; but on the matter of 'politics' he stood firm. Here he took the traditional liberal view that 'politics' should be kept out of sport. Of course, this view translates, according to some critics, as 'keep the politics of sport the way they are' (Whannel 1983, 19). Rous' personal version of it had been cemented in the late 1930s. To much FA indignation, the English

Trades Union Congress had organized a picket of the England Germany match at Tottenham Hotspur's White Hart Lane in 1935; Sir Charles Clegg of the FA told the TUC that Germany's visit had been 'none of their business'. No such rebuff, however, was issued to Sir Neville Henderson, British ambassador to Germany, when in 1938 he advised the FA that, for the return match in Berlin, it would be 'normal courtesy' for the England players to give the Nazi salute before the game. Rous, however, consulted the England players, leaving the decision to them but suggesting that refusal might bring a hostile atmosphere; not surprisingly, perhaps, the players did as they were advised (Rous 1978, 63–4; Beck 1982).

Rous carried his uneasiness about the overtly political use of sport into his work with FIFA. The FA had become a dominant presence in FIFA after rejoining in the late 1940s: the Englishman Arthur Drewry became its President in 1956 and Rous took the presidency on Drewry's death in 1961. Both Drewry and Rous believed that, politics and commerce notwithstanding, football remained 'a game' (Rous 1978, 131) and they promoted it as such around the world. Rous, in particular, felt it essential 'that FIFA decentralise rather than become a vast bureaucracy based on Europe and out of touch – or thought to be out of touch – and unsympathetic to the needs of other continents' (Rous 1978, 130). Regional confederations followed. These confederations, ironically, became the political base from which England was relieved of her central role in international football. Rous lost the FIFA presidency in 1974 to the Brazilian entrepreneur Joao Havelange. Havelange had lobbied extensively in the Third World and accused Rous of favouring the Anglo-Saxon countries (Tomlinson 1986, 95; Rous 1978, 41). His victory was procured with votes from Africa and Asia, continents which Rous had helped to enfranchise and which he now accused of bringing politics into football (Rous 1978, 158–61). However, Rous had also been undone, as he himself acknowledged, by his insistence in 1973 that the World Cup qualifying match between USSR and Chile be played in Santiago. During the right-wing military coup of that year Santiago's National Stadium had reputedly been used for the torture of political prisoners and the USSR had pressed for a neutral venue for the game. Rous' refusal had meant Soviet withdrawal and had delivered the support of the USSR and her satellites to Havelange (Rous 1978, 200–1).

The Havelange regime at FIFA makes a striking contrast with the paternalist, public service approach of Rous. For Havelange football is not primarily, as it was for Rous, a decent and pleasurable activity to which the peoples of the world might be drawn; it is a *marketing operation* and, by any standard, a vast one – 26 billion people watched the World Cup of 1990 on TV (Murray 1994, ch.1). Like Silvio Berlusconi in Europe and Rupert Murdoch in the UK, USA and Oceania, the basis of Havelange's wealth is in the mass media: he owns newspapers and a TV station in Brazil. Like them, he understands *globalization*: he knows the importance of the new markets for consumer goods in the Third World, that expanding TV ownership has helped to bring into being. Since his accession to the FIFA presidency he has set about the commodification of international football. For the World Cup of 1978 in Argentina, Havelange struck important deals with Adidas, the

German sportswear firm: Adidas bought billboard space, selling it at large profits, and all players in the tournament wore Adidas boots. In 1986, when the World Cup Finals were staged in Mexico, Havelange worked closely with his friend the Mexican broadcasting magnate Escaraga, whose Miami-based company Univision controlled hotels, stadia, TV stations and Spanish-speaking radio networks. Escaraga, also a FIFA official, participated in a profit-sharing committee with FIFA (ITV *World in Action* 1986). And football's biennial World Youth Cup, inaugurated by Havelange in 1977, has resolutely avoided the old Anglo-Saxon nations, being staged successively in Tunisia, Japan, Australia, Mexico, the USSR, Chile, Saudi Arabia and Portugal; all these tournaments were sponsored by Coca Cola. Kodak and Mars also sponsor FIFA extensively. Moreover, the World Cup Finals of 1994 were awarded to the USA, a country with thriving college and women's football but *no* professional football league of its own; the strong implication has been that, although the States have no football tradition to speak of they nevertheless lead the world in marketing. As usual, Havelange relies here on sponsorship, merchandising and world-wide media deals (see chapter 10).

During the 1970s, the English FA began tentatively to embrace some of this commercialism themselves. There were several reasons for this. The Football League had relinquished its maximum wage ceiling in 1961 (Wagg 1984, ch.8) and the now prosperous England players could no longer be treated as they had been in the 1950s, when they had been paid a minimal fee and frequently had their travelling expenses disputed (Watson 1964, 50–1); the Football League, with many of its constituent clubs now hard pressed financially, had begun by the late 1960s to welcome sponsorship (Hardaker 1977, 58); and the World Cup of 1966 had demonstrated conclusively to the FA the commercial possibilities of football. Nevertheless, in an increasingly competitive leisure market, money would be needed to promote and foster the game in England. Rous' successor at the FA had been Denis Follows, a former amateur footballer and a bureaucrat by temperament. On his retirement in 1972, however, the FA sought a person who would carry more weight in the worlds of commerce and professional football. Ted Croker, a businessman and former professional footballer, had these credentials. Rous' world was not Croker's world: 'No amount of pontificating about playing the game for the game's sake', he wrote later, 'will alter the fact that sport is about trying to win' (Croker 1987, 59–60).

The year after Croker's appointment, Sir Alf Ramsey was dismissed as England team manager. Ramsey, as Croker later made clear, had not only paid the price for England's failure to qualify for the World Cup of 1974 (with the resultant loss of advertising revenue, broadcasting fees and so on), but had proved uncooperative in the increasingly important field of 'press and public relations' (Croker 1987, 82). He is also known to have opposed commercial ventures like the Adidas deal, to which the FA and the England players were party (Wagg 1984, 135). Ramsey's replacement, Don Revie, was associated with a robust Northern professionalism, which he had applied successfully as manager of Leeds United but which was, culturally, new ground for the FA. Under Revie and Croker the fees paid to England players were increased, a shirt sponsorship deal was signed and an England international was advertised on TV for the first time (in 1975). By 1986 the FA were receiving annually over £1 million for the rights to broadcast England matches.

The present FA Secretary, Graham Kelly, therefore inherited a far more commercially oriented organization when Croker retired in 1989. By this time, the Football League had seen the full effects of the freeing of its labour market in 1961. Several major clubs had emerged to dominate domestic competition in recent decades; Liverpool, indeed, were outside the top two of the League only twice between 1973 and 1992. On the continent of Europe, too, between the late 1960s and the mid-80s, English clubs had held sway, their progress interrupted by the horrific events at the Heysel stadium in Belgium in 1985 and the subsequent banning of English clubs from European club competition. Thus deprived of a vital source of revenue, the leading clubs – notably, the Big Five of Arsenal, Everton, Liverpool, Manchester United and Tottenham Hotspur – began to press for their own media deals, outside those negotiated by the League (Goldberg and Wagg 1991). There were threats that these clubs would secede from the League, whereupon the Football League and the FA drew up parallel proposals for a separate Premier League, with its own sponsorship and media coverage agreements. The FA's plan was adopted. Their Premier League, now called the Premiership, began in 1992. It is sponsored by the lager company Carling and B Sky B, the satellite TV channel owned by News International, has paid £300 million for the right to show live matches over a five-year period. To appease public opinion, since satellite TV still serves a small minority of homes in England, a subsidiary deal gives recorded highlights to the BBC, the public service channel. English football's cultural transition from people's game to television show, begun in the 1960s (Wagg 1984, ch.9), seems virtually complete.

The annual turnover of the FA, until the 1970s a stronghold of amateurism and anti-commercialism, has moved from £14 million in the late 1980s to £30 million in 1993 (Williams 1993). As the oldest administrative body in the football world, the FA has become a part of the burgeoning heritage industry – a licensing authority which commodifies its own historic place in England's culture: at the time of writing even the FA Cup (founded, like the FA itself, in 1863) now has a sponsor: Littlewoods.

Scotland: rocks and hard places

The problems which faced English football authorities in the 1980s confronted administrators of the Scottish League somewhat sooner. Many Scottish League clubs were situated in towns of no more than a few thousand in population. By the 1920s a number of these found themselves under threat of extinction. As in England, religious and political conviction ruled certain commercial options inadmissible. There was a steadfast refusal to consider pools income and, in the early 1930s, the town clubs which dominated the SFA and the Scottish League forbade dog racing at Scottish football grounds because it involved gambling. Clyde and Celtic were also refused permission to open special turnstiles for the unemployed (Crampsey 1990, 92–5). A third of the adult male population of Clydeside was unemployed at the time.

'The Scottish game', observes the League's historian, 'was caught between the rock of finance, of business prudence, and the hard place of sentiment' (Crampsey 1990, 83). Several Scottish League clubs folded before the Second World War. There was serious talk of a Super League in Scotland as early as 1946, the idea being to restrict the League to a maximum of 16 clubs, with ground capacity a major criterion of inclusion (Crampsey 1990, 133). The idea came to nothing but by the beginning of the 1960s match attendances, as in other countries, were declining sharply. One founder member of the League, the Clydeside club Third Lanark, went out of business in 1967. By 1970, other League clubs in the Clydeside area, of which there were several beside Rangers and Celtic, were in serious difficulties (Crampsey 1990, 182).

In 1970 the Scottish League turned cautiously to sponsorship. Two new (shortlived) competitions were introduced, sponsored respectively by the oil company Texaco and Dryborough, the brewers. By the summer of 1974 it was agreed that a Premier Division should be formed, consisting of ten clubs only. In 1977 Hibernian became the first Scottish League club to adopt shirt advertising. Television, warily admitted to Scottish League matches in the late 1950s, was now made more welcome and in 1979 Bell's Whisky agreed to sponsor the Scottish League Cup. Attendances at Scottish League and League Cup matches, however, had meanwhile continued to spiral downward from 6,338,000 in 1956–7 to 4,443,000 in 1969–70 to 2,870,000 for 1980–1 (Crampsey 1990, 211). By 1983, nine Premier Division members were said to be so angry about the power exercised by the smaller clubs that they, like their English counterparts, were prepared to countenance leaving the League. This was averted, largely through the obtaining of sponsorship for the Scottish League itself: Fine Fare, the supermarket chain, took this on in 1985, followed in 1988 by B & Q, the chain of D.I.Y. shops

The Scottish League entered the 1990s still, in a nation of only 5 million people, maintaining 38 clubs; this compares with 92 clubs to 50 million people in England and Wales. As Moorhouse points out, the Taylor Report which followed the deaths of 95 Liverpool supporters at the Hillsborough Stadium, Sheffield in 1989 requires modifications to football grounds that few Scottish clubs can afford (Moorhouse 1991, 214–18). Since several of them attract regular crowds of a few hundred only, it is likely that for some of them the rock of business imperatives will once again confront the hard place of sentiment. One option, in theory, would be the merging of ailing clubs but experience suggests that attempts to pursue this strategy will founder – as with the plan to combine Clyde and Hamilton Academicals in 1970 (Crampsey 1990, 182–3) and the move in 1990 to amalgamate the two Edinburgh clubs, Hibernian and Heart of Midlothian (Moorhouse 1991, 211–13). Public feeling runs high in such situations and traditional club loyalties have proved unshakeable.

At the other end of the scale, according to observers such as Moorhouse,

Glasgow Rangers stand alone. In his view, no other Scottish club now competes with the playing strength or business wherewithal of Rangers. While English clubs were exiled from European competition Rangers established themselves as a side attuned to international football. Rangers' financial power enabled their manager of the late 1980s, Graeme Souness, to begin reversing the historically long-established trend of good footballers moving to England by signing several England internationals. In 1989 the club also moved to challenge the religious bigotry of many of their Protestant supporters by signing the Catholic, former Celtic player Maurice Johnston. The resultant protests were firmly rebutted. The Scottish press meanwhile talked of the incompatibility of religious bigotry with a 'European Super League'.

Rangers, it seems, stand ready to join such a league, when it forms. Other Scottish clubs, including Rangers' great rivals Celtic, do not. Rangers are run by David Murray, a modern media tycoon in the Berlusconi mould, who represents a post-industrial Glasgow. Under him Rangers 'call Scottish football to a new identity; towards managerialist, multinational modernity'. On the other hand, Celtic, it is said, represent the older, unregenerated, sectarian Glasgow. The club is still run by the same families that have run it for much of this century; they lack the resources to match Rangers and increasingly they invoke 'community' – Irishness and Catholicism – against the 'mercenaries' of Rangers (Moorhouse 1991, 208).

If this is the case, then it marks a significant transformation in Scottish football culture. During the late 1960s and early 1970s, the period when in Scotland as elsewhere in Europe economic difficulties began to preoccupy national leagues, Glasgow Celtic were Scotland's leading team, by some margin. During that time they won nine consecutive national league titles and, in 1967, they became the first British team to win the European Cup, beating Inter Milan in Lisbon. All this was achieved under the managership of Jock Stein. Scotland's national football culture has been inherently fractured: some players attracted hostility because of their religion, others, like Dave Mackay, Denis Law (see Holt 1994) and Kenny Dalglish, the holder of most Scottish caps, because they were 'Anglos'. Stein was, arguably, this culture's one unambiguous hero and a central figure in the forming of modern Scottish football identity.

In football, as in other cultural realms, Scottishness, like all national identities, is contested terrain. There is some agreement, though, that Scottishness consists in an opposition to the English. 'Anti-Englishness', writes Moorhouse, '[is] the essence which defines "Scottishness" . . .' (Moorhouse 1991, 203), and the writer Stuart Cosgrove has expressed it thus: 'Football is simply the most significant national activity in Scotland. On the street corners, on television, at Hampden Park [the national football stadium in Glasgow] but most importantly on the bi-annual trips down to Wembley [for the England game in the Home International tournament, now defunct] football is the respirator' (Cosgrove 1986, 99). The biennial away games in England dated back to the late nineteenth century and accounts suggest that, for much of their history, they were cheerful occasions when Scottish families came South for a day out in London, or wherever (Moorhouse 1987). In the

1960s and 70s, however, the event was associated with mayhem: after the games of 1967 and 1977, Scottish supporters ripped out pieces of turf from the Wembley pitch. On the latter occasion the goalposts were dismantled. These incidents fed back, on both sides of the border, into powerful myths of the Scottish – myths which Stein, who went on to manage Scotland and died on the bench at a Scotland match in 1985, tried to confront.

Central to these myths is the 'tanner ball player'. The 'tanner ball players' mingled skill on the ball, aggression and cheek. They enjoyed the impudent gesture – notably, when playing against England – and displayed enormous virtuosity with a football, but fiery temper and bad judgement often undid their good work. Off the field such men were frequently partial to drinking and fighting. In the post-war era Billy Bremner, who came to England to play for Leeds in the late 1960s, and Jimmy Johnstone, the Celtic winger of the same era, stand out: they were often being sent home by an exasperated Scottish management. The most cherished moment in the post-war era, for most Scottish supporters, was when, during Scotland's defeat of England at Wembley in 1967, the Scotland wing half Jim Baxter stopped and sat on the ball, inflicting the definitive humiliation on the English. Baxter, thought to be a heavy drinker, left football soon afterward. This ultimate porousness was felt to lie at the heart of Scottish football. It was also seen as reflecting broad strains of working-class masculine culture in Scotland, especially on Clydeside: in popular myth the Glaswegian working-class male, however gifted, for the most part simply got drunk, fought, was sectarian and hated the English. Stein opposed these tendencies and sought to preserve only what was best, and potentially modern, in the Scottish game. He insisted that the Irish tricolour, which flew over Celtic's ground, should be replaced by the flag of the Scottish Football League. His Celtic teams preserved the artistry of the 'tanner ball players' but they were consistently successful too. He used Celtic's achievements as a basis for recovering a pride in Scottish football, long since eroded by decades of migration to England (Crampsey 1990, 179). But this pride was tempered with rationalism. For Stein, qualifying for the World Cup was more important than beating England.

It has been suggested that Stein, like others among the leading British football managers of the 1960s and 70s (Busby, Shankly, Clough), stood for a kind of 'labourism': getting the best deal for the working class and working with the most positive elements in its culture (Cosgrove 1986, 108). Indeed, the football grounds of post-war England have been described as 'the Labour Party at prayer' (Fishwick 1989, 150). But the heavy industrial economy that brought the working classes of Clydeside and other Scottish cities into being has largely disintegrated. Shipyards, mines and jute mills have closed; computer-based light industries have opened up – part of Central Scotland is now called 'Silicon Glen'. Transnational corporations come and go in the search for inexpensive labour (the US-based watchmakers Timex closed their factory in Dundee in 1993, blaming wage costs) and oil companies, one of whom was the first sponsor of Scottish football, have been drilling off Scotland's East coast since the 1970s. Widespread concern about the wealth being taken out of the country has seen a resurgence of Scottish nationalism and this has occasionally been glimpsed in football culture: in 1977, for instance, when Scottish supporters took away lumps of earth from England's stadium, they chanted 'Give Us an Assembly and We'll Give You Back Your Wembley' (Cosgrove 1986, 107).

Although opposition to the British Conservative government is manifestly strong in Scotland, there is still no national assembly and, meanwhile, the Scots are trying to develop new tertiary industries, such as tourism – Glasgow, for example, was declared a 'City of Culture' in 1990. The Scottish football world, according to Moorhouse, is struggling – and often failing – to adapt. Although, as he argues, no Scottish club currently rivals Rangers in modernity, the reduction in the number of teams that would seem necessary to enhance competition has little popular support; in fact, in 1991, Scottish clubs voted to increase the number of teams in the Premier Division. Rangers manager Graeme Souness quit and, like so many Scotsmen before him, moved to England.

Ireland: a game of two halves

Nobody can suppose that football is unaffected by religious or political sectarianism in the North of Ireland. Northern Ireland consists of six counties in the North East of the island. This territory has, since the late seventeenth century, been predominantly Protestant and loyal to the British crown, although there are significant Catholic and Republican minorities. Since partition it has been a dependent nation within the United Kingdom. Longstanding discrimination against Catholics in the job and housing markets led to a civil rights movement in the late 1960s, which in turn provoked a Protestant backlash. Paramilitary death squads from both Republican and Loyalist communities have been active since the 1970s and the British army has been garrisoned in Northern Ireland for much of that time, ostensibly as a peace-keeping force.

Inevitably, perhaps, football clubs in the province have acquired sectarian identities. During the inter-war years, when Belfast Celtic, an accomplished team and the northern club with the biggest Catholic support, played either Linfield or Glentoran, both clubs with large Protestant followings, serious crowd violence usually ensued. In 1948, after a match between Belfast Celtic and Linfield at Windsor Park in Belfast, the Celtic players were set upon by spectators; the club seceded from the Irish League at the end of the season. Catholic interest has since focused successively on Glentoran, who employed Catholics, Distillery and, in the late 1970s, Cliftonville. There have been heavy policing and sporadic sectarian affrays at games between these clubs and sides from Loyalist areas, but the most conspicuous victim of what are universally called 'The Troubles' has been Derry City.

Derry City had played in the Irish League since 1929. The city of Derry (or Londonderry) where it is situated is mostly Catholic but it has traditionally attracted support from both communities. Derry's ground, The Brandywell, is near a strongly Republican district called the Bogside and persistent rioting in the area from 1969 into 1971 persuaded club officials to leave the Irish

League. In 1985 they joined the League of Ireland (the Republic's league) and in 1989 became the first side to represent two national leagues in the European Cup – in 1965 they had played in the competition as winners of the Irish League.

In the final analysis, given the increasingly global economy, sectarianism may be fought most effectively by commercial sanction: in 1992, Thorn-EMI withdrew their sponsorship of Linfield, whose manager had declared he would not sign a Catholic player, and Coca Cola threatened to stop funding the IFA (Sugden and Bairner 1993, 78, 82–6).

Selection for the national side in Northern Ireland has not been sectarian. Some of the country's leading players in recent times have been Catholic: goalkeeper Pat Jennings, for instance, Northern Ireland's most capped player, was from a Catholic family in Newry, and Gerry Armstrong and Martin O'Neill, two prominent players of the 1980s, were former Gaelic footballers. But the fissures of Northern Irish society have affected support for the team: because of serious unrest between 1972 and 1978 the team played all its home fixtures on the British mainland and, in the 1980s, with many Unionists paradoxically contemplating an independent Northern Ireland (to avoid reunification), the loyalty of Catholic players has been questioned on the terraces (Sugden and Bairner 1993, 75–8).

Although Northern Ireland qualified for the World Cup Finals of 1982 (when they progressed beyond the first round) and 1986, their best team is said to have been the one that achieved their only previous qualification, in 1958. The captain of that side, Danny Blanchflower, also led the Tottenham Hotspur team that won the Football League and FA Cup double in 1961. Blanchflower was a gifted player and caustic wit and on his death in 1993 there was much public nostalgia in the British football world for the more skilled game of his era. All the 1958 side, bar one (Peacock of Glasgow Celtic) played their football in England, as have most subsequent Northern Ireland internationals. Ireland's failure to qualify for the World Cup Finals in the 1960s or 70s meant that George Best, regarded by many as the most naturally talented British outfield player of the post-war period, was never seen in major international competition. Best, a Belfast Protestant, played for Manchester United in the late 1960s and early 70s and was a member of their European Cup winning side of 1968. (The opting to play for Wales of the current Manchester United player Ryan Giggs, whom many compare to Best, may have similar consequences. Wales did not qualify for the World Cup Finals of 1994 and several of their better players, for whom they have no obvious replacements, are unlikely to be around in 1998.) Since the disbanding in 1984 of the British Home International tournament, the Irish FA has suffered a loss of income and consequent decline. Lately there have been calls for a united Irish team; this was unthinkable until peace talks in 1993–5 made it a remote possibility.

The Republic of Ireland were the only national side from the British Isles who qualified for the World Cup Finals of 1994 in the USA. The Republic does not have a strong football tradition: rugby football and Gaelic sports are at least as popular there. As with the other 'submerged' British nations, most of their better players made their living and their name in England,

notably with Manchester United and Arsenal. These two clubs, as I
observed earlier, have strong Irish links and the latter draws on the London
Irish community, among other communities, for its support. The best
Southern Irish players of the 1960s, Shay Brennan, Tony Dunne, Noel
Cantwell and John Giles, played for Manchester United (although Giles
went on to play his best football with Leeds) and their leading players in the
1980s – Liam Brady, perhaps the best player to come out of the South
of Ireland, David O'Leary and Frank Stapleton – were at Arsenal. Brady
spent a lot of the later 1980s at Italian clubs, while Stapleton moved to
Manchester United.

The Southern Irish side had its occasional achievements in the post-war
era: to its defeat of England in Liverpool in 1949 it added two victories over
West Germany, 3–0 in Dublin in 1956 and 1–0 in Dusseldorf in 1960. But
the most accomplished side to represent the Republic is, in essence, the
current one, which has been assembled by the ex-England player Jack
Charlton, the manager since 1986. This team qualified for the European
Nations Championships in 1988, during which they defeated England; the
then England manager Bobby Robson later described the Republic as one of
the top four sides in the world – not the outlandish judgement that it was
branded by an impatient English press. They qualified for the World Cup
Finals for the first time in 1990, progressing to the Quarter Finals and,
although they didn't make the European Championship of 1992 in Sweden,
they were World Cup finalists again in 1994.

There have been two principal factors in their success, both the object of
much, largely hypocritical, criticism in England. First, Charlton has taken
advantage of FIFA's liberalized eligibility rules (see Duke 1991) which allow
parentage and grandparentage to be considered. Several of the present
Republic team were born on the British mainland but of Irish families: Irish
migrant workers have, after all, been coming to England since the early
nineteenth century. This has given rise to such jokes in the English football
world as, 'FAI stands for Find Any Irishman', or 'If you've drunk a pint of
Guinness, you qualify for Ireland', and so on. Second, Charlton has adopted
a 'long ball game' with balls frequently aimed upfield for the tall centre
forward, Niall Quinn. This is attacked in the English football press as crude,
but many European football people see this same crudeness as a
characteristic of the English game too.

In any event, despite the comparatively weak cultural base that football
has in the South of Ireland, the exploits of Charlton's side, with the attendant
television coverage and publicity, has created much interest in southern Irish
society for the team and the game.

FOOTBALL IN THE BRITISH ISLES: THE STATE OF PLAY

Football in the British Isles, then, faces a painful and uneven transition to
full modernity. In England, the FA, an historical bastion of amateurism and
anti-commercial high-mindedness, has now embraced the market, hoping to
use its new-found wealth to promote and enhance the English game. In

Scotland, Glasgow Rangers lead the way towards a European Super League, at present still on the drawing board. The modernizers, though, have to deal, in the football cultures either side of the border, with the atavistic tendencies of their opponents. In England, a brand of football condemned by coaches in numerous other countries as 'kick and rush', appears to prevail (and is undeniably popular with overseas television audiences), while the English football press, fixated on the glories of an imagined past, blames the team manager. In Scotland, traditional loyalties bar the way to possible rationalizations of the League structure.

In Wales, the national sport of rugby may be ailing. The breeding ground of the game – the working-class areas of the South Wales coalfields – could grow barren, following the closure of many pits in the 1980s and the resulting decay of communities (Williams 1994). Much of football's future lies with television. In that context, football is a more popular sport than rugby and so it may prove for the rising generation of young Welsh. The Welsh football team recently transferred their matches to the Cardiff Arms Park, the national stadium previously used only by the country's rugby team, and they have been attracting good crowds.

Moreover, the geo-politics of the world game may be working to strengthen association football in Wales, albeit in a context where serious contradictions between centre and periphery, and between commercial imperatives and national identity, have been raised. In 1991, the Football Association of Wales, concerned about the growing lobby in Africa and on the continent of Europe for a **British** team, rather than separate national sides, to be entered in international competition, proposed to begin a national football league in Wales. This, they judged, would strengthen their credibility with UEFA and, through access to European competition, bring more revenue into Welsh football. However, the main sides in Wales – Cardiff City, Swansea City and Wrexham – all negotiated exemption from this new league, agreeing to enter only their reserve sides. Furthermore, eight of the Welsh small town clubs – like Merthyr Tydfil, Colwyn Bay and Caernarfon – preferred to play in English leagues such as the Vauxhall Conference and the Beazer Homes. These leagues are at the base of the 'Football League pyramid' – that is, they carry the possibility of promotion into the Football League itself – and the clubs argued that keeping English football as the focus of their aspiration was commercially more advantageous and offered stiffer competition (Lloyd 1991). Most of them relented, however, rather than lose the recognition of the FAW. But Newport AFC opted to stay in the Beazer Homes League and were therefore forbidden by the Welsh FA to stage their home matches in Wales; they now travel 80 miles to play these. The League of Wales, meanwhile, was recognized by UEFA and obtained sponsorship from Konica, the photographic company. It completed its first season in 1993 and the winners, Inter Cardiff, entered the European Cup.

However, on the field at least, at the time of writing, it is Southern Ireland, a largely rural nation with a negligible football history, albeit their current football hero and manager an Englishman and with few Irish accents in the dressing room, that leads the way.

REFERENCES

Beck, Peter J. (1982) 'England v. Germany 1938', *History Today*, June

Cosgrove, Stuart (1986) 'And the bonnie Scotland will be there: football in Scottish culture', in Alan Tomlinson and Garry Whannel (eds) *Off The Ball*, London, Pluto Press

Crampsey, Bob (1990) *The Scottish Football League: The First 100 Years*, Glasgow, Scottish Football League

Croker, Ted (1987) *The First Voice You Will Hear Is . . .* London, Willow Books.

Duke, Vic (1991) 'The politics of football in the new Europe', in John Williams and Stephen Wagg (eds) *British Football and Social Change*, Leicester, Leicester University Press

Dunning, Eric and Sheard, Kenneth (1979) *Barbarians, Gentlemen and Players*, Oxford, Martin Robertson

Fishwick, Nick (1989) *English Football and Society 1910–1950*, Manchester, Manchester University Press

Goldberg, Adrian and Wagg, Stephen (1991) 'It's not a knockout: English football and globalisation', in Williams and Wagg, op. cit.

Hardaker, Alan, with Butler, Bryon (1977) *Hardaker of the League*, London, Pelham Books

Holt, Richard (1989) *Sport and the British*, Oxford, Clarendon Press

Holt, Richard (1994) 'King Across the Border; Denis Law and Scottish Football', in Grant Jarvie and Graham Walker (eds) *Scottish Sport in the Making of the Nation*, London, Leicester University Press

Inglis, Simon (1988) *League Football and the Men Who Made It*, London, Collins Willow

Jeffery, Gordon (1965) *European International Football*, London, Sportsman's Book Club

Leith, Alex (1993) 'Ireland's champion Jack', *Guardian*, 11 October

Lloyd, Grahame (1991) 'Eight to challenge Welsh league', *Guardian*, 29 November

Mason, Tony (1979) *Association Football and English Society 1863–1915*, Hassocks, Harvester Press

Moorhouse, H.F. (1987) 'Scotland against England: Football and Popular Culture', *The International Journal of the History of Sport*, vol.4, 189–202

Moorhouse, H.F. (1991) 'On the periphery: Scotland, Scottish football and the new Europe', in Williams and Wagg, op. cit.

Murray, Bill (1984) *The Old Firm: Sectarianism, Sport and Society in Scotland*, Edinburgh, John Donald

Murray, Bill (1994) *Soccer: A History of the World Game*, Aldershot, Scolar Press

Oliver, Guy (1992) *The Guinness Record of World Soccer*, Enfield, Guinness Publishing

Patrick, James (1973) *A Glasgow Gang Observed*, London, Eyre Methuen

Rafferty, John (1973) *One Hundred Years of Scottish Football*, London, Pan Books

Rous, Stanley (1978) *Football Worlds*, London, Faber and Faber

Smith, David and Williams, Gareth (1980) *Fields of Praise: The Official History of the Welsh Rugby Union 1881–1981*, Cardiff, University of Wales Press

Studd, Stephen (1981) *Herbert Chapman: Football Emperor*, London, Peter Owen

Sugden, John and Bairner, Alan (1993) *Sport, Sectarianism and Society in a Divided Ireland*, Leicester, Leicester University Press

Tomlinson, Alan (1986) 'Going global: the FIFA story', in Tomlinson and Whannel, op. cit.

Wagg, Stephen (1984) *The Football World*, Brighton, Harvester Press

Wagg, Stephen (1986) 'Naming the guilty men: managers and the media', in Tomlinson and Whannel, op. cit.

Wagg, Stephen (1991) 'Playing the past: the media and the England football team', in Williams and Wagg, op. cit.

Watson, Willie (1964) *Double International*, London, Sportsman's Book Club

Whannel, Garry (1983) *Blowing the Whistle: The Politics of Sport*, London, Pluto Press

Williams, John and Taylor, Rogan (1994) 'Boys keep swinging: masculinity and football culture in England', in Tim Newburn and Elizabeth A. Stanko (eds) *Just Boys Doing Business?* London, Routledge

Williams, Richard (1993) 'Is this man fit for England?', *Independent on Sunday*, 12 December

Williams, Richard (1994) 'The dying of the light', *Independent on Sunday*, 9 January

2

THE LIONS STIR: FOOTBALL IN AFRICAN SOCIETY

Ossie Stuart

INTRODUCTION

From outside the African continent the game of soccer in Africa appears to have just emerged on to the world scene. The performance of Cameroon's 'Indomitable Lions' at the 1990 World Cup is one of the few images young fans have of African national teams. Those with longer memories may remember Ghana's 'Black Stars' and their stunning performances during the 1960s and 70s. Nevertheless, the overall impression is that soccer in Africa is a recent phenomenon.

Recent world attention, however, is a poor guide to the length of time soccer has been played on the continent. Yet, there are a number of reasons why the assumption of the newness of the African game persists. Colonialism is one. The occupation of African countries and the use of their resources for white minorities and European states for half a century precluded any opportunity for Africans to pursue excellence in their own right. The poor quality of the African game, with a few notable exceptions, is another reason.

It is not enough to explain this late recognition without asking further questions. First of all, in what way did colonialism limit the development of African soccer? Soccer came to Africa through colonial conquest. The colonists' refusal to invest in key universal African social institutions, such as education, ensured that the game would remain the sport of the rich, the fortunate or the elite until the end of the colonial period.

The lack of investment in education and health also partially explains why the game remained of poor quality when it was played in Africa during the first decades after independence. Countries north of the Sahara dominated the African game for this reason. Egypt, Algeria and Tunisia, until recently, benefited from the early strength of their social institutions, as compared with their peers south of the Sahara. Likewise, three of four black African nations south of the Sahara dominated the international game for the first three decades after the first independence movement. These original Princes of

African soccer – Zaire, Ghana and Sudan – had enjoyed a degree of investment in sport by their colonial masters which was not so forthcoming in other colonies. At independence they were able to reap the benefits accordingly.

Today, none of these countries can reproduce past form. They have failed to maintain the investment necessary to ensure continued success. In contrast, the paupers of African soccer have begun to emerge with significant soccer riches. They now challenge Africa's former soccer princes. Cameroon is a case in point. However, other former soccer minnows, such as Zambia, Cote d'Ivoire and, most recently, Zimbabwe, are now reaping the benefits of relatively stable economies, free universal primary education and investment in rudimentary, but comprehensive, health systems.

The success of Cameroon in Italy was significant because it was a sign that, at last, sub-Saharan Africa had put in place the structures vital to produce consistently world class players for the future. This pool of soccer talent is no longer the product of the fading colonial period. Rather, it represents the new structures created by societies which have shaken off colonial legacies and who are preparing for the twenty-first century.

HISTORIC LEGACY

The game of football has been played on the African continent for almost a century. Soccer came to Africa when Europeans first began to colonize the continent in the latter half of the nineteenth century. European powers raced to grab land and exploit the wealth they found. They benefited enormously from the exploitation of Africa. What they gave in return has been of questionable value.

Today, the same countries still compete for African assets. One of these is the skills of African soccer players; one by one, they are being enticed to play their soccer in Europe rather than in Africa. The most accomplished African soccer players are being attracted to the top soccer clubs in the national leagues across that continent. As in the past, the development of African soccer is dependent upon this new 'trade'. The future strength of the African game will be strongly influenced by what is returned to Africa from Europe.

Among the resources returned to Africa are knowledge of the game, the latest expertise, training methods, management skills and, most important of all, money. How they are exploited depends upon the priorities of each independent African nation, not the former parasitical colonial administrations of the past. Today, for every African player abroad, many thousands of others seek the prestige, wealth and social mobility which goes hand in hand with soccer. The success of the African national team in the international arena also depends upon the performance of African players abroad. African governments, keenly aware of the benefits the game brings to their nations, know they ignore the sport at their peril.

This chapter will focus on the history and modern development of soccer not in one of Africa's soccer principalities, but in Zimbabwe. Zimbabwe is a good choice because it has had long history of domestic soccer. It has also been confronted with all the problems of developing the game in an economy outside the rich North. However, this does not mean that other nations will be ignored. Examples of the contribution to the development of the game made by other nations in sub-Saharan Africa will be included. The absence of reference to soccer nations north of the Sahara is deliberate. The greatest improvement in the game has taken place in sub-Saharan Africa. At the 1992 African Nations Cup Tournament, for example, not a single team from North Africa remained in the competition by the Quarter Finals stage. So this will focus on the development of sub-Saharan soccer.

THE ARRIVAL OF THE WORLD GAME

All change

Colonialism and the struggle to overthrow it still continues in Africa. The enduring legacy left behind by three-quarters of a century of European rule has been a radically transformed African continent. Prior to the arrival of the colonists popular culture in Africa was also very different. Sport performed a number of functions in agrarian communities found across the continent. For example, it served to reinforce the identity of the community. It was also used to introduce the young to adulthood. Wrestling, stick fighting, swimming and dance each played this role. Though more popular in some regions than in others, these activities were found all over Africa. (Baker and Mangan 1987).

The colonial experiment wrought havoc with pre-colonial African society. Agrarian societies bore the brunt of dramatic change in the face of colonial expansion. No region was spared the destruction of traditional African agriculture. The introduction of European land ownership, taxation and the wage economy forced men and, much later, women off the land and into wage labour in the new cities and mines. As colonial rule was extended deeper into the heart of Africa, more and more men were forced to migrate and join the wage economy to meet their colonial tax demands. The families they left behind were evicted from the richest lands to make way for European settlers. Those families ended up on arid lands, not even suitable for subsistence farming (Palmer and Parsons 1983).

This great population transfer created the African cities which sprang up during the first four decades of the twentieth century. Packed into them were migrant workers, living in squalid and overcrowded conditions. In search of precious cash, these workers received no assistance, save what was necessary to keep them alive and productive. In the South African diamond and gold mines, for example, migrants were prey to gamblers, gangs, illness and prostitution in the mining compounds. These conditions went hand-in-hand with dangerous working conditions and very poor wages.

European employers and colonial governments had only a very limited interest in the welfare of their black inhabitants and employees. In order to survive, individuals had, first, to depend upon their families – cousins, brothers, uncles. Also, those who spoke the same language, came from the same village or from the same territory looked to each other to survive.

The ethnic groups we know today in Africa are not primordial institutions with traditions which stretch back a thousand years. Rather, they are a recent phenomenon, based on the mine or the city and created out of necessity. One of their roles was to ensure an individual's survival. Membership of a group provided an individual with a rudimentary social service where there was none. They were the difference between getting and not getting a job. The stronger the ethnic identity, the higher the chance of survival. Though Africans used the cultural resources from their agrarian experiences – religion, language, selected traditions, medicine and so on – these ethnic identities were created and made real by circumstances in the city. Hence, initially at least, these identities only had relevance and meaning in the city (Ranger 1987).

The game arrives

It was into this urban environment that soccer was introduced. The game was brought to the attention of Africans in a number of ways. European settlers taught the game to, and competed against, local African populations in the towns. European soldiers did likewise with Africans recruited as baggage handlers and to fight in colonial wars. Schools specifically established for the African elite played soccer rather than rugby. Finally, missionaries found soccer to be an ideal form of recreation for pupils at their mission schools. Furthermore, the promise of a game after the service helped to boost their African congregation.

Soccer was introduced to Africa for the benefit of European settlers, however. No thought was given to its likely impact upon the African population. No attempt was made to develop the sport into a universal form of recreation; in fact, this was discouraged. Perhaps the best example of this was in Cameroon. This German colony was taken over by both the British and French governments as part of the territorial settlement of the First World War. The French, given administrative control of Cameroon, encouraged its nationals, mainly from the lower middle class and the *petite bourgeoisie*, among whom soccer is still very popular, to emigrate and run the colony. Yet the number of French settlers so assigned was very small. To administer the territory satisfactorily the French turned to Africans already accustomed to European norms and practices. Rather than look to the local population, the French chose to recruit Africans from other French territories to complement their own nationals. These came from Senegal, Sierra Leone and Gabon and became the supervisory personnel. Immediately they assumed the position of an African expatriate elite in Cameroon. Once established in large numbers they were also recruited to play European-run soccer. The isolated settlers were too few to make up single-ethnicity soccer teams, so they turned to the African elite to make up the numbers in the local soccer league (Clignet and Stark 1974).

As more French settlers arrived, soccer was again largely restricted to those of European origin. Only a very few Africans were allowed to play in this mixed arena. Those chosen still came from the elite of the African expatriate population. In the 1920s, the club 'Estoile Sportive' of Yaoundé had two teams: one exclusively white, the other open to Africans, most of whom were expatriates. The visits by the French Navy in 1929 and 1930 were occasions for celebration in Cameroon. Part of the activities consisted of a soccer match between a Navy side and a local team, usually 'Sporting Club' of Douala. On each occasion the opposing white teams played each other first, and only afterwards were Africans allowed to take the field (Clignet and Stark 1974).

The small number of Europeans in areas outside the major cities of Cameroon meant that racially integrated teams did indeed exist in the smaller towns. Yet, as one got closer to the larger cities they disappeared. European-only teams were not sufficiently skilled to play with or beat African teams. So, in the racial atmosphere of the day, the chances of black and white teams playing together remained remote. Nevertheless, the colonial background to Africa's introduction to soccer has had a lasting impact upon Cameroon society (Clignet and Stark 1974).

Access to soccer for Africans within a colonial society was dependent on an individual's exposure to privileged contacts with European culture. It is no accident that the majority of Africans playing for the largest clubs, even after independence, came from the few elite schools and colleges in the capital. Soccer still retains the aura of an elite activity in the Cameroon today, rather than being a game of the urban poor and the working class, as in Northern Europe. It enjoys a different social position in both Cameroon and right across the African continent.

Soccer remained an activity of the privileged throughout the colonial period. First, it was found in the elite African schools and later in the towns. Soccer never became a universal sport in colonial Africa. Those who played the game were always the fortunate few in societies where the vast majority of people could afford neither to feed their children, nor to educate them.

Football comes to southern Africa

The story of the arrival of soccer in colonial Zimbabwe begins in South Africa. Though rugby was the game played predominantly by whites, soccer was also played as early as the 1870s (Couzens 1983). The Natal Football Association was founded in June 1882, to which white clubs, such as the Natal Wasps, the Durban Alphas and the Umgeni Stars affiliated. These were all-white clubs which subsequently came together in 1891 to form their own segregated association.

Soccer played by Africans in South Africa developed in parallel with white-run soccer. Elite African schools lead the way. The education institutions established for privileged Africans in South Africa were Zonnebloem and Adams College in Natal and schools such as Lovedale, Healdtown and St Mathews. By the second decade of this century these institutions attracted pupils from the very top of Southern Africa's African society. At the same time a collegiate soccer tradition was developing. Teams from these schools and colleges played each other in regular competition. They also sought out African teams in the nearby cities and mines, with whom they established regular fixtures.

One particular school, Adams College, was typical of the colleges of this time. The schools' missionary founders, from the United States, were quick to recognize the value of soccer and encouraged it among their pupils. In the 1890s, Adams College – then known as Amanzimtoti Institute – had a senior team called the Shooting Stars and a junior team called the Flying Stars. Players from these teams regularly played against other schools and against worker and local town teams. This close relationship between the elite teams and the city clubs formed the basis of the formation of Durban and District Football Association in 1907.

While education brought soccer to the elite, the colonial army spread the game among the labouring population in the cities. The British Colonial Army was the way many Africans first discovered soccer. British soldiers passed on the game to African workers trapped with them during the defence of the besieged towns of Ladysmith and Mafeking during the 1899–1902 Boer War. In turn, the game was passed on to other migrants throughout the region and on to areas of the Transvaal, including Johannesburg. The Rainbows, Ladysmith and the Invincibles were some of the earliest African teams in Natal. The Royals of Pietermaritzburg, another turn of the century team, probably took their name from the Royal Engineers based in that region before and throughout the Anglo-Boer war (Couzens 1983).

Many other teams were established in Durban at this time. Most were based upon the workplace or sprang up in the African quarter in the poorest areas of the city. For example, the Africans who worked for Natal Government Railways named their team the NGR. Teams such as the Vultures, the Wanderers, the Native Swallows and the Mzinyati mission team called the Willows were typical of the Clubs of the day, being based on the workplace, the mission or the street. The Condors played in New Scotland, the Natal Cannons in Inanda while both the Corinthians and Jumpers played in Verlum.

Similar teams proliferated throughout the big industrial urban areas in South Africa. Football began a little later on the Johannesburg Reef than in Natal. It was not until the second decade of the twentieth century that Witwatersrand District Football Association was formed. Most of the teams were based around the gold mines. Employers were happy to encourage the game amongst their African workers. For the employer it had a number of advantages. Soccer raised morale among the workforce. Players remained sober throughout the weekend. It filled in the non-work time of the workforce, diverting them from gambling, complaining about poor conditions and low wages. So important did mine owners consider the game that they competed to recruit star players, which gave the most accomplished players the opportunity to obtain the best jobs available (Couzens 1983).

Location communities such as Sophiatown, Eastern Native Township,

Western Native Township and Pimville played a different form of soccer. This was organized on the basis of the Yard or street. Each Yard would choose its team and challenge a neighbouring one. Street soccer matches were regularly played for a cash jackpot collected prior to the match. Eventually Yards merged to form clubs. For example, the Doornfontein club, made up of the best players of the local Yards, was called the Rangers. They played similar clubs from Pimville and Vrededorp on the flat tops of mine dumps, the only space available (Couzens 1983).

All this unofficial activity did not escape the attention of the authorities in South Africa. The early 1920s was a period of intense and violent industrial strife among both black and white workers. The former were perceived to be of greater threat by the authorities. In response, they followed the example of employers and began to use sport, soccer especially, as a form of social control. Like the mine owners during an earlier period, they hoped soccer would divert bored young men from militancy, drunkenness and increase their efficiency at work as well.

Outside the mines the Johannesburg Municipality formed the Johannesburg Bantu Football Association in 1929. Its aim of 'controlling all football grounds to be set aside for [Africans]' and of 'placing football amongst [Africans] on a sound footing and to eliminate gambling and other objectionable practices' (Couzens 1983).

This set the basis for the dramatic growth of soccer in South Africa. For example, by 1937 the Johannesburg Bantu Football Association [JBFA] had registered 435 senior and junior African clubs. This heralded more intense competition from the mines, who were reluctant to lose players from the mining compounds to the JBFA leagues. However, the organization to challenge the JBFA was the Johannesburg African Football Association [JAFA]. Clubs joined one or other of these organizations. Teams run by the mines or big business joined the 'Africans'. The residential locations for Africans were run by the Municipal Council, so their teams joined the 'Bantus'. It was from this that the political and racial division which created modern soccer in South Africa began.

It was into this burgeoning activity that scholars and labourers from colonial Zimbabwe came. Since the first diamond was discovered, South Africa has always been at the centre of the southern African regional economy. Millions of Africans have been drawn to South Africa from countries as far away as Tanzania, Angola and Zambia. In South Africa the best wages available on the continent are to be found. Zimbabweans also undertook this trek to the south. There they too discovered the game of soccer and took it back with them.

Some of the first northern migrants did not seek employment. Instead, they went to South Africa to receive higher education, which was impossible in colonial Zimbabwe until the Second World War. During the 1920s and 30s elite Zimbabweans were found at Zonnebloem, Adams and Lovedale Colleges. (Nationalist leader, Joshua Nkomo went to Adams College in the late 1930s.) As a consequence, they also discovered soccer, as did their colleagues who went in search of employment. For example, C. Lobengula, a grandson of late Ndebele King, was a student at Zonnebloem at the turn of the century. He played centre half for the College between 1905 and 1907 and, later, became its club secretary (Couzens 1983).

However, it was while working in South Africa that the majority of Zimbabweans discovered soccer. This was the case for Benjamin Burombo, one of the important nationalist figures of the 1940s in Zimbabwe. He perfected his football while in Johannesburg during the previous decade. There, he lived in Alexander Township, and worked in Johannesburg as an assistant chef. Of the two teams organized by Zimbabweans in Alexander at this time, the Mashonaland Club and the Home Sweepers, Burombo played for the former. On his return to Zimbabwe in 1937, Burombo set up and coached a team on a pitch next to his home in Selukwe. This team played against teams from Selukwe Mine as well as local schools (Bhebe 1989).

Burombo was typical of his generation. The game was taught at the few Zimbabwean primary schools for Africans which were run by missionaries, such as Seventh Day Adventist and American Board Missions. Yet it was mass migration south which introduced Zimbabweans to the range, depth and popularity of African soccer in South Africa. They participated in the soccer leagues there and improved their skills. Most important of all, migrants adopted many of the methods they found in South Africa and brought them back to Zimbabwe.

The beginnings of soccer in Zimbabwe

African migrants were not the only ones from colonial Zimbabwe to take an interest in soccer as it developed in South Africa. White settlers also took the game north when they trekked into what is now Zimbabwe during the last decade of the nineteenth century. Clubs called Police, Kopje and Causeway played in Salisbury (Harare) in the early 1890s. The latter two clubs later changed their names to Alexandra and Salisbury respectively. Settler clubs such as these played in the colony's first league overseen by the Salisbury Association League, whose first President, J.H. Deary, donated a cup for this competition.

The Salisbury Association League had changed its name to the Mashonaland Football Association in 1908. In that year a national team was selected from the Matabeleland and Umtali (now Mutare) and the Mashonaland Association, and sent to South Africa to compete in the Currie Cup. In 1929 the first international match was played in colonial Zimbabwe when an English Football Association team, led by Jimmy Seed, visited the colony.

The usefulness of the game as a form of social control in South Africa had not escaped the attention of Zimbabwe's colonial authorities. In Zimbabwe, as in South Africa, colonization had pushed African communities off land to make way for whites to develop substantial cattle and maize farms. The dispossessed were forced into colonial Zimbabwe's developing industrial sector and had to endure the accompanying urban ills. At Wankie, in northern Matabeleland, for example, a massive mine and its accompanying labour compounds had been established in the west of the colony. Elsewhere small gold mines were also developed. At the centre of all this activity was Bulawayo. Here, the railway had been forced through from South Africa during the first decade of this century. With it came commerce, speculators and supplies from South Africa and Britain.

Bulawayo, as the colony's primary import and export city, attracted most of colonial Zimbabwe's main industry. The marshalling yards of the newly established Rhodesia Railways were located there and mine engineering firms proliferated in the town, as did engineering firms in support of the local agricultural industry. This economic activity placed Bulawayo at the heart of the colony's economy for most of the colonial period. Bulawayo's importance reached its zenith during the decade after the Second World War. At that time tens of thousands of African labourers migrated to Bulawayo to work in this industry. There they found African labour from all the neighbouring colonies, including South Africa. There were also migrants from the most remote regions within Zimbabwe itself, including the rural areas bordering Bulawayo. The conditions were similar to those common in the South African gold mines and industrial centres. As in South Africa, migrant workers were forced to live in squalid, putrid and overcrowded compounds and locations. Yet these were the fortunate ones. Employers and Bulawayo's Municipality refused to invest in housing for its African population, so the growth of shanty towns, a common feature in the big cities in South Africa, was repeated in Bulawayo.

These impromptu 'villages' were without facilities, without even clean water. They harboured disease and death was ever present. The harshness of life in Bulawayo created a community spirit within the many yards, compounds and squatter camps, which took the form of ethnic-based self-help associations. Each provided some of the essential social services for those forced to live and work in the town. They also provided access to jobs in the ethnically divided workplace.

As in South Africa, the authorities in Zimbabwe feared the potential for social discord and industrial action among its urban-based African workforce. As the Great Depression reached its height in Southern Africa, violent and prolonged riots broke out in Bulawayo during the Christmas vacation of 1929. This sent officials from colonial authorities scurrying south to learn about the methods employed there to impose a degree of social control over their burgeoning urban African population. It was during one of these trips that the idea of adopting state-run sport, particularly soccer, in colonial Zimbabwe was considered.

The game had already been introduced by returning migrants such as Burombo. However, they had little equipment, having to rely upon rudimentary balls made of bark covered by animal skin. The game spread in an unplanned, haphazard way. Nevertheless, by the end of the 1920s soccer pitches had sprung up in remote villages and towns across Zimbabwe. Yet it was not until the authorities took an interest in the game that a coordinated league structure was first established. Again, it should be remembered that this was not a policy to provide universal sport in Zimbabwe, rather its sole purpose was the town's social control.

Soccer's introduction in Bulawayo was a great success. A former African trade union activist reluctantly agreed that organized sport had a great impact upon Bulawayo's African inhabitants when it was first introduced in the 1930s. Bored young men were the main constituency for the militant trade union in Bulawayo of that day, the Industrial and Commercial Union (ICU). They were also the most enthusiastic converts to soccer. Participation in sports such as cycle racing, soccer and basketball gave these young men the chance to win cash prizes and equipment. Sport quickly had an impact on the intensity of mass worker militancy as well as street fights and drunkenness. As weekend sport became established, attendance at ICU meetings fell away dramatically.

By the end of the 1930s soccer was flourishing in colonial Zimbabwe's main urban centres. The African Welfare Society (AWS), entrusted by the authorities to run black recreation, took the credit. Run by a Methodist minister, the AWS was a benign organization, allowing African soccer teams a degree of freedom to organize and compete in the local leagues of each province. One of the most successful branches of this charity was the Matabeleland AWS. This branch allowed the local African teams to organize their own association, called the Bulawayo African Football Association. By 1938 it was competent enough to run all soccer in Bulawayo. In that year control of the junior African football clubs in Bulawayo was handed over to the African Football Association.

One year later soccer in Bulawayo was almost completely African controlled. The Association itself was run as an autonomous organization responsible only to the Management Committee of the Matabeleland AWS. It had its own constitution, bank account and African officials, and came under the direction of only the Welfare Society's welfare officer. By 1941 the football season lasted for nine months and consisted of 16 teams competing in the local league regularly each weekend.

The Mashonaland African Welfare Society established and sponsored the Governor's Cup competition for Salisbury's (Harare) African soccer teams. So popular was this local competition, teams outside the City also wanted to take part. In 1933 the Secretary of the Umtali District Native Football Association protested to the Prime Minister at the failure to invite teams represented by his organization to participate in the Cup competition. Indeed, the organization of football – around the Governor's Cup in the Salisbury province and, nationally, around the Osborn Cup (which was donated by the Governor in 1937) – was the AWS's most significant achievement (West 1990).

Bulawayo's Football Association and league remained the most dynamic in Zimbabwe. It jealously guarded its independence. The names of some of the clubs in this local league were the Matabeleland Highlanders, the Mashonaland Club, the Northern Rhodesia Club, the United Africans Club and the Home Sweepers Club of Western Commonage. There was also a town team, known as the Red Army. The Red Army forged links with teams all over Southern and Central Africa, regularly playing teams from Johannesburg, Bechuanaland, Mashonaland and the Belgian Congo.

SOCCER AND PROTEST

Despite the popularity of soccer among Africans, the state's use of the game as a form of social control failed. Labourers were not diverted from protesting about the low wages and oppressive conditions they had to endure in the towns. Both in South Africa and colonial Zimbabwe these protests took the form of strikes. The soccer teams were at times the focus of these protests after the Second World War. The clubs had an elite background, but also drew in many workers. It may be reasoned that from the post-war period onwards, soccer, at different times, became an embodiment of the political aspirations of the African people.

The soccer club was one of the very few African-run organizations that the colonial authorities would tolerate. Trades Unions, political organizations, even ethnically based 'home' societies were either banned altogether or very carefully controlled. In the soccer crowd there was a refuge for political and nationalist leaders constantly in fear of government spies or arrest. Soccer, popular among both the labouring classes and the African elite, became an ideal tool with which to win mass support from the majority of the population. African political leaders were not slow to exploit soccer in this way. Even today politicians in Africa always ensure that they are closely associated with the most popular teams in their country.

Finally, it should be remembered that the soccer clubs were a feature of the urban areas, so they usually represented one or other of the major ethnic communities, themselves creations of the city. Clubs invariably had a close identity with the people in that part of town where they were located. The success or failure of a team was also that of the ethnic group it represented. Soccer became the embodiment of the African experience in the city. Thus, in the decades that followed its introduction, soccer became an African possession. It was part of the experience of living in Bulawayo, Johannesburg, Lagos or anywhere else that it was played across the continent. The game was wrested from European control and used by the African population to assert their new urban identity. The game became an expression of defiance towards the state and of independence from their colonial oppressors.

Protest took the African game into the modern era. In colonial Zimbabwe this was explicitly the case, as demonstrated by a soccer boycott which began among black players in Bulawayo in 1947 and lasted two years. The issue that sparked the boycott was the question of 'ownership' of the game in colonial Zimbabwe.

Organized soccer was controlled by the colonial authorities. Its purpose was just another tool of social control. From the authorities' point of view, along with the Pass Laws, compounds, taxation, segregation and the restriction of the right to vote to the white population, sport was simply another control weapon in their armoury.

Black Africans now demanded to take full responsibility for the game they considered to be their own. Prior to the boycott, the most educated from the black population were allowed merely an unpaid advisory role in the running of soccer. No decision was made outside an all-white committee, from major financial matters right down to the all-too-frequent disputes between clubs. Even the officials, referees and linesmen were selected by this white-controlled committee. Finally, all the pitches on which games were played were owned by the municipality. The elite players wanted a greater say than this.

The meagre power of the African-run Bulawayo African Football Association depended upon the willingness of the welfare societies to continue to oversee African soccer. Direct control by the local authority would sweep away even this meagre influence enjoyed by African clubs, a fact that the players were patently aware of.

But, in 1947 the Bulawayo African Football Association was told that at the beginning of the new season control of all African soccer would pass from the AWS to the municipality forthwith. This change meant a dramatic reduction in the players' influence on their game. They would now have to make representations to a junior welfare officer, who would, in turn, report these to the municipality's recreation committee if he so chose. This committee, the weakest within the local executive, was an unsatisfactory guardian of African soccer. The municipality held punitive powers over the clubs. It owned all the pitches on which African league games were played. It collected all gate money. The kit worn by the top clubs was purchased and dispensed by the municipality and the quality of the facilities depended solely upon it.

Rather than bend to the will of the new controllers of local African soccer, the clubs chose to fight. Their tactic was to boycott indefinitely all municipal organized soccer. This strategy of confrontation was in keeping with other events taking place in Bulawayo at this time. In 1945 a week-long strike by African railworkers had paralysed the rail network as far as the Copper Belt in what is now Zambia. The concessions won by these workers inspired the rest of the city's workforce. For the next two years wildcat strikes erupted all over the city, causing great disruption. Two city-wide African trades unions were established in the year following the rail strike and they spent the next two years squabbling over who had the ear of the workers. Finally, in 1948, a city-wide general strike called for by all the black labourers turned into a two-day total strike which engulfed the entire colony.

It was in this atmosphere that the strategy of a soccer boycott was decided upon. The two charismatic leaders of the two large unions, Benjamin Burombo and Sipambaniso Manyoba, were also involved in the soccer protests. Burombo's history has already been described, while Manyoba's has not. He was not only the captain of his local team, the Matabele Highlanders, he also captained the city team, the Red Army. To him, as a soccer player, this attack by the municipality was consistent with their treatment of the entire black population within their jurisdiction. It was the largest employer in the city and had primary responsibility for administering by-laws established to control the local black population.

Initially, the municipality was not concerned about a prolonged soccer boycott. Its welfare officer reported that he was confident that with the right level of inducement selected teams would be persuaded to join the municipal league. With the blessing of the recreation committee, this officer offered individual teams substantial material and financial bribes, such as new kit and balls as well as generous prize money, if they joined the new council-run league. However, by the end of the first league season the boycott held firm. Not one team had agreed to play for the municipality.

1948 saw more confrontation between the colonizers and colonized than any year since the 1890s. The municipality was determined to make an example of the soccer players and to impose the municipal league on them. To this end they raised the bribe to selected clubs. This time the municipality also offered to maintain and improve Barbour Fields (the principal location of the city's soccer pitches), supply all sports equipment free of charge, meet all travelling expenses and even provide compensation for injury. In return for what appeared to be a generous offer, the African Football Association had to surrender its financial independence to the municipality. This proved completely unacceptable to the clubs. Throughout 1948 the boycott held firm and no soccer was played in Bulawayo for a second season.

This exceptional year of African defiance culminated in a colony-wide general strike. African sport, which was supposed to be a central tool of colonial social control, had become another weapon with which Africans could challenge the authority of the colonial state. What really scared the local authority was that this protest was beginning to spread to African soccer associations in other towns.

To end the dispute, the municipality capitulated at the end of 1948. They agreed to accept the independence of the soccer clubs and their Association. They then entered into negotiation to agree the status of the Association and the extent of its new authority. Thus the soccer players achieved a remarkable victory. Nothing of the kind had ever taken place before in the history of the colony.

After protracted negotiation it was agreed, first, that both the Football Association and the municipality would establish a joint body to oversee the use of Barbour Fields, though no definite lease would be given. Second, and most important, the League would be allowed to charge gate money on the understanding that it would be entirely self-supporting in regard to the purchase of equipment and clothing. In effect, the Football Association had been given what it had wanted; it was now solely responsible for soccer in Bulawayo.

The independence of the Association was recognized on 9 March 1949. The success of the Bulawayo soccer players was quickly emulated elsewhere in the colony. In Mutare, Harare and Gweru soccer associations broke away from their municipal masters and established independent organizations. The Rhodesian Bantu Football Association, as it was first called, had its constitution formally accepted in 1953. In that year a national Football League was established to which all clubs were affiliated.

The establishment of a fully independent African-run football association should not blind us to the facts of soccer life in the colonial period. The popularity of the game and its expansion in colonial Zimbabwe was not enough to ensure its universal appeal. Nor did it mean that the majority of schoolchildren were exposed to it at school. Also, even the best players earned very little from the game.

While the formation of the Football Association may have been politically significant, detaching the state from the running of the game may have fatally retarded the development of the African game in Zimbabwe. The tiny African Football Association would never command the resources to match the levels of investment colonial authorities in Kenya, Ghana, Sudan or Nigeria, for example, put into African sport. The colonial period remained the real impediment to any dramatic development of soccer in Zimbabwe, as in the rest of Africa. We shall now turn to the post-colonial period to see how this situation was transformed.

AFRICAN SOCCER IN THE MODERN ERA

Without an appreciation of the rich and varied history of the game of soccer in Africa, it would be difficult to understand its role on the continent today. Unlike soccer traditions in Europe, soccer has always been a universal game in Africa – one which transcends class, ethnic and even gender divisions. Soccer, like the African nation-state itself, had to be wrested from the colonial master. The game is closely associated with the bloody struggle for independence and the creation of the nation-state. As a consequence, it has become an integral part of the identity of Africa's population.

The African struggle for independence has always been a fight to join the world community of nations. From the beginning, a desire has existed among all Africa's nation-states to be recognized as fully mature and able to make a significant contribution to the modern world. For this reason, soccer has always been considered to be one of the most important modernizing forces of the continent. The degree of competence an African state has achieved is measured on the soccer pitch. Games between neighbouring states and against Western teams are treated as an unofficial assessment of a state's progress. The boycott of South African sport probably had a bigger impact on that country than any other sanction. The World Cup Tournament, the ability to compete at the highest level, has become the ultimate measure of progress.

Ghana: dazzle and decline

Modern soccer in Ghana is a case in point. Soccer became one of the dazzling symbols of a newly independent Ghana. Ghana has long been considered one of Africa's princes of soccer – a reputation that was well deserved. Ghana's Black Stars won the African Cup of Nations at consecutive tournament finals in 1963 and 1965. In these finals they defeated Sudan 3–0 in Accra and Tunisia 3–2 in Tunis. The next tournament, held in Addis Ababa in 1968, again saw the Black Stars reach the final. This time they had to be satisfied with the runners-up medals, losing 1–0 to Zaire (then known as Congo-Kinshasa).

Players such as Osei Kofi, Mfum and Odametey personified Ghanaian success throughout the heady 'liberation years' of the 1960s, not to mention the coach C.K. Gyamfi. Victory after victory on the international soccer field propelled the Black Stars to a level of fame never before achieved by an African soccer team. The Ghanaian state and people basked in reflected glory. This appeared to confirm the promise of a golden era not only for Africa's first independent sub-Saharan state but for the whole of Africa. Yet, these successes have been eclipsed by the teams of other African states and are now merely 'memories', as described by Ben Dotsei Malor (Malor 1991).

The success of the Indomitable Lions of Cameroon at the 1990 World Cup in Italy was welcomed fulsomely by Ghana, as by the rest of Africa. Yet in Ghana the success of their near neighbours also left a lingering sense of national failure. As Ben Malor suggested, the feeling in Accra was '. . . if The Lions could go that far, why not the twinkle, twinkle "Black Stars" of Ghana!' (Malor 1991). In contrast to the Lions, Ghana's Black Stars have had abysmal World Cup campaigns. The Ghanaian experience in the two most recent World Cup tournaments neatly summarizes this ill-fortune.

Ghana's journey to the 1990 World Cup Finals was halted, in the opinion of most Ghanaians, by the Lone Stars of Liberia, prior to that country's sad decline into civil war. Defeat ensured Ghana's elimination at the pre-liminaries stage. Four years later this pattern has been repeated and Ghana has already exited the 1994 United States' World Cup Finals. This time the Black Stars needed to beat Algeria to progress to the second round of the African section of the preliminary rounds. Despite the presence of the African Player of the Year, Abede Pele, and Nii Lamptey Odartey, Ghana lost the game 2–1 in Algiers. The seeds of this West African disaster were sown in an earlier match which the Black Stars lost 1–0 to Burundi in Bujumbura. Pele Ayew is thought of as the most accomplished player on the African continent. His absence from the World Cup Finals is a tragedy for both Ghana and African soccer.

Such a stunning reversal by a team thought to be one of the most accomplished in Africa has caused a great deal of soul searching in Ghana. Success in the continent-wide competition, particularly the African Cup of Nations, has offered scant consolation for the Ghanaian public. The Black Stars played magnificently to reach that tournament's final in 1992 only to be narrowly defeated by Cote d'Ivoire in a penalty shoot-out. In fact, far from creating a sense of pride in Ghana's national side, such a performance only makes World Cup failure harder to accept.

Success on the sports field and national progress and pride are inseparable, which means that soccer failure can very quickly be perceived as political failure. The reverse may also be true. In the case of Ghana, success on the soccer field coincided with rapid economic and political progress and a sense of national strength. Now, defeat brings introspection and a sense of decline. In Ghana today a national debate is underway to identify the cause of this soccer malaise.

There is a perception that the two principal clubs in Ghana, Accra Hearts of Oak and Kumasi Asante Kotoko, may be too dominant. In the opinion of some, not only do they monopolize the domestic trophies, their fans are too partisan. It is quite common for the supporters of one club to rejoice at the elimination of their rivals from international competition, such as the Africa Cup of Champions. This is called the 'against factor'. Fans of Kotoko, for example, took to the streets in celebration when their rivals, Hearts, were defeated at the quarter-final stage of the 1990 African Cup Winners Cup (Malor 1991). It is thought that such intense rivalry between these traditional opponents has prevented players from other clubs gaining the experience necessary to contribute to the national squad.

Match fixing, financial mismanagement and bitter boardroom power struggles are as common in Ghana as in many other nations. The prevalence of such factors is a sign of the close link between local politics and sport. The body politic in Ghana is keen to use soccer as a political weapon with which to destroy rivals, reward friends or enhance popularity. As local commentators observe, it is hardly surprising that top international players have little commitment to the Black Stars when they see their paymasters behaving in this way (Malor 1991). Until the International Federation of Football Associations (FIFA), football's governing body, changed the rules concerning the participation of foreign-based international players in national teams for the 1994 World Cup campaign, Ghana found it almost impossible to persuade her top internationals to represent their country regularly.

The explanations for the decline and fall of Ghanaian soccer are varied. One of the most plausible causes is government complacency. This had set in after the victorious 60s and has continued up to the Jerry Rawlings administration. Successive governments have failed to invest adequately in the sport and the dire straits sporting facilities have fallen into are a national scandal. It has become commonplace for spectators and important dignitaries alike to receive serious injuries from collapsing stands and falling masonry while watching games in stadia kept in an appalling state of repair. In 1989 four people were killed in the Kumasi Sports Stadium, the home of Kotoko, when a portion of the terrace railing collapsed. Along with the Kumasi stadium, the top athletics tracks in Accra have fallen behind the standards of the rest of the world. These infrastructural weaknesses have undermined Ghana's sports effort.

This financial malaise has been belatedly recognized by the Rawlings government. The sight of Cameroon gaining world acclaim at the expense of Ghana has galvanized his government into diverting scarce resources into sport, of which soccer has received an important share. Resources for domestic and international soccer have been channelled through, what has been appropriately called, the 'Soccer Recovery Programme'. This initiative is a sign of the importance of the task of regaining national soccer pride (Malor 1991).

This effort to improve the performance of the Black Stars appears so far to have failed. The team was defeated, albeit in the final, at the 1992 African Cup of Nations finals. Nor were they present at the 1994 World Cup Finals in the USA. However, what should not be overlooked is the performance of Ghana's national youth team. In Scotland in 1989, at the Barcelona Olympiad in 1992 and, most recently, at the Youth World Championships in

Australia in 1993, the team played to its full potential and defeated significant opponents. Perhaps here, with Ghana's future international players, is where the benefits of this investment shall be reaped. This cannot but bode well for the long-term future of national and international soccer in Ghana.

The majority of people in sub-Saharan Africa would quickly recognize what the average fan in Ghana has had to endure. The decline of national soccer in other leading African soccer nations has been as rapid and would evoke a similar level of concern. As in the case of Ghana, this has remained an inward-looking exercise, the assumption being that a remedy lies with this or that action, this or that policy. Included in this exercize is the acknowledgement that soccer suffers, like everything else in Africa, from the ravages of prolonged and painful economic decline. Despite this, little attention has been paid to the most important external reason for the relative decline of the soccer's best African teams – i.e., the general improvement in the standard of soccer all over Africa, and especially in southern Africa.

Despite obvious impediments, soccer has continued to develop and thrive right across Africa during the last four decades. The gap between the very best and very worst national teams has narrowed accordingly. The victory by Cote d'Ivoire over Ghana at the 1992 African Cup of Nations has already been mentioned. National teams as obscure on the soccer map as Burundi can now provide a stiff test for the very best in Africa. The game equalizes individuals from dramatically differing backgrounds; by the same token, it helps to equalize large and small nations. So, players from Liberia, Guinea Bissau, Mozambique and other similar small, poor nations are found in Europe's soccer clubs alongside Ghanaians, Nigerians and players from the Cameroon. The largest African soccer nations no longer have a monopoly on Africa's available playing talent.

A large part of the explanation for this is the spread of free education in Africa's former colonies. With it has come soccer. For the first time children have the opportunity to learn and play the game in numbers approaching their peers in Europe and Latin America. Universal education has been one of the main African success stories. Without it, the associated growth in the numbers who know how to play soccer on that continent would have been much slower.

Accompanying the spread of schools' sport, has been the huge expansion of media coverage of soccer and athletics in Africa. The rewards to be gained through participation in sport are there for everybody to see. Soccer has become a principal route to wealth, social status and mobility for many. This message is reinforced each time the game is beamed into the homes of millions of Africans. International success is a prerequisite, even in the poorest state, and with it comes the dream of personal fame. Soccer can create a modern-day prince. It has a critical part to play in the school yards right across the African continent. Africa's soccer paupers are now seeking to take the crown long held by the princes.

The tragic destruction of Zambia's national team in the air disaster of 28 April 1993 is a case in point. The plane crash killed all 30 people on board, including 18 players and 5 officials. The leading internationals, Kalusha

Bwalya (African Player of The Year in 1988), Johnson Bwalya, Charles Musonda, Kenneth Malitoli and Gibby Mbasela, all of whom are foreign-based players, were not aboard the plane and will form the core of a rebuilt team. Prior to the disaster, Zambia's 'Dream Team' had been one of Southern Africa's strongest sides. Though poverty stricken, Zambia's pool of first class players has continued to grow over the last two decades. Zambian players are to be found in the leagues of Europe, the Middle East and in South Africa. In the 1980s the national team emerged and began to reach the finals of the African Nations Cup on a regular basis. Great things were expected from the squad in the campaigns for both the last World Cup and the African Nations Cup tournaments. Indeed at the time of the disaster the 'Dream Team' was well placed and confident of qualifying for the World Cup Finals for the first time. The assumption that such an achievement was now beyond Zambia would not have been unreasonable, yet this was not the case.

After an appropriate period of grieving and reorganization, Zambia's national team has resumed both competitions with performances as good as, if not better than, the previous team. First, they brushed aside the Senegalese challenge in their latest World Cup Qualifier. To confirm that they are still a force to be reckoned with in African soccer, they then comprehensively defeated South Africa in Lusaka in their latest qualifying match for the African Nations Cup Finals.

The ability of the Zambian national team to recover so quickly from such a tragedy is a tribute to the previous investment in the game which has taken place in earlier decades and which has left Zambia with a large pool of high-calibre players. Furthermore, the desire for success may have been enhanced by the unexpected reverse. For a new generation of players, international soccer has arrived when they least expected it and the importance of the game in Africa means they will certainly not let this opportunity pass them by.

Zimbabwe: the pauper wishes to be prince

As one of the few states which can be described as partially industrialized in Africa, it is peculiar that Zimbabwe's national soccer team does not enjoy a higher profile. The explanation is simple. Zimbabwe only emerged as a nation-state in 1980, the year it achieved political independence. Its national team, the Warriors, has had very little experience of international soccer compared to the majority of African states. This is reflected in its performance over the decade. Until very recently, the Warriors enjoyed little success in either international or continental competitions, failing to reach any finals stage. The sole exception was in 1985. In that year the team managed to defeat Kenya 2–1 to win the Confederation of Central African Football Associations Cup (CECAFA) in front of 30,000 people in Harare's Rufaro Stadium.

Zimbabwe is still perceived to be a pauper among Africa's soccer princes. Although Zimbabwe's Warriors did not reach the 1994 World Cup Finals, this impression is rapidly changing. First, Zimbabwe has maintained, if not enhanced, her political and economic importance in the Southern African region. Until the recent drought struck the area, Zimbabwe was considered a model African economy. Zimbabwe was a net exporter of maize to hungry continental neighbours. As important, Zimbabwe enjoys an open political tradition and a multi-party democratic system, which is also in stark contrast to many of its African peers. Zimbabwe's nine million people have looked to the national soccer team to reflect this political and economic strength. They have never been content with the status of a soccer pauper, desiring rather to be recognized as one of Africa's soccer princes. Furthermore, the recent political change from colony to independent state has made sporting success all the more pertinent. Until it is achieved, the journey from independence to political maturity is incomplete.

Second, today, outside music, Zimbabwe's major stars and heroes are soccer players. Moses Chunga was the first black Zimbabwean to play in Europe, Peter Ndluvo the latest. Bruce Grobbelaar played for one of England's top clubs, Liverpool, and is now with another, Southampton. In Zimbabwe each has come to epitomize the rewards which can follow soccer success. Though they are the best known players who play their soccer abroad, many other Zimbabweans are found in the minor leagues of Europe, mainly in Belgium and Germany. More so than any other celebrity, the soccer star evokes the image of individual success through talent and hard work rather than through nepotism. The abundance of talented players and a moderately stable economy has meant that, at last, Zimbabwe's national team is playing the kind of soccer which is threatening the very best of Africa's leading soccer nations.

The performance of the Warriors is beginning to reflect the potential for success. In August 1992 they soundly beat South Africa in a qualifying round of the African Cup of Nations. Subsequently, the Warriors enjoyed an unprecedented run in the preliminary rounds of the forthcoming World Cup. In the quest to reach the finals in the USA, they even managed to overcome Egypt, the clear favourites in Zimbabwe's first round group.

So Zimbabwe found itself in an unfamiliar position. For the first time the Warriors were on the threshold of qualifying for both the World Cup and the African Nations Cup finals, of 1994. This happy position was a clear demonstration of the improvement of the Zimbabwean game in recent years. Yet it does not mean Zimbabwe has been free from the ills which have afflicted soccer in the rest of Africa. Ironically, international success has been achieved at a time when Zimbabwe's domestic game has been beset by massive administrative problems.

Maladministration, alleged corruption, struggles over the control of top clubs, political interference and crowd violence are a fact of life of Zimbabwe's domestic game today. These factors cannot be understood properly without also taking note of the positive influences upon the game. These include a strong league structure, encouragement of the game at school level, support of national youth teams, comprehensive local sponsorship, the involvement of industry in the sport, government patronage and, finally, strong media interest in both domestic and international soccer.

Organized sport

Soccer is the national sport of Zimbabwe. In the years since Zimbabwe achieved independence the Zimbabwean game has enjoyed a turnover of more than $1 million. Despite only a population of just over nine million, attendances at Zimbabwe's major grounds in Harare and Bulawayo can reach between 30,000 and 45,000 for major league clashes, important cup matches and internationals. The premier league consists of 14 clubs, some semi-professional, of which no one club can be described as pre-eminent. All this activity is overseen by the Zimbabwe Football Association (ZIFA), which replaced the Rhodesian African Football Association of the earlier colonial period. Yet the game's success depends upon the many thousands of people who play soccer just for pleasure right across Zimbabwe.

Domestic soccer in Zimbabwe is organized on both a local and national basis. At the local level it is played right across the country. In each province, in both the rural and urban areas, soccer is played in schools, clubs, the streets and fields by children of all ages. The growth in popularity of soccer among schoolchildren was given a significant boost at independence. In 1980 the government introduced a policy of free primary education and expanded secondary education. This resulted in a rapid growth of enrolment. By the middle of the last decade nearly three million children were attending either primary or secondary school. On the back of this expansion went youth sport, and soccer especially. This new school structure ensured that the game now reached more children than was ever possible during the colonial period.

Beyond school, local leagues have become an intrinsic part of the national structure. Organized on a provincial basis, the local leagues are found in each of Zimbabwe's eight provinces – Matabeleland North, Matabeleland South, Midlands, Masvingo, Manicaland, Mashonaland East, Mashonaland Central and Mashonaland West. This ensures that the momentum achieved in school is maintained once youngsters reach school-leaving age.

The provincial leagues are brought together and linked to the national league structure via league Division Five, the lowest division in that structure. Those teams which succeed at the provincial level compete for entry into either the Northern or Southern sections of the national league lower division. So, it is possible for the smallest clubs in each of the provincial leagues to progress right up to the premier division of the national league, the Super League. The Super League has been the top division in Zimbabwe since independence. However, at the end of the 1992 season the Super League was superseded by a new premier league structure, which will be discussed later.

Rivalry among the top clubs in the Super League has been intense and competition is of a high standard. The Super League received sponsorship from the multinational company BAT, which has significant investments in Zimbabwe. The cup competitions have also enjoyed similar support from major companies who have invested heavily in the Zimbabwean economy. As a result, lucrative prize money is available for the winners of the various competitions throughout the football season. The important Northern and Southern Division Ones receive sponsorship from Rothmans.

The Super League championship lasts eight months, from February to November, and coincides with Zimbabwe's cooler dry season. Fourteen teams compete for the title of League Champion. The three major annual cup competitions are the other prizes available during the season. For the 1992 season, these were the National Foods Africa Day Trophy, for which the winners received 75,000 Zimbabwean dollars [Z$], the Z$175,000 Natbrew Castle Cup, and the Independence Trophy. The names of the two former tournaments demonstrate the level of involvement major companies have in domestic soccer in Zimbabwe. The latter trophy is a reminder of political requirements of the game.

In the early days after independence one or two clubs dominated the premier league. However, today, and in contrast to countries like Ghana, the competition is much more open. During the 1992 season the Black Aces made Zimbabwean history by winning the BAT Super League championship for the first time under the guidance of the veteran Zimbabwean coach, Peter Nyama. What made this achievement more notable was that the Black Aces achieved this during their first season in the Super League, having been promoted from Division One, Northern Region, the previous season. This achievement is a clear demonstration that, at last, smaller clubs are now able to challenge effectively for domestic soccer's highest league and cup honours. As the pool of competent players from Zimbabwe's schools increases, the weaker becomes the stranglehold of the four or five top clubs on the championship and trophies.

In the cup competition in 1992, it appeared that normal service had been resumed. One of the 'big clubs', the Highlanders of Bulawayo, won the African Day Trophy. This was followed by the success of another glamour club, CAPS United, who won the Independence Trophy. This team had built up a fearsome reputation in the cup competitions, and well deserved its folk name 'Cup Kings'. CAPS were also runners up in the Super League for the fourth consecutive year. Yet big club monopoly of the premier soccer trophy, the Castle Cup, had finally been broken when another outsider managed to win in 1992. This time it was a club owned and run by a textile company, Darren T, who pushed past the 'Cup Kings' to take Zimbabwe's most prestigious trophy.

Clubs up, clubs down

Bulawayo and Harare teams have dominated both league and cup competition in Zimbabwe since independence. Harare, the capital of Zimbabwe, is the largest city in the country, having a population of about 700,000. Bulawayo is Zimbabwe's second city. Though no longer Zimbabwe's largest industrial city, Bulawayo is still an important economic centre in Matabeleland. Bulawayo has a population estimated at over 500,000. The city has close associations with both ZAPU, one of the main nationalist parties, and Ndebele ethnic identity. In contrast, since independence the ruling ZANU (PF) has been predominant in Harare, the other main nationalist party, which has close associations with the Shona tribe.

Of the major clubs resident in Harare, the Dynamos is the leading one, and the dominant club in the south is Bulawayo's Highlanders. Each of these clubs, at one time or another, has enjoyed a period of domination in Zimbabwean soccer. Though rivalry between clubs in Harare is strong, it cannot match the intense hostility between the fans and players of Zimbabwe's two top clubs, the Dynamos (known locally as the 'Glamour Boys') and the Highlanders.

This rivalry is based upon regional, political and ethnic factors. First, they are the top clubs in Zimbabwe's two principal rival cities. Second, they are enmeshed in the web of politics and sport. The two main nationalist parties have adopted the respective clubs as ways of identifying with the mass of the population in each city. Finally, support is akin to ethnic allegiance. Each club has a long history of association with the two main rival ethnic populations in Zimbabwe, the Ndebele and the Shona. For a time in the early years of Zimbabwean independence, political allegiance went hand-in-hand with ethnic identity. This meant support for one or other of these clubs was part of partisan political expression.

They are the only clubs in Zimbabwe able to survive on gate takings alone. Each draw crowds of 10,000 to 30,000 on a regular basis. With this kind of support the clubs are financially strong and can attract the best players available. At one stage, as in the case of Ghana, they threatened to monopolize both the league championship and the major cup competitions. Between them they shared all the available trophies during the first five years after independence. The vast majority of players in the national team came from the Highlanders and the Dynamos.

Only in recent years has this duopoly been broken. Today other teams have begun to enjoy a greater share of league and cup success, and have had their players represent the country. The underlying reason for this relative decline in the dominance of the Highlanders and the Dynamos has been the recent structural change within Zimbabwean soccer. This is a reflection of the emergence from the colonial past where resources were concentrated on a minority at the expense of the majority. Today, resources such as education are spread more evenly throughout society. Alternative centres of power have the opportunity to develop and survive. Sport, and particularly soccer, has benefited from this process.

More young players of a higher quality are now available. At the same time, more sponsorship and other resources have been put into the game. Clubs beyond the Highlanders and the Dynamos can afford to obtain higher quality players, a luxury which was once only available to the strongest clubs in the country. The rise and fall in the fortunes of the Dynamos is indicative of this change.

In 1995 the Dynamos will celebrate their 30th birthday. The club was established immediately after Ian Smith's rebel Southern Rhodesian Government imposed UDI in 1965. The Dynamos have always had a political identity. The club also has a proud record of playing soccer to a consistently high standard and has won more trophies and championships than any other soccer club in Zimbabwe. Located at Rufaro Stadium in the Mbare district of Harare, its huge popularity has been sustained by an almost religious following from fans from the poorest areas of the city. Its location in the poorest district of Harare means that the Dynamos are perceived to be the people's team and are affectionately called 'De Mbare'.

Guaranteed gate takings and the huge popularity of the club has always attracted Zimbabwe's very best players. The pinnacle of the domestic career of the most talented players was to play for the Dynamos. Of those, only the best players ever make it into the first team to earn the accolade of being one of Zimbabwe's 'Glamour Boys'.

The fortunes of the Dynamos have reflected the political climate of the day. The club was established as a direct challenge to the Ian Smith regime and the imposition of proto apartheid policies. The excellence of the sixties team made the Dynamos and the people of Mbare impossible to ignore. However, in the opinion of many, the team reached its pinnacle between 1975 and 1979 – the time when the guerilla war had begun to turn against the Smith regime. Dynamos' games became the medium through which urban Africans were able to demonstrate their defiance and strength to the fading white minority.

Today the Dynamos are a pale shadow of those heady years. The club still enjoys partisan support, but the team's performance on the field has been very disappointing. They failed to win a single trophy in the 1992 season, whereas just one season earlier the Dynamos were the Super League Champions and Castle Cup victors. This slump in performance can be attributed to a very vicious boardroom struggle that has raged for two seasons – a struggle which at one point brought into question the very survival of the club.

By the middle of the last season there were, in effect, two rival executive committees, two rival chairmen and also two teams – one recognized by ZIFA, the other not. The senior players demonstrated their allegiance to the committee which was not recognized by ZIFA and spent the rest of the season playing friendly matches. The remainder of the weakened Dynamos playing staff followed the chairman supported by ZIFA and saw out the league obligations. The fans made their views known by beating up the players supported by ZIFA and demanding the resignation of the ZIFA-backed executive.

This off-the-pitch wrangle was about the financial control of the wealthy club and it all but destroyed the Dynamos. It accounts for the poor performance of the team on the playing field and has brought into question the way in which the officials run Zimbabwean soccer. This dispute is just one symptom of a wider crisis in the Zimbabwean game. In this crisis the very authority of ZIFA has been fatally undermined.

At the beginning of the 1992 season a new ZIFA executive was voted in to control and manage domestic Zimbabwean soccer by the nation's largest soccer clubs. This change was welcomed as a break with the past. The old ZIFA executive had been in control since independence and had lost the confidence of the clubs whose interests they were supposed to oversee. In the opinion of many, the old executive had been inclined to use their association with soccer for partisan interests rather than to promote the game. Indeed, because the new chairman had extensive experience as a former player and coach, many hoped that a modern, professional executive would guide domestic and international soccer in Zimbabwe into the future.

Unfortunately, allegations of corruption and discord within the ZIFA executive marred this promising start. This was compounded by suspicion that the association was keeping a larger share of the gate takings from domestic league games than it officially stated. Finally, outrage and anger was expressed when it became clear that ZIFA had not only failed to resolve the Dynamos dispute but had chosen to intervene and take sides. The spectacle of a government minister resolving a dispute within ZIFA's province fatally undermined the last vestige of confidence the largest clubs had in the newly elected executive.

As a consequence, the clubs have turned their backs on plans ZIFA had to establish and oversee Zimbabwe's first professional league. Instead, they established their own 16-team National Premier Soccer League. This league is independent of ZIFA control and, most important of all, a larger portion of the monies raised from gate receipts will remain within the clubs. This overturns the old system whereby ZIFA oversaw and collected all gate receipts and allocated a percentage to the clubs. The new arrangement deprived ZIFA of its income and weakened its influence on Zimbabwean soccer. It remains to be seen what role Zimbabwe's official link with world soccer will have in the domestic game in the future.

This battle was put into sharp relief by other developments in the domestic game. The 1992 Super League Champions were the Black Aces. This success confirms the improvement in the general level of play in the Zimbabwean game. In addition, the Aces is Zimbabwe's first all-professional team. The club's modern approach to training, player welfare, health and security has given it a significant advantage. The rivalry and infighting hid the fact that Zimbabwean soccer is no longer dominated by a few clubs who monopolize available resources.

ZIFA's virtual demise is a lesson for those who think it is still possible to impose an autocratic administration on the running of domestic soccer. The structure of Zimbabwean soccer has changed and there are new lessons to be learnt. The primary one is that other clubs will also have to embrace professionalism as without it they will be unable to keep up with the Aces; nor will they meet the rising expectation of the many young, talented, players now leaving Zimbabwe's schools.

Playing for the Dynamos is no longer the pinnacle of a player's career, rather it is merely a stepping-stone to richer pastures. The dispute which struck the team has left some players very disenchanted. Vitalis 'Digital' Takawira, the 21-year-old Dynamos and Warriors striker, is a case in point. A top striker in the tradition of Dynamos players David Mandigora, Japhet Mparutsa and Moses Chunga, Vitalis is no longer content to wait for a call from European soccer. Instead, he has let it be known that he is willing to trek south to play soccer in South Africa.

More and more players from the biggest clubs in the country are following Takawira's lead and moving south. There are a number of motivations for

Zimbabwean players to make such a move. The wages on offer in the south are not matched in Zimbabwean soccer; the general standard of living for soccer players is higher; and the sports facilities are also better. Yet moving south does have its disadvantages. Unlike European soccer, the standard of South African soccer is very poor. This means that the loss of players to South Africa will not be compensated by an infusion into Zimbabwean soccer of new techniques and knowledge of the game when they return. Furthermore, this movement is happening just as Zimbabwe has begun to exploit its investment in its own domestic soccer and address management weaknesses and the misuse of resources. The Zimbabwean game looks as if it is on the threshold of great things, but the situation in the south may undo a great deal of the work done over the past decade.

The management hot seat

Whatever happens on the domestic scene, success on the international stage will be the defining influence. It will directly affect the fortunes of many hundreds of players and their chances of playing in Europe. For hundreds of clubs in Zimbabwe, international success will mean additional resources from increased gate-takings, sponsorship and from the sale of players.

The person responsible for the national squad is the team manager. In Africa this has always been a very controversial position to hold. Prior to the final match of the eighteenth African Cup of Nations, the Cote d'Ivoire manager, Yeo Martial, held a news conference. At it he dedicated the final to African coaches. He then pointed out that of the semi-finalists, only the Cote d'Ivoire had an African manager. For Ghana there was the German Otto Pfister; for Nigeria, Clemens Westerhof from Holland; and Cameroon had Phillip Redon from France. Yeo Martial said he wanted an Ivorian victory as a slap in the face for his opponents who employed foreign coaches. His wish was granted.

The implication behind Martial's words is a little misleading. His feat of guiding the Code d'Ivoire to victory should be applauded, yet of the eighteen Africa Nations Cup championships, an African coach has guided his team to victory on eight occasions. The Ghanaian team's four victories have all been overseen by an African coach. On three occasions, in 1963, 1965 and 1982, the Black Stars won the tournament with the great C.K. Gyamfi at the helm. Nobody else has even come close to his record.

Nevertheless, the appointment of Europeans to manage either the national team or domestic clubs is a controversial issue in Africa. In the past, due to Africa's enforced isolation from the soccer world, foreign coaches were the only option for countries anxious for swift improvements to their domestic game. Sending African coaches to obtain coaching certificates in Europe was costly and a very slow process. It represented a substantial investment for the future. On the other hand the recruitment of foreign coaches was a cheap short cut to soccer expertise. They also created the convenient impression of a soccer administration willing to leave no stone unturned to achieve soccer success.

Today, this option is no longer tenable. These highly paid individuals can bring nothing more to the African game than an African coach could achieve. Yet the foreign coach is still of value in the African game. First of all, the expense of sending an African to a European coaching clinic is still prohibitive. Scarce foreign currency limits impoverished Africa. The choice of a national coach is always a highly charged political decision. The position has a high status and an important profile, not to mention the substantial income. It means that the post is rarely given on merit. Governments and football associations have political promises to meet or friends to reward. The political nature of such an appointment may mean that on occasions the sacking of an African coach might provoke a political crisis.

The appointment of a foreign coach can avoid accusations of corruption or nepotism. Furthermore, if and when things go wrong the foreign coach, who is without a political base, is easily made the scapegoat and sacked. Martial's criticism does ignore the fact that the best foreign coaches have grasped of the needs and demands of the African game. Many have spent a substantial proportion of their careers working with clubs and national teams on the continent. This has given the best of them an unmatched knowledge of African soccer.

The fortunes of two such coaches, Wieslaw Grabowski and Reinhard Fabisch, characterize the experience of the average foreign coach in Africa. Grabowski cut his teeth as assistant coach to the Polish national team before masterminding Zambia's national team's rise to prominence in the early 1980s. In 1984 he guided Zambia's national under-20 side to victory in the Confederation of Southern African Football Associations Cup (COSAFA). He was dismissed and replaced by Colonel Brightwell Banda who reaped the benefits of an improved national team, then known as KK-XI.

The Zimbabwe Football Association, thoroughly dissatisfied with the quality of their local coaches, turned to Grabowski after the Warriors failed to qualify for the 1984 African Nations Cup Finals. As the nation's first foreign coach a lot was expected of Grabowski, especially after his work with Zimbabwe's arch soccer rivals, Zambia.

The decision to recruit a foreign coach appeared to have been justified when Zimbabwe's Young Warriors promptly won the COSAFA Cup in July 1985, defeating favourites Malawi 1–0 in the final. Grabowski failed to repeat this success with the Warriors, which cut short his career as Zimbabwe's national coach. Though he managed to get the Warriors to the verge of qualification for the finals of the 1986 African Nations Cup, it was not good enough. The team imposed on him by the ZIFA executive lost the final match in this competition against Senegal. Their principal striker, Jules Bocande, played an instrumental role in dismantling Zimbabwe's controversial team. Grabowski was blamed and promptly sacked for this reversal.

This was not the end of Grabowski's career in Zimbabwe. After years as coach to different domestic clubs, he was appointed coach to Darren T – a highly motivated team from Chitungwiza, a new town just outside Harare. He was appointed in 1991 when the club was going through off-the-pitch power struggles which eclipsed those at the Dynamos in their ferocity. The subsequent results have been impressive. The pinnacle of Darren T's season was the defeat of CAPS United 4–0 to win the Natbrew Castle Cup.

The highs and lows of African soccer have been Grabowski's training school and he has learnt his lessons well. At the end of the 1992 season he was offered the post of coach to the South African national side, an offer he would surely have accepted five years earlier. On this occasion he turned it down, citing the political uncertainty in that country as a reason. It would not be too surprising if his reference to 'politics' meant the soccer, rather than the governmental kind.

In contrast to the career of Grabowski, that of Reinhard Fabisch could not have been more different. He became coach to Zimbabwe in August, 1992. Of his job he said, 'as a coach, my job is to coach the national team according to what I know to be best for them and not according to what people [ZIFA?] think is best.' It would have been impossible for any previous Zimbabwean national coach, Grabowski included, to make so clear a declaration of independence. No other coach has been fortunate enough to work under the conditions enjoyed by Fabisch.

Fabisch, from the west of Germany, began as a player in the Bundesliga, playing for Borussia Dortmund, and went on to coach the second division teams, Berlin and Cologne. His first experience of African soccer was with the Kenyan national team. In 1986 he was invited to help prepare the national side to qualify for the pending African Nations Cup finals. In that year, Kenya's Harambee Stars qualified for the finals for the first time. Between 1987 and 1991 he coached in the Middle East, Liberia, Nepal and the Philippines. His first assignment in Zimbabwe was as assistant to the Zimbabwean John Rugg, the coach to the national under-23 team. Rugg's task was to prepare the team for the All Africa Games, held in Cairo in 1991. FIFA appointed Fabisch as an instructor to conduct coaching clinics worldwide in the name of the organization. Though his initial role in Zimbabwe was to set up coaching clinics for young players, he received the blessing of his own soccer association to accept Zimbabwe's offer to take up the post of the national team's coach.

Since appointment, the record of Fabisch as national coach has been extremely impressive. In August 1992 the Warriors achieved an historic and sensational victory over South Africa. His African Nations and World Cup campaigns have also been very productive to date. For the first time in Zimbabwe's football history, the Warriors have a real chance of qualifying for the two premier tournaments on the African international calendar. The excellence of the Zimbabwean national side is the main reason for this positive situation. However, Fabisch has also received a substantial amount of the credit for this achievement. It means that, unlike his predecessors, he is in a very strong position as national coach.

CONCLUSION

This chapter began by questioning the assumption that the game of soccer was new to Africa and ended on an optimistic note, suggesting that the

African game is on the threshold of becoming a world force. These contrasting views illustrate the fact that African soccer is, perhaps, at the end of a phase of development which has seen a rapid but painful transformation of the game from a popular domestic pastime to an important leisure industry. Participation by African countries like Cameroon and Nigeria in the World Cup Finals of recent years, has provided a dramatic boost to this process.

As in the past, whether the African game benefits from this process depends on the future social and economic development on the continent. It is likely that this will always remain patchy and inconsistent, with one region enjoying success at the expense of another. However, the key to the continuing improvement may be soccer in South Africa. Only this economy has the potential depth and strength necessary to meet the aspirations of the rising numbers of player in the south of the continent. The invitation to the South African Football Association to join the continent's Confederation of Football Associations in 1992 would lead an optimist to say that the first decade of the twenty-first century will be Africa's decade.

REFERENCES

Baker, W.J. and Mangan, J.A. (eds) (1987) *Sport in Africa: Essays in Social History*, New York, African Publishing Company

Bhebe, N. (1989) 'B. Burombo', *African Politics in Zimbabwe*, Harare, College Press

Clignet, R. and Stark, S. (1974) 'Modernisation and football in Cameroon', *The Journal of Modern African Studies*

Couzens, T. (1983) 'An introduction to the History of Football in South Africa', in Belinda Bozzoli (ed.) *Town and Countryside in the Transvaal*, Johannesburg, Raven Press

Malor, B. (1991) *Focus on Africa*, vol.2, no.3, July/Sept, BBC Magazines

Palmer, R. and Parsons, N. (1983) *The Roots of Rural Poverty in Central Southern Africa*, London, Heineman

Ranger, T.O. (1987) 'Pugilism and pathology: African boxing and the black urban experience in Southern Rhodesia', in Baker and Mangan, op. cit.

West, M.O. (1990) 'African middle-class formation in colonial Zimbabwe, 1890–1965', doctoral thesis

3

DON'T STOP THE CARNIVAL: FOOTBALL IN THE SOCIETIES OF LATIN AMERICA

Maurice Biriotti Del Burgo

INTRODUCTION

To imagine a World Cup without the Latin Americans* is to imagine a World Cup without the blend of flair, rhythm and unpredictability which marks the football of Latin America as a phenomenon apart. It is to imagine a competition devoid of New World 'colour' and of 'carnival'. For the European football fan, it is simultaneously to remove the greatest threat and the greatest thrill that the contest proffers.

Latin-American football has become synonymous with passionate, exuberant crowds, breathtakingly talented players, and a catalogue of successes by the 'big three' national sides – Argentina, Brazil and Uruguay – which has often signalled an unchallenged dominance on the international stage. Football is the national sport of most of the region. As such, both as a participatory and as a spectator activity, it holds sway over Latin America. However, it is only in recent years that serious attention has begun to be paid to the sport by sociologists, ethnographers and historians. This chapter attempts to explain the immense social importance which football has acquired in Latin America and the way in which the sport has become inscribed in national political processes, as well as addressing the development of a style of playing which has become emblematic of these nations' performances.

IMPORTING THE GAME

There is no doubt that the unique character of Latin-American football owes much to the social make-up of the continent and to the early history of the

---

* Latin America here is taken as including the Spanish-speaking countries of the Americas and Brazil. All references to 'the continent' in this article mean this geographical area.

game. When the Spanish, and later the Portuguese and other Europeans, 'discovered' the Americas, they found peoples who had already developed a number of ball games. But football itself was brought over by the English in the latter part of the nineteenth century. In fact, apart from England, Argentina, with the Buenos Aires Football Club founded in 1865, has a longer footballing history than virtually any other nation.

It is of course impossible to outline adequately the footballing history of nations with such divergent sporting and socio-political traditions. By and large, however, it is fair to say that throughout Latin America, the game became, and developed as, the preserve of the English and migrant European communities who lived in the emerging Latin-American metropolises. The case of Uruguay, for example, is fairly typical. William Poole, an English professor at Montevideo University, is credited with bringing the game to the country and the first two clubs which were established have strong English links: in the case of Albion Football Club, the name speaks for itself; while Peñarol, still a potent force in the Uruguayan domestic game, was originally set up by English workers in the Central Uruguayan Railway. This sort of pattern is repeated in Brazil, Chile and other footballing Latin-American nations. The first clubs throughout the continent were exclusively for migrants.

URBAN DEVELOPMENTS

Industrialization, often controlled by companies from Europe or the United States, brought about a shift in population from the country to the cities. Urban centres began to attract workers anxious for jobs in the new industries and prepared to live in densely populated *barrios*. As the process of urbanization began to take hold of Latin-American societies, and as their citizens found themselves confined to a very different and much more restricted social and physical space, the game took on a radically different character. Sailors from England and other parts of Europe would land in the booming ports which emerged around the turn of the century and, spontaneously, football matches developed between them. The rules of the game were gradually taught to the locals, eager for entertainment and distractions from the rigours of city life. It is in this sense that, even today, sociologists of Latin America talk of football having provided a new living-space in the urban context. Teams developed which reflected the new urban divisions: neighbourhood played neighbourhood; factory workers challenged dockers; gangs of street kids would battle it out on makeshift pitches with balls made of stone weights wrapped in rags.

Over this period, a new face of football emerges in the cities. The genteel English aspirations of the middle classes find their counterparts in the working-class celebrations of flair and exuberance which emerge almost spontaneously. The football of the streets and of the ports offers a space for social interaction to the poor and the dispossessed. Football diversifies as the complex ethnic mix of Latin-American societies is reflected in its new-found and enthusiastic devotees. As opposed to the structured and circumscribed club scene of the English game on the continent, with its myth of the 'sportsman' (the amateur athlete who embodied aristocratic sporting values), the new spontaneous football arena provides a forum for mass involvement, mass entertainment, and the ostentatious display of physical prowess.

Street football provides a radical contrast to the predominantly white pastime of the migrant amateurs. Importantly, it provides, perhaps for the first time, an arena for sporting interaction involving the socially disenfranchised: black descendants of former slaves in countries like Brazil; young men from indigenous families newly arrived in the cities in countries like Mexico and Bolivia; the forgotten multitude of mestizos (mixed race Amerindian and European peoples) throughout Latin America. Inevitably, what emerges is a dramatic tension of opposites: the game of the leisured classes versus the football of the poor; the white preserve of the Europeans versus the ethnically diverse, non-white contests played out in ports and slums; the playing fields hosting organized games between clubs in leagues versus the urban sites and makeshift battlegrounds of spontaneous competition.

It is precisely the spontaneity of the popular game, in its early twentieth-century origins, that makes football in Latin America a unique phenomenon. The specific cultural references are different for each Latin-American nation, but the importance of understanding football in terms of its popular working-class cultural roots remains the same. In Brazil, as Matthew Shirts has pointed out, football must be interpreted in a very particular cultural context. It is, he argues, 'part of the characteristic and unique popular culture that emerged in Brazilian cities around the turn of the century [. . .] As such, *futebol* [. . .] should be grouped not with other sports, but within a tradition that includes cultural manifestations such as carnival, Afro-Brazilian religions, popular music and Catholicism' (Shirts 1988). Of these, the notion of carnival is the most useful analogy throughout the continent. Across Latin America, carnivals adorn the calendar, igniting social passions and suspending the seriousness and drudgery of everyday life. In carnivals (most famously the Carnival in Brazil and the Day of the Dead in Mexico) the drama of social interaction is played out in masks and pageantry, in the complex physical language of dances and marches, in the symbols and codes and in the sheer energy of mass participation. The new football *is* carnival. It takes on the character of public festival. It encodes and plays out enmities and conflicts. It suspends solemnity in a frenzy of mass enthusiasm.

HARNESSING CARNIVAL

The ordered world of the established clubs and this carnivalesque development in Latin-American football could not have been more different. The racism and elitism which dominated social attitudes throughout the continent inevitably prevailed in football too. For instance, '[f]or years after the British brought football to Brazil, blacks were barred from Brazilian clubs, and mulattos who wanted to play powdered their faces to look whiter'

(Kuper 1994, 198). The lines were drawn. Football developed its own Latin-American apartheid.

But the new football generated its own momentum, and became a social force in its own right. In the early years of the century, many old-style establishments – not only football clubs but also factory management boards and the like – representatives of Latin America's elite, made attempts to form relationships with working-class teams. At times this took the form of patronage, with an established club funding an affiliated local team. At other times, it took on other dimensions – managers encouraging the creation of football sides among the workers to engender company loyalty and, perhaps more importantly, to divert employees' attentions away from the more damaging spectre of industrial unrest. In these early relationships, forged between the elite and the masses in football, can be seen the origins of one of the most compelling arguments in the analysis of football in Latin America: that football serves as an opiate of the masses, an instrument of mass control, a social adhesive binding the most volatile and precarious of ethnic and political mixes.

Football emerges, through the first few decades of this century, as a potent and at times rather unpredictable force in Latin American societies. In many ways, the history of the game on the continent is the story of a conflict between the spontaneity of a game played in streets, in backyards and in the heart of the sprawling cities on the one hand, and the attempts to harness and control those energies on the other.

FIRST DIVISIONS AND SUPPORTERS UNIONS: FOOTBALL AS A SPECTATOR SPORT

As the early decades of the century wore on, the power of the old-style clubs waned, and in many cases had been totally eclipsed by the inter-clan rivalry which divided the working-class inhabitants of urban centres. Interest in football as a spectator sport swept many nations, and stadia were built which could accommodate the new demand. In Lima, for instance, as the city expanded beyond its traditional colonial boundaries, the migrant workers from rural areas constituted an eager audience for the game. By the 1920s, it was common for crowds of up to 25,000 to gather and watch the sport.

In the emergence of club loyalties and the subsequent processes of collective identification, social divisions were, and in many cases still are, sharply focused in Latin America. Communities from divergent ethnic backgrounds and representing different socio-economic groups vied with each other as they watched games in which passions ran high. Amílcar G. Romero identifies the main characteristic of the football clan, at its most virulently antagonistic in Argentina, as its warlike desire to defeat other clans, cohesion between supporters depending more on their united opposition to a common enemy than on the establishment of social links among themselves (Romero 1986).

The potential for establishing cohesion, however, was from the outset as evident as the articulation of social divisions which the emerging sport afforded. Even cohesion achieved at the expense of rival groups was nonetheless cohesion, and the football clubs that attracted supporters in the cities of the continent often developed a social function quite unlike that of their European equivalents. As Janet Lever has shown, football clubs in Brazil operate like social clubs, welcoming not only the devoted fan, but also the neighbour who simply wants to use the benefit of low monthly fees and good facilities to stave off the loneliness and isolation of city-dwelling (Lever 1983, 1988). The opportunity for identifying with a discrete group in the process affords the club member a chance to integrate into complex urban structures.

With the dynamic potential for collective identification on the one hand, and rivalry between neighbouring factions on the other, came dangers and opportunities. The dangers were ever more alarming: unrest that developed between fans of opposing teams became as potent a force in civil disobedience as strikes and riots. The opportunities meanwhile were there for the taking. Since the end of the nineteenth century, spectators to football matches on the continent had been charged an admission fee. As interest in the sport grew, football became lucrative business.

All of this demanded organization, and throughout Latin America national leagues were established which took charge of arranging matches and controlling the sport in a centralized and coordinated way. This was not always a smooth and seamless process. In many countries, notably Argentina, rival governing bodies jockeyed for position in the 1920s and 30s in an attempt to control a national league whose popularity was self-evident. Furthermore, the attempt to organize the sport at a national level in some way contradicted the very spontaneity upon which the Latin-American game, in its twentieth-century incarnation, was founded. This tension was to be exacerbated by two developments: the establishment of national representative teams, and the legalization of professionalism.

IDENTIFYING WITH THE ENEMY

As teams took each other on across the country, the dynamics of collective identification were altering. Supporters of rival teams from the same state or region were prepared to lay down their enmities in the interests of a neighbouring team defeating one from another region. In her analysis of the main teams of Rio de Janeiro, Janet Lever shows how supporters from Rio get behind a local team regardless of their allegiances. When Botafogo plays a São Paulo team, it receives mascots from all the other big three local sides: Flamengo, Fluminense and Vasco da Gama (Lever 1988).

The possibilities of allegiances extending beyond the boundaries of the specifically defined local community and of the establishment of a national administrative structure made the idea of international representative football in Latin America appealing remarkably early. The structures for international rivalry had been put into place as early as 1901, when a representative side from Argentina took on one from Uruguay, initiating a tradition of 'derby' encounters which has yielded more matches than any other in the world. The

South American championship played by the 10 members of CONMEBOL (Confederación Sudamericana de Fútbol) is the longest running tournament in world football, the first contest having taken place in 1910. The other championship which includes Latin-American nations, CONCACAF (Confederación Norte-Centro-americana de Fútbol), had its origins in the 1924 Congreso Deportivo Centroamericano. The link between football and international competition has long roots in this part of the world.

The prospect of national sides opens up the possibility of football as a means of national identification, but also sees the beginning of links between the sport and its organization on the one hand, and the wider political context of the nation on the other.

ALIANZA LIMA

To represent one's nation is always to take on a status beyond that of a sports person or athlete. It is always in some sense also to act as an ambassador. The question, in the complex make-up of Latin-American societies, arises: who shall represent the nation? This question strikes at the heart of issues such as race, class and citizenship. In the early years of the game's development, the amateur status of all players suggested that the honour be reserved for those who embodied the European ideal of the gentleman-athlete. But, as the football of the streets yielded the staggering talents for which Latin American teams have become famous, the inclusion of black or working-class players became imperative. The desire for footballers both to 'give the right image' of their country and to succeed, could lead to conflict, and risked serious breaks with the carnival tradition.

One notable exception, cited by Steve Hein, is the case of the famous Lima team Alianza (Hein 1988). This was a team which in the 1920s had developed firmly within the tradition of football's carnivalesque street origins and had generated keen local support. It consisted mainly of black players of considerable skill, who had made a sensational impact on various national competitions. Increasingly co-opted into the official circuit of Peruvian football, the team's performances became legendary. In 1929, when Peru entered the South-American Cup, a number of Alianza players were picked to represent the nation. Peru, like many Latin-American societies, was heavily influenced by the cultural models and attitudes of nineteenth- and early twentieth-century Europe. Though made up primarily of indigenous and mestizo peoples, Peruvian society maintained in the early part of the century a systematic prejudice against blacks. It became clear that, because of their race, the Alianza players were not to be given treatment equal to that of their non-black colleagues, either on a personal or a professional level. When they withdrew from the national squad in protest, Alianza was expelled from the National League and barred from competing in official events. Alianza, at first, far from caving in, simply reverted to the traditional makeshift spaces with which football had been so closely associated only a few years earlier, and entertained crowds whenever they played. Their brilliance was matched only by the abject failure of the national team. This example amply demonstrates the potential for conflict. On one side, there is the development of a national sport and the necessary establishment of an institutional grip on the game. On the other, there is the carnivalesque, working-class manifestation of football, which ironically had made the sport so successful in the first place.

The story of Alianza, however, ends with a triumph for the establishment: football was going professional. It was not long before the Alianza players ate humble pie and offered their apologies to the authorities, who were chastened by Alianza's success and were eager to reintegrate them into the national structures. For the most part, the players' willingness to comply was based on the financial opportunities with which doing so presented them. Professionalism meant playing could not only become a way of life, but a lucrative one at that, and with professionalism came new sorts of control. Throughout the 1930s the dynamic between the game's organizing structures and the players altered beyond recognition.

PROFESSIONAL FOUL PLAY

In the 1930s and 40s, the desire to comply with the standards being set by football's international body FIFA and to compete at the very highest level, forced the Latin-American footballing nations to embrace professionalisation wholesale. In most countries, some kind of *ad hoc* remuneration had already been allowed for players, and, just as it had throughout the world, the issue of *shamateurism* had given the lie to the old amateur ideal. Professionalism made it possible for those who were not of the leisured classes to devote themselves full time to football. But it required more layers of control and administration, and, thus, took Latin-American football a little further from its roots as a spontaneous form of cultural expression.

The process was not always smooth. Many had, and indeed continue to have, a powerful dislike of professionalism, and the dispute between supporters of the professional game and its detractors in the early days was often very public and very damaging. Some structures simply could not cope. In Mexico, for instance, the league which had been formed in 1927 to control the national scene (the Federación Mexicana de Futbol Asociación) did not survive the change and was promptly supplanted by another organization, one which was not ideologically opposed to making official payments. With professionalism came inevitable blood-letting.

This kind of conflict was typical of the experience in the early 30s of many Latin-American nations. Uruguay had been the most startlingly successful country in the years of amateur football. After the introduction of professionalism, however, only Peñarol and Nacional, the two most prominent teams, could afford proper remuneration. Quality footballers demanded remuneration worthy of their talents. With the lure of the two big teams within Uruguay, and a host of wealthy teams around the world, other teams simply could not compete, and saw their failure to do so merely compound their financial difficulties. For the next 20 years at least the domestic game was dogged by financial and administrative chaos. Even in Brazil, whose footballing strengths during the middle years of the century have become legendary, it was not until the 1940s that professionalism stopped being the cause of rifts and divisions in the game, and instead began to form a basis for greater organization.

Still today, throughout Latin America, there remains a nostalgia for the amateur game; for its value of 'playing for playing's sake'; for its autonomy; for its privileging of pleasure over profit. The nostalgia is no doubt reminiscent of similar emotions the world over. However, in Latin America, it carries with it a dual implication: traces of the European athletic ideal, and folk memories of the spontaneity and carnival atmosphere of early working-class contests. Nostalgia can therefore take very different forms: a reactionary desire to purge the game of its working-class overtones and return to the days of white middle-class supremacy; or, more commonly, a popular *cri de cœur*, calling for the reinstatement of the values of street football: love, passion, magic.

Professionalism has had undoubted benefits, but it also brought discord. With it came endless administrative wrangles and the spectre of mercenary involvement with the game. For some countries this signalled chaos – the relentless jostling for position in the emerging institutions of the game's internal structure. Players' strikes and messy conflicts over organizational arrangements, coupled with the financial lure of other leagues, have frequently led to the migration of star players. At times, the beneficiaries of national troubles have been other Latin-American nations, but the European leagues have often cashed in too: first-rate Latin-American players are now a regular feature of the game at the top level in Spain and Italy. The loss to Latin America has at times been acute. The fate of the legendary Alfredo Di Stefano is a case in point. When Diego Maradona was hailed recently as the greatest Argentinian footballer of the century, he protested, not without justification, that Di Stefano was better still: in the annals of sport history, Di Stefano ranks as one of the finest footballers of all time. Alfredo Di Stefano left Argentina during the players' strike of 1948 and made his name with the great Real Madrid side of the late 50s and early 60s. In international football he later represented not Argentina but Spain.

THE GOLD OF *EL DORADO*

There was also the potential for the game's domination at the hands of powerful representatives of the continent's vested interests. Increasingly, money became a strong factor in determining the course of the game, in attracting and in retaining the best players. In the most shocking cases the result has been little short of chaotic. No country can epitomize the potential for disaster lurking in the heady mixture of power, money and football, than Colombia. In the 1950s, shortly after the adoption of professionalism, Colombia entered a period known as *El Dorado*. Benefiting from strikes in Argentina and Uruguay, a rebel league, Di Mayor, outraged the world by attracting an unprecedented array of international footballing talent. Footballers from around the world, including the England international Neil

Franklin, were drawn to Colombia by offers of money far above wage levels in their domestic leagues. The major team, Deportivo Municipal of Bogota, was nicknamed Los Millonarios, indicating the extent to which its success was bound up with the strength of its financial backing. Franklin, England's centre half at the time, signed for Deportivo's rivals Santa Fe in 1950 and, thus, missed England's World Cup Finals campaign in Brazil that year. (Football League players Billy Higgins of Everton, Charlie Mitten of Manchester United and Franklin's teammate at Stoke City, George Mountford, also went briefly to play in Bogota; they all received suspensions from the Football Association on their (rapid) return to Britain, since Colombia was not then affiliated to FIFA.)

The effects of this period lasted beyond its four-year heyday. The national game was greatly weakened by the influx of foreign talent, which left the home-grown game depleted. Even after the serious attempts to rectify that situation had restored the Colombian game to respectability (and latterly some notable successes), the link between football and powerful financial backers has remained a major problem in a country beset by the conflicts and rivalries of the drugs cartels. The rumours are often substantiated by events: of players paid off to win or lose, as massive investment or gambling intensifies the bitterness of partisanship. As recently as November 1989, the influence of the drugs barons, and of the high financial stakes which have become a feature of Colombia's football, came to the attention of the international community: when Daniel Ortega refereed a match on which a large bet had been placed by a drug gang, his decisions, unfavourable to the cartel in question, led to his assassination.

The case of Colombia is extreme. But it serves as an illustration of the potential for damage caused, both to the game and to society at large, by the massive importance, both social and financial, which has been invested in the game. Even more powerful, however, are the forces that link football to the consolidation of nationhood.

COMMON GOALS

The nineteenth century in Latin-American history is characterized by a breaking away from the strictures of colonial rule. The twentieth century sees a consolidation of the idea of nationhood throughout the continent. This is manifested by a tireless quest for 'identity' both on a political level and in the field of cultural production. Articulating the nation in paintings and novels, in speeches, in the establishment of museums and other national institutions, becomes a political imperative throughout the continent. Football duly takes its place within a process that sees nationalism asserting itself again and again in the discourses of Latin-American statehood.

For many nations in the region, the very diversity of social and ethnic backgrounds that make up the citizenship can be problematic. Football rapidly becomes one of the central means by which a notion of unity can be inscribed in the national consciousness. Hecht affirms that 'football is without doubt one of the principal factors in bridging the gap between the white and colored races' (Hecht 1968). Aspirations united in support of a common purpose allow a nation to coalesce. Even in cases in which the national team cannot be expected to do well, leading club sides often act as a focus for nation-wide support. The fortunes of Olimpia in Paraguay, for example, have acted as a national rallying-point as they battle it out for the various club trophies of Latin America. Their victories in the prestigious Copa Libetadores (played between clubs across Latin America) in 1979 and 1990, and their defeat of Malmö in the World Club Championship in 1979 united the whole nation behind them, bringing glory not only to one local team, but to the nation as a whole.

A NATION OF FOOTBALL

The claims that can be made of football's ability to influence the national consciousness can go further still. Janet Lever shows how Brazil's military government used the national obsession with football to instil in the people a sense of that country's vast and sprawling geography. National and social cohesion are predicated on some notion of what precisely constitutes the nation. Many remote parts of Brazil were previously known to few of its urban inhabitants. In 1969, the Sports Lottery was set up and was devised not only to raise huge amounts of revenue for social projects, but also to include football results from remote provinces. For the majority, unaware of the extent of Brazil's borders and even of the existence of some of these areas, the football results constituted, literally, their first contact with the shape of their own country. The football network becomes the grid upon which a geographical understanding of the nation is sketched, and football becomes inextricably bound up with the idea of nationhood itself.

Above all, the relation between football and the nation articulates itself not at the club level but at the international level. The national team, selection for which becomes, as in all footballing nations, a matter of intense debate at every level, is public property, especially in the more successful Latin-American countries. Scenes of Eva Peron surrounded by footballers, or being snapped 'kicking off' at important games, show how much capital could be gained for the publicity-conscious political dynasty. In the 1962 World Cup in Chile, when Brazilian winger Garrincha was sent off in an early game, a telegram was dispatched by the Brazilian prime minister Tancredo Neves to FIFA president Sir Stanley Rous, urging him to rescind the decision: this episode demonstrates clearly how important it is for governments to associate themselves with their national team, and to be seen to speak for millions of their citizens' distress when their side's fortunes threaten to wane.

STAGING THE CARNIVAL

Football could also bring prizes of a tangible and direct kind: Latin-American nations have, six times, acted as host to the greatest carnival of them all – the World Cup. Uruguay staged the first final tournament in 1930, the centenary of Uruguayan independence from Spain, and the Centenario stadium in Montevideo, which was built for the tournament, was also a celebration of Uruguay's nationhood. Brazil were hosts in 1950, Chile in 1962, Mexico in 1970 and 1986, and Argentina in 1978. The importance of hosting the contest is difficult to overstate. First there is the money. Then there is the prestige, as the world's attention, particularly in the age of television, is focused sharply and uninterruptedly on the nation. And finally, there is the potential, particularly for those countries which find themselves in a state of difficulty and crisis, for achieving legitimacy either in the eyes of their own people, or in those of the world at large. A case in point is Chile, which was ravaged by a violent earthquake before hosting the Cup in 1962. Millions of dollars of public funds were invested in making the occasion a success. Although some might have argued that the money would have been better spent on other projects, the move to invest in the competition nevertheless met with general public approval. 'Chile must have the World Cup because we have nothing', was the popular slogan and it expresses aptly the desire to be offered the contest which has often led to a single-minded pursuit of nomination.

Getting it right once nomination has been achieved, becomes a matter of grave public concern. There is a grim determination about the way in which Argentina's military junta, compensating for the inadequacies of the previous Peronista Governement, appointed the Ente Autarquico Mundial to oversee the preparations for the World Cup of 1978. Its leader, General Omar Actis, was assassinated on his way to the first press conference. The Argentinian case makes depressing reading. Amid horrific repression by the state, in which many had 'disappeared', and many more had been tortured or murdered, investment in the World Cup multiplied (Glanville 1993, 211). 'A smashing *Mundial* won by Argentina, they reasoned, would make up for the occasional death at home. [. . .] The Junta's slogan, "25 million Argentinians Will Play in the World Cup", was soon popularised to "25 million Argentinians Will Pay for the World Cup."' (Kuper 1994, 174) Despite this, the Montoneros, the left-wing guerrilla movement operating in Uruguay and the Argentine, gave the World Cup free passage, declaring it to be 'a festival of the people.' Rumours abound that, in addition to lavishing huge amounts of public funds on staging the competition, the Junta bribed Peru, whom Argentina had to beat in a second-round match by 4–0 to reach the final. Argentina eventually beat them by an extraordinary 6–0 margin. The running of the Cup is a major political issue and can take on the dimensions almost of a military campaign.

These examples serve to illustrate the importance of being seen to control the football carnival, of using the display of international football to legitimate a regime or even a nation, and to galvanize a population. To watch the contest is a political act; to watch it in one's own country is an act of national affirmation. Through football, in Latin America, citizenship and spectatorship intertwine. Nowhere has this been more evident than in Mexico – twice in recent years hosts to the competition.

On both occasions – in 1970 and in 1986 – Mexico provided excellent facilities, although in 1986, the competition might (and some say should) never have been awarded to Mexico. It had been offered to Colombia, but that nation's rather troubled political record and insubstantial public funds meant that by 1982 FIFA was unwilling to go through with the arrangements. Money, political influence, and above all the enormous power of the Mexican television network, Televisa, whose president, Azcarraga, held a key position in the negotiations, brought the World Cup to Mexico despite strong bids from other nations, and despite the evident problems of altitude and heat (Glanville 1993, 271).

The Aztec Stadium in Mexico City, drenched, in name and in architecture, in the symbols of Mexican, and by extension Latin-American, cultural history became an icon of Latin-American football in its own right. To paraphrase the Mexican intellectual, Carlos Monsiváis, the stadium becomes emblematic of football itself, of Televisa, of the modern way of using common land, of the excitement of young aficionados and, in a sense, of the Mexican nation. Monsiváis demonstrates how, in the celebrations of 1986, in the cultural display of national pride and in the semiotics of the competition, Mexico's citizens were offered a feast of patriotic excess (Monsiváis 1987). The stadium articulates pride and progress. The world's gaze is focused on Mexico. The Mexican wave bids farewell to invisibility and marginality and ushers in the dawn of Mexico's acceptance and integration into the hyper-reality of television's global community.

In the World Cup stadium, politics and football become blurred. The confrontation of teams becomes a contest between nations; the clash of styles, a conflict of ideologies. For countries relegated in the textbooks to the Third World, nations which often feel that they have not been invited to the banquet of twentieth-century international affairs, presiding over the greatest cornucopia of international rivalry is a rich prize indeed. It can serve to lend legitimacy to the country's claim on modern nationhood. Football in Latin America becomes a kind of supplement to history: at times amplifying the historical consciousness; at times replacing it altogether. In 1966, Uruguay's team manager had asserted that 'other countries have their history, Uruguay has its football'. Hosting the World Cup in this context is like hosting world history. As Monsiváis suggests in an amusing subtitle: 'we've always said it, the World Cup should be the new United Nations' (Monsiváis 1985).

'NOTHING CAN STOP US NOW'

If hosting the contest represents legitimacy, winning it represents unbridled joy – and, of course, big political capital. When Brazil triumphed at the 1970 competition, the national team was asked to stop over at Brasilia to receive an official welcome from President Médici. A national holiday was declared. The palace doors, closed since the *coup d'état* of 1964, were thrown open to the public. The players were each given a large cash bonus at a celebratory lunch. Photographs of the president surrounded by the victorious team appeared in all the national newspapers. The World Cup song became the military regime's anthem. Médici's declaration lacked any ambiguity: 'I identify this victory, achieved in the fraternity of sport with the ascension of faith in our struggle for national development.' A poll conducted in 1970, shortly after the victory, found that some 90 per cent of lower-class respondents associated Brazilian success in soccer with nationalism (cited in Lever 1988, 95). Ryszard Kapuscinski reports the feelings of a Brazilian exile at the time: 'The military right wing can be assured of at least five more years of peaceful rule.' (Kapuscinski 1990).

Pelé, whose fame extended beyond Brazil, became a hero of the nation. Inscribed on a photograph of the hero leaping up after scoring, the legend 'ninuem segura maís o Brasil' (no-one can hold Brazil back now) became a significant rallying call in the bid to manipulate the forces of nationalism by the ruling body. In Pelé's biography were encoded the values and aspirations of Brazil. Edson Arantes do Nascimiento (Pelé was merely a nickname) embodied the myth of the ordinary man made good through extraordinary talent and extraordinary application. The boy who would collect peanuts which fell from passing trains and sell them to buy football shirts for his team, became one of the richest men in Brazil celebrated on a special postage stamp to commemorate his one-thousandth first-class goal; indeed he became ubiquitous, an international icon. By appropriating his image, the Brazilian government was cashing in on one of the most potent symbols of success. In the poster campaign, Pelé was Brazil: the footballer had become the nation. Brazil by implication was the once-poor and forgotten child now on the brink of unequivocal international acclaim.

Appropriating football is a political imperative in Latin America. For the politician, to associate oneself with football is at once to align oneself with the people, and to cash in on the fever which football ignites. Soon after Carlos Menem became President of Argentina in 1989 he appeared at the national stadium in Buenos Aires, fully attired in the colours of the Argentine team and kicking a ball around with them. Similarly Menem has made much of his support for the Argentine football club River Plate – an endorsement which carried some risk for a populist politician since River Plate have a strong association with the country's elite. For most Argentinian working-class voters, however, Menem's love of football was more important than his club affiliation and, in general, this political appropriation of the game is not the preserve either of the right wing or the left. It is simply a political fact. Football wins support in Latin America.

FOOTBALL AS RESISTANCE

The sort of manipulation which has been illustrated above is to a greater or lesser degree typical of Latin-American nations. To an outsider, that is a striking phenomenon. Kapuscinski, registering a note of European surprise, relates what he has been told about the region: 'In Latin America, [. . .] the border between soccer and politics is vague' (Kapuscinski 1990). However, the relationship between football and authority in Latin America is complex. For one thing, as da Matta has argued, football marks out a space in which it is precisely possible to escape the rigidity imposed by strictly hierarchical societies (cited in Shirts 1988, 102). Football as it is played in Latin America, with its rich variety of movement, of athletic expression and of surprise, represents a kind of antidote to the regularity and circumscription of everyday life. Once again, one feels the influence of the early manifestations of the Latin-American game, of the myth of spontaneity articulated against the imposition of authority.

Even Brazil's unmistakable appropriation of football to bolster the authority of the state is not without ambiguity. Pelé himself, as Paulo Mendes Campos, the Brazilian poet, observes, is important because he is a *safo*, a man who does forbidden things, who can perform deeds on the field which defy the imagination. To read Pelé merely in the context of the political capital that was made of his success and his career is to miss a central point. Pelé is, as Kuper has suggested, a *malandro*, a working-class, resourceful confidence trickster, who can 'dribble past life's difficulties' (Kuper 1994, 198). The Latin-American style of football defies authority because it is precisely defiance that is encoded within it. As Latin-American players dodge and weave their way past better-fed, better-schooled opponents, the crowds go wild. As in the Brazilian dance/fighting style, the *capoeira*, in which knives are used but each opponent tries to win through trickery and guile, Latin-American football at its best is a carnival of resistance (Kuper 1994, 198–9).

THE *MACHO* AND THE CULT OF THE INDIVIDUAL

This exuberance is culturally determined. Latin-American football is characterized by improvization and individual inspiration. Although football is a team game, it 'allows for maximum exposure of personal merit on the field of contest' (Dealy 1992). The cultures of Latin America are cultures based on individual power, the power of the *caudillo*, or chief. The cult of the *macho*, the man who establishes his honour and authority by articulating his superiority over other men, by winning physical or verbal skirmishes, and over women through the prowess of his conquests, remains fundamental. In football, exhibitions of manly feats of daring, extraordinary displays of cunning, and ostentatious displays of talent are central both to the enjoyment of the game for the spectator and to the rationale for engaging in the sport for the player.

The game in Latin America emphasizes manoeuvring and dribbling rather than the 'scientific' values (especially latterly) upheld by the European style. Players display their ability to perform outrageous acts of courage, elasticity and surprise – right under the noses of their opponents. They display *picardía*, getting away with the unthinkable and doing the impossible. Playing football is about being in the limelight, about bolstering one's self-esteem, about pride, about manhood. The Latin-American footballer *par excellence* is never cowed. He is a hero because he embodies the potency of individual resistance. The importance of the individual cannot be overstated: most Latin-American nations have produced heroes who seem to transcend the fortunes of their team's performances: in Mexico, there is Hugo Sánchez; in Bolivia, the star of the 1963 South American Championship, Victor Ugarte;

in Ecuador, there is the hero of 1966, Alberto Spencer; in Peru, Teofilo Cubillas; in Uruguay, there is Victor Andrade. These names, and those of many other notable individuals, more than the teams for which they played, command respect among the millions of people who watch football in Latin America.

The potency of the great player is akin to sexual power. The great player in Latin America transcends those boundaries which are nominally laid down. Like the *macho* in Catholic culture, he knows the rules and knows too that his task is to break them. Indeed, the individual player will treat the game itself as a demonstration of sexual potency: in Brazil, the player must 'caress a football', 'be good to her' (cited in Hecht 1968). The football genius is the embodiment of manhood. As such, he can command the respect and admiration of his male audience. But he can also – indeed he is expected also – to be a prolific lover. Images of the Argentinian, Diego Maradona, for instance, accompanied by attractive young women became the staple of the world's gossip columns in the 1980s.

THE PLAYER OF THE PEOPLE: GARRINCHA

The great player, then, is someone who captures that mixture of manhood and daring, cunning and tenacity which is enshrined in the values of the Latin-American under-dog. He typifies instinct, spontaneity, variety, surprise. It is perhaps most clearly in the image of Garrincha, the Brazilian star, the 'Joy of the People', that we can see the epitome of the popular image of the great Latin-American player (Lopes and Maresca 1989). Famous for his sexual antics as well as his football, Garrincha, unlike Pelé with whom he often played, was as inarticulate off the pitch as he was eloquent on it. His game was characterized by a Chaplinesque naivety, an almost childlike sense of wonder at the twists and turns of the game. If Pelé was 'the king', Garrincha was the people. His style, full of intricate variations of speed as he seemed almost to hover before bemused opponents, creating space with the extraordinary accuracy of his timing, had all the hallmarks of the Latin-American game. His appalling handling of his professional career itself bespoke a kind of inspired amateurism, redolent of those early mythological days of spontaneity and pleasure. Garrincha's almost animal-like agility and lack of intellectual pretension singled him out as the representative of the brilliant instinctiveness of the popular game. With Garrincha, the game was always played for the sake of the game. There is something wild and untameable about the qualities encoded in Garrincha. To control the strange, unpredictable, almost mocking energies of the game played this way is to neutralize those energies themselves. As in the carnival, it is the body here, with its desires and its powers, its demands and its contradictions, which is uppermost. It is the very negation of order and imposition, a challenge to authority itself.

The spirit of Garrincha perhaps best sums up the specific spirit of the Latin-American game, its opposition to the values of science, or graft, of well-drilled elitism. Mane Garrincha was a man of intuitive guile, but he died in poverty. By the 1970s, the authorities in Brazil attempted, disastrously, to alter the shape of national football. The military regime's efforts to control the style of play which had become the national team's hallmark, and to 'whiten' teams (excluding black players in a racist bid to consolidate its self-image) after 1970, resulted in a noticeable weakening of the team's performances. It is significant that the policy of excluding black players and favouring instead the white middle-class golden-boys who could so easily have belonged to a European national squad, also coincided with the rejection of the style which became associated with Garrincha. In 1978, the Brazilian team manager, Claudio Coutinho's

> derogatory remarks on the dribble ('a waste of time and a proof of our weakness') and his support for European styles and terminology, such as 'overlapping', drew the reply from one ex-manager that 'overlapping is what Garrincha does by himself'. While Brazilians still hoped their team would win in 1978, they realized that it did not play like champions and did not deserve to be champions. (Humphrey 1986)

Through the 1970s and 80s, Brazil remained a force in world football, but precisely in its government's efforts to control that success something of its quintessential exuberance was sacrificed. To control the carnival is also to stop it.

FOOTBALL AND THE DIVINE

Latin-American culture is dominated by another force which goes beyond politics: Catholicism. There are some 600 million Catholics in the region. The sight of Latin-American players crossing themselves before undertaking the next breathtaking piece of wizardry is a familiar one. A victory in the game, rather like a victory in a religious war, provides justification for the winning team and legitimacy for its supporters. When Brazil beat England in 1970, 'the Rio de Janeiro paper *Jornal dos Sportes* explained the victory thus: "Whenever the ball flew towards our goal and a score seemed inevitable, Jesus reached his foot out of the clouds and cleared the ball." Drawings accompanied the article, illustrating supernatural intervention.' (Kapuscinski 1990) In Latin America, the whole sport can become imbued with a superstitious, quasi-religious significance.

But it is the great player himself who seems most evidently touched by the hand of the divine in these cultures. The great player does things beyond the ordinary, pushes the boundaries of the possible. Many great footballers have had the title 'genius' bestowed upon them. Some seem to be touched with more than even that. They seem to be divine. Catholicism's basis in the insistence on the *embodiment* of divinity is at the root of these beliefs: the Latin-American football star acts as a manifestation of the greatness of Spirit incarnate.

There can never have been a player about whom this was more true than the Argentinian hero, Diego Maradona. Maradona may be denounced as a cheat and a drug-taker, despised in Britain as an Argentinian, or reviled in northern Italy for his associations with Napoli, a southern Italian team. But, despite the allegations, the arrest on drug charges, the eventual expulsion from World Cup '94 after failing a dope test, and the sheer arrogance of the man, few dispute the supreme ability and talent he displays on the field. In a British guide to the World Cup of 1986, which appeared before the contest had taken place, Maradona was described as follows: 'When Maradona has the ball, he seems to be a god: a god capable of breath-taking dribbling, lethal shooting or a telling pass; a genius that can often transfix opposing players.' (Evans 1986). Or indeed: 'When you are blessed with a genius such as Maradona, anything is possible.' (Evans 1986, 137).

Maradona, the playboy, the alleged drug-taker, the star on the verge of physical collapse, whose body is a kind of defiance of all laws and norms, has become emblematic of the individual genius of Latin-American football. He has become superhuman. Like a god, he transcends the realms of the possible. Suspended in majestic liminality between the possible and unimaginable, the acceptable and the forbidden, the consummate perfection of the body and its decay, Maradona is the most compelling of all contemporary Latin-American icons.

WHEN GOD LENDS A HAND

To an English audience, at least, Maradona will always be remembered for one particular incident. In many ways it can stand as a summation of this description of the socio-cultural and political forces at play in Latin-American football. It took place, of course, in 1986, as Argentina met England on their way to winning the Championship. The incident, by now part of footballing legend, is charged from the start not only with the heavily loaded expectations placed on Maradona, but also with the sporting and political history which lay behind the match. In the first place, there was the fact that the Argentinians learned the game from the English. Much of the flavour of the Latin-American game is owed not so much to England, however, as to an articulation of opposition to the English game and all that it stood for: the elitism of the gentleman player, the athletic amateur ideal. England constituted the old enemy, the symbol too of the style of European play against which Latin-American football was so sharply contrasted. Second, there is the fact that on the way to winning the 1966 World Cup, England had been met in the Quarter Finals with a barrage of fouls by a team later to be described by Sir Alf Ramsey as 'animals'. 'Civilization' had wagged an angry Old-World finger at New-World 'barbarism'; from the start, questions over such issues as 'fair play' and good conduct were uppermost. And finally there was the Falklands conflict, fresh in the memory of the teams and their supporters, with passions still running high about both sides' conduct during the War; for Argentina, horror at the outcome. This was a football match which could not ignore its social, cultural, historical or political context.

England and Argentina met in the Quarter Finals of the 1986 contest in an atmosphere already heavy with the implications of the game. When

Maradona's first goal landed in the net, it seemed obvious to all except the referee that it had been punched in and should therefore have been disallowed. Shocked, the England players were treated shortly afterwards to a piece of vintage Maradona skill, and the second goal sealed England's fate in the competition.

Afterwards, Maradona, famously, declared that the first goal had been due to 'a little bit of the hand of God, a little bit of the head of Maradona'. The player, revelling in the success, cites divine inspiration in his explanation of the incident and in doing so invokes the notion of a just cause, the inspirational qualities of his own prowess and the divine accomplishment of his own body. When one of the Argentinian daily newspapers focused the issue on nationhood and on the Falklands, the picture was complete: 'We blasted the English pirates with Maradona and a little hand. He who robs a thief has a thousand years' pardon' (cited in Arnold 1986).

In this incident the political and socio-cultural dynamic of the Latin-American game is sharply focused in all its contradictions. The great Latin-American player is great because he represents the aspirations of millions. He can represent those millions because he plays alone. He can be subsumed into the authority of the discourses of nationalism because of his defiance of authority: the authority of a referee, of the Law, of the colonial nation *par excellence*. He is divine because he is human, a genius because he is 'one of us', full of the joy of the game almost because of his contempt for it. Maradona's second goal, scored fairly, one of the most memorable moments of the game's recent history, underscored the fact that, ultimately, this affair was not a simple matter of cheating. It was as much about transcendence as it was about transgression.

BEYOND EXPLANATIONS: A DIALOGUE (WITH SÓCRATES)

In many ways, that episode ties things up very nicely. At the scene of a great conflict between the Latin-American game and the English, one of the world's finest individual performers articulates in body, in deed and in word the spirit of the Latin-American game, demonstrating along the way the complex interplay of nation, culture, class and religion with which the game is shot through in the region.

But it has not been my intention to leave the reader with the impression that football in Latin America can be understood only in terms of the socio-cultural forces which sweep the continent. Although informative as far as it goes, it does not seem to me to be sufficient to understand football as a function of 'more important' political forces. Many such attempts have been made, 'explaining' football in Latin America as an opiate of the masses, as a cultural phenomenon, as a social adhesive, as an urban living-space. These accounts fail to take into consideration the fact that football is not a *tabula rasa* on which other social processes make their mark, but is a social phenomenon in its own right, which may in turn have implications for the world beyond the game. It is a phenomenon, moreover, which enters into a dialogue with society at large.

This it seems is especially true in Latin America. Amílcar Romero, in his description of crowd violence in Argentina, has shown the extent to which the spectacle of football takes on a logic of its own, the acts of violence becoming inscribed into it. Suicides induced by the result of a football match are not unheard of in the region. In addition, Latin America boasts the only 'Soccer War'. The war, fought in 1969 between Honduras and El Salvador, was caused in part by territorial disputes between the two countries. But it was precipitated by a football match, a qualifier for the World Cup Finals in Mexico the following year, suggesting that football can have a profound effect on society at large – and not simply *vice versa*.

In an excellent article on Brazilian football, Matthew Shirts has shown how the ludic principle of football played in the carnival tradition of Latin America, the brilliance of the game played by a master exponent, can take on a kind of cultural autonomy all of its own and can even have socio-political consequences (Shirts 1988). In 1982, on the eve of elections at the São Paolo club Corinthians for a new club president, a group calling itself Corinthian Democracy found itself opposing the representatives of the old-style closed administration and positing a new openness, a new freedom in football management. At the head of the campaign, the Brazilian national star (and medical doctor) Sócrates, articulated his beliefs about football:

I'm struggling for freedom, for respect for human beings, for ample and unrestricted discussions, for a professional democratisation of unforeseen limits, and all of this as a soccer player preserving the ludic, joyous, and pleasurable nature of this activity. (Cited in Shirts 1988, 100)

If Corinthian Democracy did not win the day, and the opposing faction backing the right-wing Order and Truth candidate were to pull it off, Sócrates would withdraw from the club. Sócrates' campaign spilled over from the politics of the club to the national issue of greater democratization. Corinthian Democracy won. In the 1984 attempt to secure free elections, Sócrates' involvement was less successful, but the point is that he came to have an important voice on such matters, not by virtue of being a fine orator who happened to play football, but by virtue precisely of being a footballer. It is not that Sócrates' playing simply embodied the (pre-existing) values of free thought and free speech, but rather that his playing actually helped to forge those values in the context of 1980s Brazil.

The history of soccer in Brazil is such that it ended up as more than a sport. Closer to carnival, it has generated an identity that has served as a sort of unofficial citizenship in the country. A form of cultural expression, futebol interprets the world around it, but the aesthetic dimensions of the game as it is played in Brazil has been all but ignored by analysts of sport and society. The result is a sociological analysis of a cultural manifestation that ignores content and form, and consequently collapses culture into politics and economics. Corinthian Democracy was able to draw on the tradition of the game and on the identity generated by soccer in Brazil to effect its political critique precisely because it did not make this same mistake . . . and because Sócrates, Casagrande, Wladimir & Co. played great soccer. (Shirts 1988, 109)

This article has attempted an (impossible) act of cartography, mapping out the key areas of influence and of tension which characterize the Latin-American game. It is not a social history of Latin-American football. Such a thing would be impossible. In the end, football cannot be reduced to socio-cultural explanations; too much depends on the game itself, the narrative of a match unfolding in ways that are often dictated by the inexplicable, the imponderable or the just plain puzzling. Like a literary text, the football match cannot simply be understood in terms of its social context: something always seems to spill over the edge of such an analysis. Perhaps this is especially true of the football of Latin America, where the unexpected is inscribed into the very fabric of the game, where attempts to harness the game, to tame it for political or financial gain have often led to chaos, or bad football. As the study of football in Latin America establishes itself in the academic world, let us hope that attempts to master the game intellectually do not have similar disastrous consequences.

ACKNOWLEDGEMENT

Thanks are due to Patrick Quinn for his invaluable assistance in collecting information, and to Sophie Manham for her support and encouragement.

REFERENCES

Arbena, J.L. (ed.) (1988) *Sport and Society in Latin America*, Westport, Connecticut, Greenwood Press
Arnold, P. (ed.) (1986) *Mexico 1986*, Leicester, Windward Press
Dealy, Glen Caudill (1992) *The Latin Americans*, Boulder, Westview Press, p.135
Evans, P. (1986) *World Cup 1986*, London, Knight Books
Glanville, Brian (1993) *The Story of the World Cup*, London, Faber
Hecht (1968) in C. Veliz (ed.) *Latin America and the Caribbean*, London, Anthony Blond, p.743
Hein, Steve (1988) in J.L. Arbena (ed.) op. cit., pp.63–84
Humphrey, John (1986) 'No holding Brazil: football, nationalism and politics', in Alan Tomlinson and Garry Whannel (eds) *Off the Ball*, London, Pluto Press, p.136
Kapuscinski, Ryszard (1990) *The Soccer War*, London, Granta Books, p.159
Kuper, Simon (1994) *Football Against the Enemy*, London, Orion Books
Lever, Janet (1983) *Soccer Madness*, Chicago, University of Chicago Press
Lever, Janet (1988) 'Sport in a fractured society: Brazil under military rule', in J.L. Arbena (ed.) op. cit. pp.85–96
Lopes, José Sergio Leite and Maresca, Sylvain (1989) 'La disparition de la joie du peuple' in *Actes de la recherche en sciences sociales*, no.79, Sept, pp.31–36
Monsiváis, Carlos (1987) *Goool! Somos el Desmadre in Entrada Libre*, Mexico, FCE
Romero, Amílcar G. (1986) *Muerta en la Cancha*, Buenos Aires, Editorial Nueva America, p.8
Shirts, Matthew (1988) 'Sócrates, Corinthians and Questions of Democracy' in J.L. Arbena (ed.) op. cit.

4

UNAMERICAN ACTIVITY? FOOTBALL IN US AND CANADIAN SOCIETY

David Waldstein and Stephen Wagg

During the Cuban Missile Crisis of 1962, United States government officials, examining aerial photographs of Cuban fields, missed an obvious clue about their use. It took a German-born American, Henry Kissinger, to realize the significance of these fields. They were football pitches, and the Cubans, he knew, did not play football; they played baseball. The Russians, however, were dedicated footballers. Few Americans would have known this in the early 1960s, despite the long history of soccer on their continent.

Association football in North America is considered to be a relatively new phenomenon, and the decision to stage the 1994 World Cup Finals in the United States has been seen as an effort to bring the sport to a nation that has relatively little experience of it. But the history of football in North America is a rich one and goes back hundreds of years. Although the game never flourished in the manner of the uniquely American games like baseball, basketball and American football, it has maintained a kind of folklore existence, an almost underground tradition that has fluctuated in popularity and achievement since the seventeenth century when the American colonies became the first overseas territory of the British Empire to play varieties of football.

Around the world, the US is considered to be a non-footballing nation, and yet it participated in the first two World Cups, reaching the semi-finals in the inaugural tournament of 1930. As holders of the 1991 Women's World Cup, the US also lays claim to a world championship.

Despite the fact that there is no professional league to speak of in the United States, football is still a high participation sport, with an estimated 16 million players, of all ages and both sexes, playing across the continent. But because the game has always endured a muted popularity in America, it has never succeeded in penetrating the national consciousness. No single match has ever given the nation pause nor diverted attention from other sports. Even its participation in Italia '90, after 40 years of not qualifying, generated only curiosity, certainly not the near paralysis produced in other countries. This lack of awareness has allowed the potential of 16 million players to flounder, while a country such as Uruguay with a total population of only 3 million can claim two World Cups and 13 South American Championships. Canada, though culturally closer to Britain and Europe than its Southern neighbour, has not embraced football either. Although they have baseball (Canadian teams play in the US Major League) and play their own version of American football (called Canadian football), ice hockey has prime place in the country's sports culture. Professional association football leagues have seldom been sustained for long, least of all when there was no cooperation from the US, whose own attempts at professionalism were less than successful.

Nevertheless, as has been said, despite its lack of impact on the popular imagination, association football in America, like a whale poking its head above the water now and again to breathe then plunging back under, has an interesting, if submerged, history.

FOOTBALL COMES TO NORTH AMERICA

Soccer in America has always had a strong international flavour to it, as immigration has provided the engine of the game's development. During the 1920s and 30s, the heyday of soccer in the United States, it was foreign-born players and fans, mostly from the British Isles and Portugal, that either dominated teams or provided their support. But the very inception of the game does have an indigenous aspect. Legend has it that in 1620 the Pilgrims found Native Americans playing a form of football in Massachusetts. The natives called it 'Pasuckquakkohowog', which translates as 'they gather to play football'.

Later in the century, the American colonies, still strongly under British influence, played games that closely resembled football. There are also reports that during the Civil War of the 1860s, prisoners of war played soccer in the camps. It was at this time that the United States became the first independent nation other than Great Britain to form a football club. In 1862, the Oneidas from Boston became the first American club; they played matches on Boston Common, where a monument now commemorates their pioneering achievements.

In Canada, the first association football match took place in 1876 in Toronto between the Carlton Cricket Club and the Toronto Lacrosse Club. Then in 1880 the Western Football Association was established in Berlin, Ontario in order to organize the disparate soccer entities of the time. On 28 November 1885, before Austria and Hungary had staged the first European international, a team from the United States and one from Canada played a match in Newark, New Jersey; Canada won 1–0. But the forces advocating soccer in the two countries, despite their early start, were never able to promote their sport beyond a second-, or even a third-, class citizenship.

Colleges and universities have always been instrumental, in both societies, in the development of football. From establishing rules and forming associations in the early nineteenth century, to becoming the primary source of talent in the late twentieth century, colleges have continuously provided a forum for football. As in the English public schools, a variety of football codes were played in the elite universities of North America in the latter half of the nineteenth century. The game adopted until the late 1870s at Princeton, Yale (who played a match against a visiting Old Etonians team in 1873), Rutgers and Columbia corresponded closely to what was by then established in England as association football. Harvard, however, dissented, and pursued a handling code – America's own 'Cambridge Rules' – as did McGill University in Montreal, Canada. These universities arranged to play two now celebrated challenge matches in 1874, one according to Harvard rules the other to those of English rugby football. The upshot was an agreed preference for rugby. The other major universities followed suit in the next few years and the game was then 'Americanized': by the mid-1880s intercollegiate American football was in being.

The context for all this was the concern of members of the American elite to forge a distinctively American national identity through sport. They sought a game that was distinct from British or European cultural influence, and instead defined and expressed 'the American way'. The new game had its critics, who argued well into the twentieth century that it was a brutal and unseemly affair. But for the proponents of American football, post-colonial and immigrant games lacked the aggressive masculinity which, they argued, was now endemic to life in the States. As the editor of the journal *Nation* wrote:

> The spirit of the American youth, as of the American man is to win, to 'get there', by fair means or foul; and the lack of moral scruple which pervades the struggles of the business world meets with temptations equally irresistible in the miniature contests of the football field. (Lucas and Smith 1978, 232–42)

So association football, with its comparative lack of physical contact and its origins in England's most socially exclusive schools, was increasingly seen as an unAmerican activity. This perception, of course, remains.

Before the turn of the century, the emphasis moved away from the colleges towards the club system that prevails in most of the world today. In 1884, the American Football Association (AFA) was formed in order to bring some cohesiveness to the regional and autonomous enclaves that had developed mostly along the East Coast. But the AFA did little else to promote the game, while overseas it was blossoming. During this crucial period the AFA never attempted to join FIFA, never attempted to expand the game beyond its Eastern stronghold and did little to organize amateur players.

In response to these inadequacies, the American Amateur Football Association (AAFA) was established in 1912, and challenged the AFA for administration of the game. The AAFA's first president, G. Randolph Manning, was a charismatic devotee of the game and his secretary, Thomas Cahill, was a capable administrator himself. The two men would have a lasting impact on the American game.

Manning, eager to incorporate the United States into the world football community and seek legitimacy for his new organization, sent Cahill as an emissary to the 1912 FIFA Congress in Stockholm. After some astute diplomacy on the part of Cahill, the AAFA usurped the AFA's position and was eventually granted formal recognition by FIFA in 1914. Soon afterwards it changed its name to the United States Soccer Football Association (USSFA).

The establishment of Canada's governing body was much simpler. The Dominion of Canada Football Association was founded, without opposition, in 1912. It joined FIFA the same year and set up a football competition, for provincial champions, that lasted until the late 1980s. By the time of the First World War, association football was verging on a mass sport in Canada. It was widely played in villages, towns and cities across Canada, particularly in the English-speaking areas, and there were thriving leagues in most urban centres. But, as in the United States, football conflicted with emergent national identity. As an historian of Canadian sport puts it: 'It was . . . recognised as a British game, in some ways an alien intruder on Canadian soil' (Metcalfe 1987, 74). This perception was compounded by the fact that many prominent Canadian football teams were run by recent immigrants, who chose club names which recalled the old country.

> Thistles, Scots, Sons of Scotland and Caledonia were to be found in Montreal, Toronto, Ottowa and Calgary. They were joined by Shamrocks, Celtics, Sons of England and several others . . . in 1915, eighteen of the forty-eight teams in the Toronto and District League had names such as Sunderland, Manchester United, Ulster United and Corinthians. (Metcalfe 1987, 78).

There has also been a tradition of ethnically based soccer teams among Italian Americans (Hall et al. 1991, 178). For this reason, association football never received much support at state or government level in Canada: few universities, schools or churches were prepared to promote it.

The early twentieth century was a vital period for the popularity and formation of soccer in America. Already baseball had established itself as a very popular sport in the United States, and gridiron football at the collegiate level was not far behind. In Canada, the National Hockey League was formed in 1917, but by that time soccer had already been relegated to a secondary sport in both countries, played mostly by immigrants before scant audiences, and with no national cohesion. Players from immigrant backgrounds, mostly from Britain, formed small clubs that were concentrated in the north-east in the United States and in Ontario, Canada.

Many of these clubs were associated with factories or mills, where the players could gain employment. In 1894 the National Baseball League financed the American League of Professional Clubs, a soccer league that would play its games in the baseball stadiums. But because most of the players were foreigners, the league ran into trouble with the departments of immigration and labour, and folded after only six weeks. This problem of incorporating foreign players into the American League of Professional Clubs was one that would be replayed throughout the history of soccer in America.

There has never been a professional league in North America that in any way resembled the leagues of Europe and South America. Only the North American Soccer League of the 1970s could claim to be truly national. Due mostly to lack of financial stability, no league was ever able to sustain a continuous existence. Neither have the various leagues ever employed the promotion and relegation system. Instead of building upon the foundation of small clubs, teams were regularly created from nothing and moved about from one city to another, a system common among the other professional sports in the United States and Canada, but incongruous with the rest of the world.

According to Sam Foulds, a US soccer historian who played, coached and administered the game for the better part of the twentieth century, soccer in the United States, like any other sport, is primarily a business and second a sport – the reverse of the rest of the world. 'Promotion and relegation would never work here', he explains, 'because sports, even soccer, is a business. The owners would never allow their team to be relegated to a lower division, not after they had invested a great deal of money in it' (Foulds, in interview).

When the American Soccer League was formed in 1921, with a significant effort by Tom Cahill who left the USSFA to organize the league, the teams, almost all from the north-east, were a mixture of existing clubs and teams that were affiliated to factories or mills. The league usually had between 8 and 12 teams, with different teams coming and going depending on their financial abilities. The major clubs were Boston, Fall River, Shawsheen Mills, Providence, New York, Brooklyn, Newark and the mighty Bethlehem Steel. Most teams drew between 4,000 and 5,000 fans, but Fall River, a fishing and mill town in southern Massachusetts, regularly had upwards of 12,000 supporters to watch their side.

Virtually every eastern newspaper in the '20s and '30s had a soccer columnist and reported daily on the sport. It wasn't uncommon for soccer to be the lead sports-page story, and for there to be more than one soccer story in the paper.

Bethlehem Steel was the best team in the early years and boasted some of the most talented players ever to kick a ball in North America. A major industrial concern, Bethlehem Steel could attract good professional players, mostly from Britain, who were given jobs in the factories and played football at the weekend. This was the foundation for the top level of football in the United States in what is considered to be the apex of the sport in America in terms of relative popularity and skill level. Some of the ASL teams and players were comparable to the best in the world.

Soccer then, in contrast to today, was still very much a working-class game in North America up until the Second World War, thriving in the mill towns and cities where there was an abundance of talent, both native and immigrant. Among the most skilled players in the 1920s was Archie Stark, who came to the United States from Scotland as a 12-year-old boy and was one of the best players in the world in his time. Stark's scoring touch made Bethlehem Steel the dominant team of the ASL for years, and on one occasion he played for the United States. Against Canada on 8 November

1925 at Ebbets Field in Brooklyn, he scored five goals in a 6–1 win. Joining Stark in the American league were many other fine foreign players, like former Scottish internationals Alec McNab and Tommy Muirhead, and the Irish international Mickey Hamill.

But there were American-born stars as well. Perhaps the best of all time was Billy Gonsalves, who played for several clubs and won many titles throughout his career. Gonsalves' parents came from the Portuguese island of Madeira but he was born in Fall River, a devout footballing region that imbued him with a love for the game. When he was in his mid-teens, Billy played in the Boston District League for the Lusitania Recs and Porto Club until he was spotted and signed by Boston in 1926. A member of both the 1930 and 1934 World Cup teams, he was one of the great stars of the ASL, and led six different teams to a total of eight United States Open Cup championships in 14 years.

In 1931, while playing for Fall River, Gonsalves, then 23, was informed that the Fall River club would be moving to New York. As it turned out, the New York Yankees, a name borrowed from the local baseball team, would only last a year in the Big Apple, but it was during this period that they contested one of the most significant matches in American club football history.

Glasgow Celtic, perhaps the best team in Europe at the time, came to the United States and on 31 May 1931 played the Yankees at Fenway Park in Boston. Eager to demonstrate to the rest of the world that American soccer players were talented, Gonsalves went out and scored three goals as New York shocked Celtic, 4–3. After the match Celtic offered a contract to Gonsalves, which he declined. He could make more money in the United States, and as he had just helped prove, the US had some of the best teams and competition in the world.

But, despite the fact that the ASL marks the 'Golden Age' of soccer in America, the league still had financial difficulties, and by the early 1930s it found itself in decline and in serious danger of folding. Jurisdictional disputes with the USSFA only compounded the problems. Finally, in 1929, the year of the great stock market crash, the league desisted. The quarrel with the USSFA and the economy in general – no longer were factories easily able to offer jobs to players – proved too much for a second-tier sport to overcome, and the league folded.

In 1931 a new league was formed with the same name, but it faced the same problems as before, and never got off the ground. The depression was very severe by the early 30s, and leisure sports in general, and marginal ones like soccer in particular, were hit hard. The stadiums were often in disrepair, with poor facilities and bad turf. Sam Foulds described how the ASL then faced many of the problems that the lower division British and South American clubs face today. His local club, Boston, were forced to play in typically unsavoury surroundings that contributed to low attendances.

Boston played at the Walpole Street Grounds, an old baseball stadium going back to 1869. The turf was terrible, there was virtually no grass, and the grandstands were all torn down. There were bleachers [benches, or cheap seats] only at one end, and railroad tracks at the other, and there were absolutely no facilities. It wasn't a family attraction and it was very difficult to get women to go there. (Foulds, in interview)

The new league, meanwhile, had additional problems. Always dependent upon foreign talent, soccer in the United States fell victim to the growing political sentiment of isolationism. Soccer was regarded as a foreign game, despite its roots and long tradition in North America, and philosophically it was considered as unAmerican. These sentiments led to restrictions on immigration which prevented overseas players and coaches from contributing to football in the United States, and eventually removed the US from a cultural interaction with the rest of the world that almost all others engaged in. It now fell to native players and the ageing immigrants already resident in the States to keep American association football alive. And they did so for a while, but slowly the game fell into decline and by the Second World War it was almost completely out of the public eye. In 1930 there had been over 200 registered clubs in the United States; by June 1941 there were only eight. Professional club soccer then lay virtually dormant until the establishment of the NASL in 1967.

THE USA AND CANADA IN INTERNATIONAL FOOTBALL

The national teams of Canada and the United States have had only limited success in international football. For Canada, a long history of attempting to qualify for the World Cup has yielded only one Finals appearance, in Mexico in 1986. Playing mostly with veterans of the NASL, Canada were thought to be a pushover in their group, but proved otherwise. Although they lost all three games – to France (0–1), Hungary (0–2) and USSR (0–2) – their level of play was impressive considering their inexperience. In fact, it required a late goal by Jean-Pierre Papin for semi-finalists France to defeat them.

After Mexico, Canada was expected to continue its progress, but has thus far been disappointing in its efforts. They failed to qualify for Italia '90, and a crucial 2–1 loss to a fierce Mexican squad in their CONCACAF qualifying match in Toronto meant an arduous road through Australia and South America lay ahead if Canada was to reach USA '94.

Ever since their international clash in New Jersey in 1885, both the United States and Canada were pioneers in international play. The US continued that tradition by participating in the first two FIFA World Cups in 1930 and 1934. In 1930 teams did not have to prove their worthiness with qualifying tournaments. In fact, FIFA had trouble filling out the field, so the entrants were simply the ones interested enough to travel to Montevideo, Uruguay. The only worthiness required was in relation to the sea, over which the Americans made the long journey to South America, training on board as they sailed.

Once on land, the Americans, far from home and the attentions of the US public, found themselves drawn against Paraguay and Belgium in group 4.

The team was led by Billy Gonsalves at midfield with Bert Patenaude (like Gonsalves, from Fall River, Mass.) and Bart McGhee, another American-born player, up front. Patenaude was the third-leading scorer of the tournament, as he became the first player in World Cup history to notch up three goals. With McGhee's contribution, the two forwards combined for five of the teams seven goals in the tournament.

On 13 July 1930, two full years after the team had last assembled to play a full international, they defeated Belgium 3–0 through a goal by Patenaude and a pair from McGhee. Four days later they met Paraguay and defeated them 3–0 as well. This time, with the same players but in a slightly different alignment, Patenaude scored two goals and Thomas Florie, moving forward from midfield, scored the third. Wilfred Cummings, the manager, decided that he liked this formation better and stuck with it for the semi-final contest against Argentina.

Unfortunately for the Americans, no alignment would help them on this day, as the Argentines dismantled them 6–1 in a savage semi-final. But Roger Allaway, who has compiled a very complete record of the United States soccer team, points out that although the 6–1 score suggests otherwise, the US was not five goals the lesser team that day. The score was 1–0 at half-time, but that would not hold up as Allaway explains.

> In the second half the US was overcome by injuries. John Douglas, the goal-keeper, had hurt his leg and could barely walk, and midfielder Raphael Tracy was playing on what turned out to be a broken leg. So, although it ended up 6–1, it's fair to say that it should have been a lot closer. (Allaway, in interview)

With no substitutions allowed in those days, both players were forced to brave it out, as ineffective as they were.

The 'vigorous, sideswiping Argentines', as manager Wilfred Cummings referred to them in his official report to the USSFA after the tournament, were not reluctant to engage in physical play or even inflict injury. Andy Auld had his lip ripped open, and while the trainer was applying smelling salts, an Argentine player reported knocked the salt into the forward's eye, blinding him temporarily. In his report, Cummings, though reserved, expressed his belief that without the injuries the US had a chance to win. He wrote:

> I honestly believe that the Argentinians were a little better team due to their having played together for many years; but believe that the unbiased footballer would have given us a good chance to win if we could have kept our 11 players in the game and uninjured.

Although it would be too generous to suggest that the United States was one of the best four teams in the world in 1930 – after all, very few European teams chose to participate – it is clear that the level of football in the States at this point was at a relative high point, even if few US citizens knew or cared. Furthermore, despite assertions that the team was composed almost entirely of foreigners – assertions that would be reiterated when the States beat England in 1950 – six of the 11 players on the team were American born, most notably the playmaker and star, Billy Gonsalves.

Following on the heels of their strong performance in Montevideo, the Americans headed north to Rio de Janeiro three weeks later where they played and lost to Brazil, 4–3. The Fall River duo, Patenaude (two goals) and Gonsalves (one goal), combined for the goals. But after that game, the US would not play again until their single World Cup qualifying match in 1934.

The 1934 World Cup was held in Italy, as was the United States qualifying match against Mexico. Aldo 'Buff' Donelli scored all four goals as the Americans defeated the Mexicans 4–2 in Rome to quality for the knockout tournament. Unfortunately they did not fare so well against their hosts in the finals, losing 7–1 in Rome, and were eliminated. They would not win another full international until 1949.

With isolationist sentiment on the rise in the United States, and with the distinct potential for war in Europe, the American team opted out of the 1938 World Cup in France. The War cancelled the tournament until 1950 in Brazil, which the US did decide to enter.

With a draw and a win over Cuba, the US qualified and set out for Brazil in June 1950 and its most shocking win of all time. They finished the '50 World Cup with one win and two losses and did not qualify for the second round, but their win, a dramatic 1–0 triumph over a great England side, was considered a minor national tragedy in England.

On 29 June the United States were drawn to play an England team which at that time featured Stanley Matthews, Alf Ramsey and Billy Wright. As underdogs, the Americans were favoured by the Belo Horizonte crowd, and the stingy US defence prevented the English from operating freely in front of goal, especially in the second half. As Matthews, who did not play in the match because it was thought that he was not needed, suggested later in his biography by David Miller, 'We could have played for twenty-four hours and not scored. The Americans fought and chased.'

Joe Gaetjens, a Haitian citizen who later disappeared and, it is assumed, was executed by the Tonton Macoute (the Haitian security force), scored the only goal of the match with a header five minutes before half-time. Many observers, particularly in England, tried to justify the result by saying that the United States was essentially a mercenary outfit, using a majority of foreigners to build the team. There were certainly foreigners in the US side – Gaetjens, the Scottish defender, Eddie McIlvenny, and Belgian midfielder Joseph Maca were not US citizens. The rest of the squad, however, was composed of Americans, and all played a role in what became one of the biggest upsets in international football history.

But the win would have no significant impact in the US. It received scant attention in the press, and even in the soccer community it provided no impetus to progress. It was merely an aberration, an unexpected spasm on a steady line of indifference. It would be 40 years before the United States would again compete on the world stage in Italia '90, though every year it tried in vain to qualify, usually being thwarted by the challenge of Mexico in the Confederation of North, Central American and Caribbean Football

(CONCACAF) qualifying group. During this period, the notion of soccer fell further and further from the consciousness of the average sporting American.

Canada, meanwhile, have made their own small, quiet contribution to world football. They were represented at the Olympics of 1904, in St. Louis, by the Ontario team Galt FC, and beat the United States in the final: although football was only an exhibition sport at these Olympics, this remains Canada's only football honour. Canada played a smattering of internationals between 1904 and 1927 but these were confined to British dominions: the US, Australia and New Zealand. They re-emerged in international competition in 1957, with their first game in the preliminaries to the Stockholm World Cup the following year; they beat the US 5–1 in what was the first international football match on Canadian soil (Oliver 1992).

In the early 1960s, prior to the setting up of the NASL, Canada had its own professional soccer league. Then, in the late 60s and the 70s, Canadian clubs took part in the North American Soccer League. In this context, attempts were made to use Canadian football's historic association with ethnic minorities and immigrant communities as a marketing device: for example, in the mid-1970s the club now known as Toronto Blizzard was called Toronto Metro Croatia, in an effort to appeal to the city's Yugoslav population. Most of Metro's players were brought from Yugoslavia itself and these were augmented by a few Yugoslav-Canadians. Canadian players were also signed by US clubs – notably Wes McLeod, who went to Tampa Bay Rowdies – and a few went to English League teams: Buzz Parsons (1969) and Bruce Twamley (1975) both played for Ipswich Town.

Canadian football, albeit as a minority sport, continues to hold its own. The country has 285,000 registered players, although only 200 of them are professionals, and another Canadian Soccer League began in 1987. Former Canadian NASL clubs, such as Vancouver Whitecaps and Toronto Blizzard, survived the break-up of that league and they attracted good players: Peter Beardsley, for example, who was one of the leading English players of the late 1980s, spent a period with the Whitecaps. They also still produce and export good players: several Canadians are currently playing professional football in England.

THE NORTH AMERICAN SOCCER LEAGUE: RISE AND FALL

After the fall of the American Soccer League and the restrictions on immigration, soccer went into a dormant period in the United States that lasted well into the 1960s. When it finally reawoke, it had changed its composition from a working-class sport played by immigrants to an upper-middle class and suburban recreational activity, played almost entirely by the young.

No longer did factories or mills sponsor teams. Gone were the days of talented Portuguese, Scottish or Italian clubs drawing several thousand on a Saturday, with a full-page report the following day in the local newspapers. Now it was primarily a polite suburban game and exclusive high schools and colleges became the foci of the game. This transformation included the attendant perceptions of the game that it was for 'sissies', girls and those afraid to play American football.

For those playing and enjoying the game, there were two problems. First, the gulf between the Golden Age of the first ASL and the present day had left in its wake a dearth of experienced coaches. Many young players were taught by coaches who knew little more of the sport than the players themselves. Second, for the most talented players there was no outlet for their skills. Without a viable pro league, college was the highest level an American could attain at home.

The problem of developing a professional league in the United States was more difficult now than ever due to the vacuum that had been created. But in the summer of 1966, following the World Cup in England, the final of which had been watched by 400 million TV viewers, three groups of businessmen, convinced that soccer could work in North America, proposed to both the USSFA and the Canadian Soccer Football Association (CSFA) a cross-continent, two-nation league. When jurisdictional disputes arose, two leagues were formed in 1967 – the United Soccer Association (USA), and the National Professional Soccer League (NPSL).

Perhaps it was too ambitious to expect high attendances in their first years, perhaps there simply was not enough interest to sustain two leagues. In any event, attendances dropped dramatically after the initial year of the two groups and it soon became apparent that rival leagues could not survive. So in December 1967 the two leagues merged and formed the North American Soccer League (NASL).

In 1968 the NASL had 17 teams in the US and Canada, many of which started out in serious financial trouble and by the end of the season only five teams remained. For the 1968 season the league retrenched and produced a low-budget operation, organized and maintained by Lamar Hunt, owner of the Dallas Tornadoes. The league adopted the US system of using foreign teams out of their own domestic season to represent its cities, and so Aston Villa became the Atlanta Chiefs, West Ham United the Baltimore Bays, Wolves the Kansas City Spurs and so on.

The NASL, always willing to experiment, tried several methods of filling gaps in schedules and raising the talent level by importing foreign teams in various forms. Gradually, starting in the early 70s, teams started to attain more stability as the league began slowly to take hold. More and more foreign players, particularly those from the British Isles who were either past their prime or too young and inexperienced for their own domestic leagues, were signed by NASL.

Many of the older players gave the league very little regard, and their performances reflected their detachment. This tended to stunt the popularity of the league and, as many have suggested, led to its eventual downfall. In order to promote American players, the NASL placed restrictions on the composition of teams. But instead of limiting foreigners, they imposed a minimum number of Americans that had to be on the field at all times, starting with one and gradually increasing. This only reinforced the perception that the game was foreign-dominated and unAmerican, and the league continued to tread water.

Of course, some people transcend nationality and Pelé is one such person. When the New York Cosmos enticed him out of retirement in 1975, the NASL and all the pro-footballing forces in the United States could barely contain their optimism. No marketing executive, no diligent organizer, no native-born player could ever do what Pelé was about to do: legitimize the NASL and add enough flair, skill and beauty – even at the age of 34 – to revitalize football in America and capture the attention of the nation. For most Americans, even today, Pelé would be the only professional soccer player they could name.

After Pelé, the floodgates opened and one after another the foreign stars joined him in the NASL. Franz Beckenbauer, Gerd Muller, Eusebio, Georgio Chinaglia, Johan Cruyff, George Best, Bobby Moore and Carlos Alberto to name but a few, came and finished up their careers in the now profitable league.

For several others, the league provided a precursor to successful professional careers elsewhere. Bruce Grobbelaar, Trevor Francis, Mark Hateley, Peter Beardsley, Graeme Souness and Hugo Sanchez all played in the NASL before going on to carve out famous careers. Even some managers, most notably Rinus Michels of the Dutch national team and the former Hungarian World Cup star Ferenc Puskas, coached in the NASL.

From Pelé's first season in 1975, the league enjoyed a dramatic upturn in interest and attendances. Once again, all the newspapers had reporters covering the teams on a regular basis and television was again involved in the show. Huge attendance figures were greeted with delight by league and soccer officials, and it was assumed that football had arrived for good. But once again there were underlying problems that festered and remained unchecked.

The lack of quality American players was a constant threat to the league's survival. Kyle Rote Jr., the first American to lead the league in scoring in 1974; Shep Messing, the flamboyant Cosmos goalkeeper who graduated from Harvard and Ricky Davis, also of the Cosmos, were the most notable American stars. But otherwise the Americans were token selections with low public profiles. Even the three previously mentioned players were hardly well-known names.

Another problem the league encountered was with the traditional powers in Association Football, particularly FIFA. In order to promote higher scoring the league experimented with new offside rules, and instituted tiebreaking rules to eliminate draws. FIFA found these rule changes an irritant and was constantly hounding the NASL to conform to international standards. Furthermore, the NASL owners, with no precedent for co-operating with international bodies, let alone the USSF (the group changed its name to the US Soccer Federation in 1974), sometimes ignored FIFA regulations and signed banned or restricted players. They believed themselves autonomous and felt no allegiance to the world body. Moreover, they kept changing the league structure and playoff format, which, combined with the constant rearranging of teams from one city to another, led to a lack of cohesion and stability.

In the end, the main problem was simply that Pelé could not play forever. On 1 October 1977 the Brazilian star played his last game in the United

States – an exhibition match against his old club, Santos, in which he played for both teams. 77,202 fans attended Pelé's touching farewell, but it was clear that the challenge would now be to turn his spark into a fire. During Pelé's reign as king of the NASL, the league, and the Cosmos in particular, enjoyed a tremendous boost in attendances. In 1975 the Cosmos attracted a total of 114,939 fans over 22 games. By 1978, their peak year, average attendance was close to 50,000 per game, with a total of 717,842. By 1981 only 35,000 were going to the games each week, a decline that would accelerate dramatically in the next couple of years. Overall, the league had an average attendance of less than 10,000 in 1975, and their peak in 1979 was just under 15,000.

By 1981 the NASL, not having addressed its problems, was facing a spiralling downward trend in popularity, the quality of players, money and, finally, the number of teams. In 1978 there were 24 teams; in 1982 there were 14; and by its final season, 1984, there were only nine. By the time the NASL suspended operations in 1985, few people were still aware of its existence. It folded and left the scene much as it had arrived: quietly and quickly. Colin Jose, a soccer historian and expert on the NASL points out that the death of the league was a serious blow to football advocates: '. . . it seemed that all hope had gone. If the NASL had failed, what hope had any other league of surviving?' (Jose 1989)

Vague remnants of the NASL still exist, including some teams like the Tampa Bay Rowdies; reporters who have now been assigned the US World Cup beat; and the potential gate receipts that the league garnered after Pelé's arrival. Paradoxically, it is possible that the NASL, despite its failures, led to the appointment of the 1994 World Cup to the United States.

FIFA COMES TO THE UNITED STATES – WORLD CUP 1994

Although conspiracy theorists claim that greedy FIFA officials foisted the World Cup on to the unsuspecting Americans, there is evidence to suggest that FIFA had to be persuaded by the American organizers to consider the US as a site. On more than one occasion, after the NASL, FIFA turned down American requests to hold the tournament.

While the NASL was in the process of disintegrating, the USSF decided that the time was ripe to apply to host the World Cup. As early as 1980 the association began a campaign to convince FIFA that it was worthy. On 8 June 1980, Gene Edwards, then president of the USSF announced the inception of an international youth tournament intended to grab FIFA's attention. 'If we can prove to FIFA we can handle this tournament well', he said in a *New York Post* article, 'we can consider it a dry run for the youth World Cup in 1983 or 1985 and maybe we can ask to host the big one in 1990.'

Two years later, the USSF had officially applied for the 1990 World Cup, and, further, expressed interest in hosting the 1986 tournament should Columbia decline, which they in fact did. Brazil was next in line, but when they dropped out, optimism among the USSF ran high. According to the *New York Post* of 10 July 1982, the announcement by Brazil to withdraw

'. . . cleared the way for FIFA to award its next World Championship to the U.S. where dollars and organizational potential await.'

The USSF submitted a 92-page proposal, listing 14 potential sites, got President Reagan to send a letter in support of the application and generally seemed assured of receiving the nomination. Werner Fricker, chairman of the USSF World Cup organizing committee, said in the *New York Post* on 11 March, 1983, 'We feel very confident that after our offer is received, there should be no other choice but us.'

FIFA felt otherwise, and rejected the application, stating that the US government seemed non-committal about the proposal. FIFA's secretary, Sepp Blatter, said in the *New York Post* on 23 April, 1983, that the US failed to meet the proper requirements or provide '. . . federal or governmental guarantees to support the federation's application'. Reagan's letter apparently was not enough.

In response to the rejection, Fricker and the USSF were outraged. 'We are not prepared to accept the decision lying down. We will appeal it.' (*New York Post*, 23 April, 1983) Of course, the United States ended up securing the World Cup Finals tournament in 1994, but only after being rejected twice.

Whether or not the United States deserved the tournament, it is clear that by the time FIFA finally relented and awarded them the 1994 World Cup, they had at least been cautious in their decision. Considering FIFA's continuous disagreements with the NASL, it is not surprising that they were sceptical of an American World Cup bid. But in the end the potential of the US – the 16 million players, the organizational capabilities, the stadia and the history of exceedingly lucrative sporting events – swayed FIFA.

Another factor undoubtedly considered was the encroachment of American sports into previously untapped European markets. American football and basketball had made significant strides in Europe and Japan in the latter half of the 80s. FIFA, knowing full well that soccer was suffering from hooliganism, low scoring averages and a general decline in popularity, was eager to fight back. If gridiron football and basketball could expand across international boundaries, why not the world's most popular game.

Working in FIFA's favour was the recent performance of the United States national team. By qualifying for the 1990 World Cup, the US team helped legitimize FIFA's decision. After 39 years of almost complete futility and obscurity, the United States, with the advantage of Mexico being disqualified from the '90 Cup, went to Trinidad and Tobago on 19 November 1989 needing a win to go to Italy. Paul Caligiuri's booming left-footed goal, referred to by some as the most important goal in US soccer history, was enough: the US won 1–0.

But the finals were a different story. Playing almost entirely with college players and directed by a college coach, Bob Gansler, the US left Italy with three straight losses to Czechoslovakia, Italy and Austria, although they did gain some valuable experience. Playing in front of a packed house in Rome, the Americans only lost 1–0 to Italy, and missed an equalizing goal by inches. By the time it was over they had learned how much rougher the play was than in American colleges, and how much more serious the competition was. They knew there was much work to do.

After Italia '90, the USSF decided to hire a new coach and they chose Bora Milutinovic, the charismatic manager of the Mexican side in 1986 and then of Costa Rica, surprising qualifiers in 1990. The Yugoslavian-born Milutinovic brought instant credibility and hope to the team, even if the lack of a professional league and good players remained a serious obstacle. So a campaign to recruit more talented players began. If no indigenous players existed, the USSF would look elsewhere. Like the Republic of Ireland and Canada, the US sought out foreign players who would be eligible to play under FIFA rules. Soon, South Africa's Roy Wegerle, Germany's Thomas Dooley and Holland's Ernie Stewart became American citizens by virtue of a wife or a deceased parent.

These foreign stars, combined with players like John Harkes, Eric Wynalda and Tab Ramos who were playing in Europe, made an immediate impact. In their first game together, in the inaugural US Cup in June 1992, they stunned Ireland, 3–1 and Portugal, 1–0. After drawing 1–1 with Italy and winning the mini tournament, people began to take notice. Perhaps with the imported stars they could compete at the international level, even without a domestic foundation from which to draw players.

Another source of hope was the success of the women's team at the first Women's World Cup in China in November 1991. A 2–0 win over Norway gave the US the championship, the first world title by any American team. There may not have been a national league, but the men's and women's national teams were making great strides, though still largely unnoticed by the public.

The strategy, then, was clear. The United States was pursuing a policy unique in the international community. It would attempt to build the game with its national team, instead of having the domestic game produce the national team the way virtually every other country had done it. It is very difficult, though, to institute a tradition from the top down.

Unfortunately, when the players returned to Europe, the team's success rate plummeted, and wins once again became scarce. But the following summer, the 'Europeans' returned, and the results were similar. A 2–0 win over an England team having an indifferent time, and a 4–3 loss to the Germans were the highlights, and once again critics began to see progress, as long as the European-based players were there. But immediately following the US Cup, the 'Native-American' team travelled to Ecuador for their first entrance into the Copa America, with unsatisfying results: two losses and a draw. The Europeans were missed.

As the US continues to rely heavily on foreign players, they remain vulnerable to the same problems that helped cause the downfall of the NASL. Milutinovic often says, 'Americans demand a winner', but the question remains, at what cost? If the team is composed of mercenaries and players who have difficulty speaking the language, will the public accept them as Americans? Having foreign-born or bred players and a foreign coach do the work and achieve the glory is an unknown commodity in the US.

With the emphasis on foreign players in what has always been considered a foreign sport, the threat remains that Americans will do what they have done more than once in the past, and turn their backs on the game. After all, North Americans have already relegated football to a long history of obscurity.

REFERENCES

Cirino, Tony (1981) *US Soccer vs. the World*, New Jersey, Damon Press

Cummings, Wilfred, 'US team's participation in the first soccer championships at Montevideo, Uruguay, South America, July, 1930' from the historic archives of the National Soccer Hall of Fame, Oneonta, New York

Hall, Ann, Slack, Trevor, Smith, Gary and Whitson, David (1991) *Sport in Canadian Society*, Toronto, McClelland and Stewart

Jose, Colin (1989) *NASL: A Complete Record of the North American Soccer League*, Derby, England, Breedon Books

Lucas, John and Smith, Ronald (1978) *Saga of American Sport*, London, Kimpton

Metcalfe, Alan (1987) *Canada Learns to Play: The Emergence of Organised Sport 1807–1914*, Toronto, McClelland and Stewart

New York Post, 2 August 1926; 7 and 8 June 1927; 18 January 1935; 22 May 1938; 10 July 1982; 11 January, 11 March, 23 April 1983

New York Times, 20 December 1979; 19 May 1982; 29 November 1991

Oliver, Guy (1992) *The Guinness Record of World Soccer*, Enfield, England, Guinness Publishing

US Soccer 1993 Media Guide, United States Soccer Federation

World Soccer (February 1990) - extracts from David Miller *Stanley Matthews: The Authorised Biography*, London, Pavilion Books; (June 1993) Colin Jose 'From Kennel Club to Simpkins'

Interviews

Roger Allaway, Frank Dell'Apa, Sam Foulds, Colin Jose, Seamus Mallon, Lothar Osiander, Bora Milutinovic, Jerry Trecker.

5

GOING TO MARKET: FOOTBALL IN THE SOCIETIES OF EASTERN EUROPE

Vic Duke

Unlike the other regions in this book, Eastern Europe constitutes as much of a political entity as a geographical one. Between the end of the Second World War and the year of Eastern European 'revolutions' in 1989, countries in this region were part of the Soviet empire beyond the Iron Curtain across Europe.

Included in this region therefore are Hungary, Poland, Romania and Bulgaria, all of which have remained intact since 1989. In addition, what was Czechoslovakia but has now split into independent Czech and Slovak republics falls within Eastern Europe. In footballing terms the old federal republic remained in existence for the duration of the country's participation in the 1994 World Cup tournament with the national team being known as RCS – Representatives of Czechs and Slovaks. The former German Democratic Republic (East Germany) is excluded from this chapter in that it now forms part of a reunited Germany.

Finally, the core of the empire, the Soviet Union itself, makes up the rest of the region. The process of fragmentation underway in the Soviet empire means that there are now 15 independent republics where before there was only the one Soviet Union. In relation to competing in international football tournaments, what was the Soviet Union became CIS – Commonwealth of Independent States (comprising 11 of the republics) – in the 1992 European Championship. For the 1994 World Cup FIFA ruled in 1992 that Russia would take the place of the former Soviet Union in the qualifying tournament. This decision was not popular with the Ukraine, the second most populous of the republics, at over 51 million, which as a result had no representation in the 1994 World Cup.

Given the enormous size of the former Soviet Union, the question arises as to exactly how far east Eastern Europe goes. Based on the traditional geographical wisdom that Europe stretches as far as the Ural mountains, there is a clear case for the inclusion of 10 former Soviet republics in Eastern Europe. These are Russia, Ukraine, Belarus, Estonia, Latvia, Lithuania,

Moldova, Georgia, Armenia and Azerbaijan. The other five (Kazakhstan, Kirghizstan, Tadzhikistan, Turkmenistan and Uzbekistan) may more appropriately be affiliated to the Asian FA in the future. What the countries of Eastern Europe had in common in politico-economic terms during the communist era was their adherence to some form of state socialist society. Among the main ingredients of such a society were: a system of central planning of all aspects of the economy (including facilities for sport and the wages of full-time sports players); a meshing of the ruling communist party and the state such that all manner of appointments were subject to political influence (including officials in sports organizations and football clubs); and an official ideology espousing the historical role of the proletariat and the predominant position of working-class organizations (including the linking of football clubs – and sports clubs in general – to party and worker organizations).

Not only did these countries possess a distinctive organization of sport, they also gave it a high profile in society. The political importance of sport lay in its potential for demonstrating the superiority of communism over capitalism by winning more trophies. In the post-communist era since 1989, the traditional socialist structure has been dismantled and sport in these countries is currently experiencing a difficult transition to a market rather than a state environment.

The early history of football in Eastern Europe, however, predates the communist era and in some cases even predates the existence of some of the present-day nation-states.

FOOTBALL COMES TO EASTERN EUROPE

Key landmarks in the development of organized football in Eastern Europe are summarized in Table 5.1 below. As elsewhere in the world, British businessmen and expatriates played a prominent role in importing football to the region.

Development of organized football was most rapid in the first two countries in Table 5.1 – Hungary and Czechoslovakia (or Bohemia as it was before the First World War). They were early in founding a football association, affiliating with FIFA (itself founded only in 1904) and competing in international matches. This early progress was to reap rich rewards in the inter-war period, as will be documented later.

Football was introduced to the Habsburg empire (of which Hungary and Bohemia were part) initially in Vienna by English expatriates in the 1890s with the first recorded match in 1894. The game spread quickly to Budapest and Prague such that the three cities became the first focus of organized football in central Europe. In the period prior to the First World War, British coaches such as Edgar Chadwick, formerly of Everton, were influential in Prague football.

In Hungary, some of the earliest teams were in fact football sections added to gymnastic clubs in the 1890s. For example, both Ujpest TE and MTK in Budapest fall into this category. A Hungarian league began very quickly in

Table 5.1 Landmarks in the development of organized football in Eastern Europe

country	FA founded	affiliated to FIFA	national league	first international
Hungary	1901	1906	1901	1902
Czechoslovakia	1901[a]	1906[a]	1925	1903[a]
Soviet Union	1912[b]	1946	1936	1912[b]
Poland	1919	1923	1927[c]	1921
Romania	1908	1930	1932[d]	1922
Bulgaria	1923	1924	1937[e]	1924

Note

a. these dates relate to Bohemia rather than Czechoslovakia which was not created until 1918
b. these dates relate to Tsarist Russia prior to the revolution of 1917
c. a national championship play off competition began in 1921
d. a national championship play off competition began in 1910
e. a national championship play off competition began in 1925

1901 but in truth all the teams in it were from Budapest until 1926. In the period immediately prior to the First World War, Hungarian football was already semi-professional.

Similar beginnings were evident in Bohemia with the setting up of football sections of multi-sport clubs in Prague. The two leading football clubs to this day were formed in this way – Sparta Prague in 1894 and Slavia Prague in 1896. A league for Prague clubs began in 1896 but a Czechoslovak league did not appear until 1925. Even then the league was dominated by Bohemian clubs with no Moravian club participating in the first division until 1933 and no Slovak club until 1935. A pertinent aside at this point is that Slovakia (an independent state allied to Nazi Germany) in the period 1939–44 played international matches and ran its own national league. Both have recommenced in 1993. Further evidence of the growing football pedigree of Hungary and Bohemia at the beginning of the century is provided by their inclusion on the itinerary for England's first ever foreign tour in 1908. Both were defeated – Hungary 7–0 and Bohemia 4–0. This early development of organized football and allied international success ultimately led to both countries introducing professional football in the 1920s – Czechoslovakia in 1925 and Hungary in 1926.

Professional footballers from both countries were much in demand in the inter-war period and their export became a lucrative business. For instance, playing in the French league during the period 1932–1939 were 59 Hungarians and 43 Czechoslovaks, totals bettered only by English and Austrians. The growing prowess of both national teams was demonstrated by the England tour of 1934. Both of them defeated England 2–1.

Football was first played in Russia in the 1880s but its development was retarded by a combination of political circumstances and the harsh winter climate. Two English brothers, Harry and Clement Charnock, formed a team at the Morozov cotton mills in Orekhovo in 1887. The team played in a set of Blackburn Rovers shirts imported from England. By 1906 the club was renamed Orekhovo SK, and later as part of the socialist reorganization in 1923 became Dynamo Moscow. Dynamo were sponsored by the state security ministry and in later years became a team of international renown.

In the period prior to the First World War, football in Tsarist Russia was predominantly a pastime for the privileged classes, although an entrance was made on to the international stage in 1912. The October revolution in 1917 and the ensuing civil war postponed the further development of organized football; then followed a restructuring along socialist lines. Although there had been city leagues in St Petersburg and Moscow at the turn of the century, there was to be no national league in the Soviet Union until 1936. In terms of world football, the Soviet Union adopted a policy of studied isolation, by not affiliating with FIFA until 1946 and not entering the World Cup until the 1950s. They reached the quarter finals at the first attempt in Sweden in 1958.

Poland was re-established as an independent state in 1918, after a century of partition into areas controlled by Austria, Prussia and Russia. Football developed initially in the Austrian part largely because any other form of popular organization was regarded with political suspicion in the Russian and Prussian domains. As a result Krakow became the pioneer of Polish football. Two of the oldest surviving clubs originated here, namely Cracovia and Wisla Krakow, both in 1906.

In the Tsarist part of modern Poland, Lodz displayed the first stirring of football activity. Here some Englishmen involved in manufacturing created the first team. Today, two of the leading clubs are still from Lodz: LKS were formed in 1908 and Widzew in 1910. After the renewed political independence of Poland, organized football developed rapidly with the founding of the Polish FA in 1919, introduction of a national championship in 1921 and the first international match in the same year.

The game of football first appeared in the Balkan countries of Romania and Bulgaria in the 1890s, but the more organized version developed more quickly in Romania than Bulgaria. For example, both the national FA and the national championships were founded 15 years earlier in Romania. However, both countries were relatively late arrivals on the international scene, Romania in 1922 and Bulgaria in 1924.

In Romania, it was foreign workers in Bucharest who introduced football in the 1890s. The main nationalities involved were British, Belgian, Dutch and German. By the turn of the century teams had been formed at the Colentina textile works and the Standard oil company of Ploesti. At this time football in Romania was played and organized mainly by foreigners. The first national champions, Olimpia Bucharest in 1910, had several British players in their team.

Only after the First World War did Romania take over the game. Romania's late affiliation with FIFA in 1930 and instant entry into the inaugural 1930 World Cup in Uruguay (one of only four European countries to attend) were the direct result of King Carol's passion for football. The King personally picked the players for the World Cup and also 'arranged' time off work for them with their employers.

A Swiss physical education teacher in Varna is reputed to have introduced football to Bulgaria in 1894. As a result Varna became the hotbed of Bulgarian football in the early years. The first inter-town match was between Sofia and Plovdiv in 1912 and the oldest surviving clubs, such as Botev Plovdiv and Cherno More Varna 1912, Slavia Sofia 1913 and Levski Sofia 1914, date from this time. Organized football in Bulgaria was finally established in the 1920s. A Sofia league began in 1921, followed by a national championship in 1925 and a fully fledged national league in 1937.

The early history of the game in the region is concluded with a brief mention of football in the recently re-established Baltic states of Estonia, Latvia and Lithuania. Representatives of British commercial firms along the Baltic coast introduced the game to these countries before the First World War. All three had flourishing leagues in the 1920s and 1930s, through to 1943. They also played regular internationals during this period and rejoined the international football stage in 1992 by entering the qualifying rounds of the 1994 World Cup.

FOOTBALL UNDER SOCIALISM

No matter what their previous history prior to communist takeover (1917 in the Soviet Union and the 1940s for the rest of Eastern Europe), total reorganization of sport along socialist lines was to provide a common pattern for all these countries in the period after the Second World War up until the 1980s. The new sports structure emphasized the historical role of the working class and was based on multi-sport clubs for worker organizations. Sport was seen as part of the cultural emancipation of the working class. Not surprisingly, the Soviet Union became the role model for the other countries.

A major feature of football in the socialist republics of Eastern Europe was that top level players were not professionals. They were registered as employees of the organization which sponsored their club. In practice, they trained and performed as full-time 'professional' sportsmen. The Union of European Football Associations (UEFA) classified Eastern European players in a hybrid category as neither professionals (in the commercial sense) nor amateurs (in the part-time sense). Not until 1988, did UEFA alter the status of footballers in Czechoslovakia and Hungary to that of full-time professionals, thereby returning them to the same position as the inter-war period.

The traditional Eastern European model was for sports clubs to be sponsored by a factory, enterprise, ministry or trade union. The players were regarded as employees of the organization concerned. Many of the leading clubs were sponsored by heavy industrial enterprises in such fields as chemicals, steel and engineering. For instance, in Czechoslovakia, Banik Ostrava were sponsored by the miners' trade union and Plastika Nitra by a plastics factory; in Hungary, Tatabanya were backed by a coal mining company and Raba Gyor by a locomotive manufacturer; in the Soviet Union, Lokomotiv Moscow were sponsored by the railworkers union and Torpedo Moscow by car workers. Eastern European leagues also traditionally contained a large number of clubs funded by the army, such as Dukla Prague, Honved Budapest, Legia Warsaw, Steaua Bucharest, CSKA Sofia and CSKA Moscow. The Dynamo clubs were traditionally associated with the secret police, but this connection has been discontinued rather hastily in the post-communist period; the best known examples were in Bucharest, Moscow, Kiev and Tbilisi.

The names of the football clubs have always reflected the political climate in the socialist republics of Eastern Europe. During the 1940s and 1950s new ideologically more desirable names were imposed on the major clubs. In Bulgaria, Levski Sofia (named after a national hero in battles versus the Turks) had to spend the period 1949 to 1956 as Dinamo Sofia. In Czechoslovakia, Bohemians Prague were obliged to call themselves Spartak Stalingrad from 1951 to 1961, Slavia Prague became Dynamo Prague from 1953 to 1965, and Sparta Prague were known as Spartak Sokolovo from 1953 to 1965. The fans continued to call the clubs by their traditional names.

The three Czech clubs cited above were able to revert to their pre-communist names in 1965 at the beginning of the 'Prague Spring'. In Hungary, the liberalization of 1956 prior to the October uprising enabled leading clubs to return to their original names. MTK Budapest had three different names between 1949 and 1956, and Ferencvaros had endured periods as EDOSZ (the food industry workers trade union) in the 1949–50 period and Kiniszi (a Hungarian hero) from 1950 to '56. The years between 1954 and 1956 also witnessed a period of liberalization in Poland. No fewer than 12 first division clubs discarded their imposed socialist name and reverted to their previous name.

The more recent ending of communist rule has led to a further spate of name changes. Three trends are discernible:

1. a return to original names. For instance, in Budapest, the army club Honved have replaced the soldier on their badge with a lion, the emblem of AC Kispest. The latter club previously played at the ground and the club's name is now Kispest-Honved. In Bulgaria, Trakia Plovdiv have reverted to Botev Plovdiv, their original name in 1912;
2. dispensing with names associated with the old communist regime, e.g. in the Czech Republic, Ruda Hvezda (Red Star) Cheb have switched to Union Cheb and in Georgia, Dinamo Tbilisi have become Iberiya Tbilisi;
3. changing the name to match that of a new sponsor, e.g. Boby Brno rather than Zbrojovka Brno in the Czech Republic, and Dunaujvaros became Dunafeer in Hungary.

Political interference in club football in Eastern Europe has also taken other forms. In Bulgaria during the 1968–69 season the government ordered six mergers involving football clubs. The two most famous were in Sofia with the merging of Levski and Spartak, and also Slavia and Lokomotiv. The latter fusion lasted only until 1971 due largely to opposition from the fans, whereas the separate name of Levski was re-established in late 1989 during the social revolution. More seriously, in Romania two previously small clubs associated with the Ceaucescu family (FC Olt and Victoria Bucharest) were remarkably successful up until the overthrow of the regime and their resultant forced demotion.

Another aspect of political control under communism involved restrictions on the transfer abroad of football players in contrast to the free market situation in the inter-war period. These transfers operated within strict limits. Footballers could move to the West only after reaching the age of 30 and if they had served the national team with distinction.

Since the impact of Gorbachev's glasnost on Eastern Europe, younger players have been transferred to the West. This trend to younger transfers started with Alexander Zavarov's move from Dynamo Kiev to Juventus of Italy at the age of 27 for £3.2 million in the summer of 1988. The flow of transfers to the West from Eastern Europe accelerated after the 1990 World Cup finals in Italy. Seventeen of the Czechoslovak squad of 22 players moved to the West and most of the Romanian squad were transferred abroad after the finals.

The *glasnost* policy of permitting official transfer to the West can be seen also as an attempt to stem the flow of unofficial defections. The most notorious case in Czechoslovakia in the 1980s was the joint defection of Ivo Knoflicek and Lubos Kubik from Slavia Prague while on tour in West Germany. After several months in hiding around Europe and a fruitless attempt to sign for Derby County in England, both returned eventually to Prague to negotiate compromise deals which took them to St Pauli (West Germany) and Fiorentina (Italy) respectively.

A more beneficial legacy of the communist era is the set of international stadia constructed in the 1950s (Prague is the exception to this with its huge stadium, Strahov, dating back to the 1930s). Most of them remain large all-seater venues, perhaps lacking in Western comforts but certainly grand in scale. The most important are Budapest's Nepstadion (72,000), Sofia's Vasilij Levski Stadion (55,000), Bucharest's 23 August Stadionul (65,000), Chorzow's Slaski Stadion (70,000) and Moscow's Centralny (formerly Lenin) Stadion (100,000). Also, the newly independent republics of Ukraine and Georgia have large all-seater national grounds in Kiev (100,000) and Tbilisi (74,000).

Apart from the few national stadia of renowned stature in international football, there is a dearth of grounds in Eastern Europe with modern facilities and an all-seater capability. For example, in Czechoslovakia, of the 15 club grounds in the 1991–92 first division (Slavia Prague are excluded in that their ground is undergoing reconstruction), only two are all-seater stadia. The average for the other 13 clubs is only 25 per cent of the capacity seated.

Given the often complex mix of ethnic groups in many of the relatively new countries of Eastern Europe, it is not surprising that ethnic conflict should surface occasionally in the football arena. As the split between the Czech and Slovak Republics became inevitable, there was a growing animosity toward the opposition at matches involving leading Slovak versus leading Czech clubs. Similar tensions exist in Romania between clubs from the ethnic Hungarian part of the country and the rest. In Budapest, the traditional Jewish football team were MTK, later known as Hungaria from

1926. The club was closed down in 1940 to prevent persecution of their supporters and reformed as MTK after the war.

Regional enmities are strong in many of the Eastern European countries, either taking the form of ethnic rivalry or provincial rivalry with the centre. A distinctive feature of Eastern European football has been the dominance of clubs from the capital cities in the national leagues. This trend is strongest in Budapest (94 per cent of championships since the Second World War) and Bucharest (90 per cent). Only Warsaw has failed to win a majority of championships during this period.

Towards the end of the 1980s there began series of major organizational changes in Eastern European football, most notably professionalization of the players, independence for the football authorities and football clubs from the state, a switch from traditional socialist sponsorship to more commercial forms, and the lifting of restrictions on transfers to the West. Taken together, this package of reforms provides both new opportunities and new problems for football clubs and players. Successful players and successful clubs are likely to benefit, but ordinary players and ordinary clubs could be facing a bleak future in the later 1990s.

Change has been more gradual over a longer period of time in Hungarian football. The first steps towards professionalism were taken in 1979 and official approval was granted in 1983. In 1989 the Football Association became independent of the state and freedom of contract was granted to the players. Similarly, many of the changes in Czechoslovakia took place before the velvet revolution of 1989, largely in response to pressures for change from within but also partly influenced by the general context of *perestroika*. However, it was not until 1990 that players obtained freedom of contract and the Football Association became independent.

The urgent need for change in Eastern European football was highlighted by a series of scandals in the 1980s. One recurring theme involved the payment of illegal bonuses to top up players' inadequate wages. Czechoslovakia provided an example of this with a financial scandal at the First Division club Bohemians Prague. The president, secretary, treasurer and 20 present/past players of the club stood trial on charges of corruption and embezzlement. Several officials were imprisoned but then released as part of the general amnesty following the velvet revolution.

A second kind of incident centred on the fixing of match results, either on behalf of a betting syndicate or in order to influence promotion or relegation issues. Hungary's major scandal of the early 1980s involved 499 players, officials and organizers, some of whom were given prison sentences. Further examples of match-fixing were evident towards the end of the 1982–83 season in Bulgaria and the 1986–87 season in Poland. Only the leading Eastern European clubs have thus far negotiated major sponsorship deals with western firms in the post-communist era. For example, in Czechoslovakia, the best supported team, Sparta Prague, were the first to secure a deal in August 1990 involving shirt advertising in return for sponsorship from Opel. Minolta of Austria followed suit by sponsoring the team from Nitra. The change of sponsor unfortunately deprives us of one of the most evocative names in European football, that of Plastika Nitra. In Hungary the best supported club, Ferencvaros, obtained a lucrative sponsorship deal with a French construction company (Bras) in 1990, but unfortunately the deal ended after only one season. Another Budapest team, Kispest Honved, now have a Belgian backer (Louis De Vries).

An interesting tendency in Czechoslovakia is for clubs to be sponsored by a wealthy entrepreneur, often an expatriate made good in the West. In September 1991, Slavia Prague were taken over by Boris Korbel, an American multi-millionaire of Czech origin. He is financing the reconstruction of their stadium. Further examples of the benevolent godfather syndrome are to be found at Viktoria Zizkov (returning to their former position in the first division after 45 years) and Boby Brno (sponsored by a former ice hockey player).

In comparison to ordinary workers in Eastern Europe, professional footballers remain well off but the austerity policies introduced by many governments are imposing hardship at all levels of society. Hence the solution for the best players is to seek a transfer abroad (i.e. to the West) in order to secure a higher standard of living, not to mention Western currency.

As an example of the level of player mobility, in December 1990 there were over 200 Hungarian footballers officially playing abroad. However, around three-quarters of them were playing in the Austrian regional third and fourth divisions. These players are semi-professionals who live in Hungary and cross the border each weekend to play for Austrian teams in return for match expenses. Austrian match expenses are very desirable as they are higher than a full-time salary in Hungary. Similarly, in October 1990 there were 170 Czechoslovak footballers officially playing abroad. Around two-thirds of them were located with lower division teams near the border in Germany and Austria. As with Hungary, these players are semi-professionals who continue to live in their home country.

The move from state socialism to market capitalism has inevitably resulted in severe economic pressures on the general population, including football spectators. Policies have often involved prices doubling (at the very least) with wages remaining constant. In terms of football, the effect is higher admission charges and a resultant decline in attendances at matches. The reduced crowds further exacerbate the financial crisis in the game, especially for those clubs without new sponsorship and the players at such clubs. Predictably, the new era of financial independence from the state is taking its toll upon the smaller clubs. Between 1988 and 1989 the number of multi-sports clubs in Hungary decreased by 8 per cent and the membership of clubs declined by 19 per cent in the harsh economic climate of democratic capitalism. Similarly in Czechoslovakia, 16 of the 593 registered football clubs closed down in 1990–91 because of financial problems.

Elsewhere in Eastern Europe indicators of football's financial health are not encouraging. In 1993 it was reported that nearly every professional club in Bulgaria was in grave financial difficulties. After the promising early growth of foreign sponsorship in Romania, several clubs have been abandoned. Italian sponsors have withdrawn from Inter Sibiu, Politecnica Timisoara and Sportul Studentesc. In the Ukraine, Dynamo Kiev are having to cope with a reduction in attendances from 50,000 for important matches in the former Soviet league to a mere 2,000 for matches in the new Ukrainian league. In desperation some clubs are returning to a form of barter economy. Hutnik Warsaw recently signed a Russian player for a television set and a video recorder.

Football is undoubtedly the leading spectator sport in Eastern Europe. It is seriously challenged only by basketball in Lithuania and ice hockey in Czechoslovakia. The average attendance is around 5,500 in Czechoslovakia for both football and ice hockey first division matches but football has over six times more clubs and players. In common with many countries in Western Europe, average attendances at football matches have more than halved since the mid 1960s. The first division average in 1965–66 was 11,910. The former Soviet Union exhibited the highest number of participants in football with a total of over 4.8 million registered players. In terms of absolute numbers, this placed the Soviet Union second only to the reunified Germany. However, when the number of players per capita is measured, higher participation rates are found elsewhere in the region, in Bulgaria and Czechoslovakia.

From the very beginning of football in the region, the national team has played an important role in national consciousness. In the inter-war period many of the countries of Eastern Europe were either new or reconstituted nations. As such, football provided an opportunity for crystallizing nationalist sentiment in an era before the penetration of modern mass media. Also, many of the early international matches in the region tended to be against near neighbours, thereby stoking the fires of popular nationalism.

In the communist years, the national football teams retained a prominent position in the hearts and minds of the nation. Support for the national team could easily be construed as support for the regime. Moreover international sport was a key arena in which to demonstrate the strength and superiority of socialism. It is for this reason that the Olympic Games football competition was taken so seriously by the communist countries, leading to a period of complete dominance from 1952 to 1976.

Among the attributes advocated and adhered to by Eastern European teams of the early communist period were an ethos of good sportsmanship (thereby demonstrating the moral pre-eminence of socialist man) and an emphasis on teamwork (thus confirming the superiority of collectivism). The national legends at this time were more likely to be teams rather than individuals.

One of the earliest legends centred on the strength and invincibility of Dynamo Moscow in 1945. In order to celebrate allied victory over Nazi Germany, the Russian team came on a tour of Britain in November 1945. This visit occurred during a long period of Soviet isolation from international competition, which made them an unknown quantity. Four matches were played of which Dynamo won two and the other two were drawn. The quality of the Russian play impressed the many spectators who flocked to see them. The attendance was 82,000 at the first game, a 3–3 draw with Chelsea, and 45,000 witnessed the 10–1 demolition of Cardiff City. The 4–3 win over Arsenal was watched by 54,000 and a further 90,000 attended the 2–2 draw with Glasgow Rangers.

After the impressive display against Cardiff, the Russians were regarded in the press not as a football team but as a machine. Their style of play was to British eyes unusual in that it was based on accurate passing along the ground, subtle interchanging of position and, above all else, teamwork. The mystique was heightened by their bizarre (at the time) kit, including long baggy blue shorts with a white rim at the base. Moreover, the legend was enhanced by the circumstances of the victory over Arsenal, who fielded England's star winger Stanley Matthews as a guest player. This match was played at Tottenham Hotspur's White Hart Land ground in a veritable pea souper fog (of the kind now seen only in Hammer horror films) and controlled by a Russian referee and two Russian linesmen, who policed a half each but both on the same side of the pitch! Upon their return to the Soviet Union the entire team were made Heroes of the Soviet Union.

The second legendary team from the region were the Hungarians in the first half of the 1950s. Known as the 'Magic Magyars', Hungary lost only one game in almost six years, covering a total of 48 games. Their misfortune was that the one defeat came in the 1954 World Cup Final against Germany, a team they had already beaten 8–3 in an earlier round of the tournament. By way of some recompense the run of victories did include winning the 1952 Olympic gold medal.

Undoubtedly the status of this Hungarian team was increased by their performances against England. In November 1953 Hungary dispelled the myth of English invulnerability by winning 6–3 at Wembley, the first home defeat for England against foreign opposition. Next year in Budapest the difference in quality between the two sides was confirmed emphatically in a 7–1 scoreline. In terms of playing style the Hungarians combined individual brilliance with collective skills, relied on finesse rather than force to dominate a match and introduced the tactical innovation of the deep lying centre forward. Sadly, the 1956 Hungarian uprising against Soviet domination led to the break-up of the side with three of the leading players (including perhaps the best of them all Ferenc Puskas, the 'galloping major' who played for the army team Honved) defecting to the West.

Given the overwhelming political influence on all aspects of society in the communist era, it is self-evident that the presentation of sport in the press and media comprised only the officially approved coverage. Naturally this version extended to strong support for the national football team in the hope that success on the field would reflect beneficially on the regime.

All the Eastern European socialist republics had a national daily sports paper (such as *Ceskoslovensky Sport* in Prague and *Nep Sport* in Budapest) in which football was given a high profile. An interesting feature of the coverage during this period was the complete invisibility of defected sports stars, including footballers, in the national press. Even where such individuals were highly successful in the West, their performances never got a mention.

Political interference in the organization of the national team was commonplace in a structure of total state control of sporting activity. In some respects this situation was to the benefit of the national team, which could demand all the players and resources they desired. The common scenario in the West of disputes between leading clubs and the national team over the availability of players was just not an issue in the East. The club versus country debate was always decided in favour of the national team.

An extreme example of interference in national team selection and administration occurred in the Soviet Union in the mid-1970s. After Dynamo Kiev became the first Soviet club side to win a European club trophy, the authorities declared that the club's players *en masse* were to become the Soviet Union national team for the next two years. This experiment was ultimately unsuccessful in that the pressures of appearing as both a club and a national side took their toll on the players' performance. In a similar vein, the Romanian FA installed their under-18 national team in the first division championship as Viitorul Bucharest for two seasons from 1961 to 1963.

ON THE WORLD STAGE

In terms of international standing, Eastern Europe has a distinguished football pedigree. The region has a record of success in the World Cup, the Olympics and the European Championship. It has provided the runners-up in the World Cup final four times (Czechoslovakia and Hungary twice each), the winners of the Olympic football gold seven times and the silver six times, plus two victories and three runners up in the European Championship. Unfortunately most of the countries are going through a difficult period currently in the transition to a market economy, and the good showing in particular of Romania and Bulgaria in USA 1994, was thus against the odds.

Czechoslovakia and Hungary were among Europe's football elite in the inter-war period and they have had their successes under communism also. Both countries fall within the Donauschule tradition (along with Austria) of football with an emphasis on passing and high technical skill.

Czechoslovakia has twice reached the World Cup Final only to lose both times. In 1934 they lost in extra time to the host nation Italy after spurning chances to clinch the match in normal time. Their second final in Chile in 1962 was lost 3–1 to the great Brazilian team, albeit lacking Pelé, who was injured. In addition, Czechoslovakia have won the Olympic gold in 1980 and lost in the final twice – 1920 and 1964. In the former case they were never awarded the silver medal after walking off the field against Belgium (the host country) before the end of the match when 2–0 down. Czechoslovakia's other notable triumph was to win the European Championship in 1976.

It is generally agreed that there have been three great Czechoslovak teams. These are the 1930s team (World Cup finalists in 1934), the early 1960s (World Cup finalists in 1962 and based heavily on the army team Dukla Prague) and the 1976 European champions. The great tradition has now been fragmented by the political division into Czech and Slovak Republics as from 1 January 1993. Czechoslovakia as a football entity ceased to exist a little later with the national team's elimination from the World Cup.

Hungary has had an equally distinguished career in international football. They have an identical World Cup record to Czechoslovakia in the sense of reaching but losing two World Cup Finals. The 1938 final was lost to the World Cup holders Italy and in 1954 the Magic Magyars surprisingly lost to

Germany (as outlined above). Hungary also has a good record in Olympic football, winning the gold three times (1952, 1964 and 1968) and the silver in 1972.

There have been three great Hungarian teams. The first was in the period immediately prior to the First World War, and the second in the 1930s which reached the World Cup Final. The last great Hungarian team was the Magic Magyars of the 1950s. In the last two decades Hungarian football has fallen below its previous high standards and as yet the decline shows no sign of abating. Failure to qualify for USA 1994 was known early in the qualifying competition.

Currently, the most powerful football nation in the region is Russia, the main inheritor of the Soviet Union's tradition in world football. That tradition is a relatively short one in that for a long while the Soviet Union pursued an isolationist policy in relation to international competition. Their first appearance in Olympic football was not until 1952 and they did not enter the World Cup until the qualifying tournament for 1958. Predictably, a political explanation lay behind this. The Soviet Union did not wish to enter the world arena until it felt confident of performing successfully and indeed had a good chance of winning trophies.

In the World Cup itself the Soviet Union never progressed beyond the semi-final stage, which was achieved in England in 1966. However, the Soviet Union has a strong record of success in the other major events. They struck Olympic gold twice in 1956 and 1988, won the first European Championship in 1960 and were runners-up in it three times (1964, 1972 and 1988).

Poland achieved little in the way of football success in the pre-communist period. It is usually cited as one of the three countries (along with Bulgaria and Romania) to benefit from the communist reorganization of football. There has been one truly great Polish team in the 1970s. This team came third in two World Cups (1974 and 1982), won the Olympic gold in 1972 and the silver four years later in 1976. Following the team's last success of 1982 there was an exodus of players to the West. Since then, the Poles were runners-up in the 1992 Olympics.

Bulgaria also benefited from the improved training facilities and technical standards under communism. However, its only major success was to win the Olympic silver in 1968. Around the same time Bulgaria achieved its best run in the World Cup by qualifying for four consecutive final tournaments between 1962 and 1974. The Bulgarian traditional style of play is a passing game involving a slow build-up from defence.

The Romanian national team has had no major successes in international football. They have qualified for the final stages of the World Cup on five occasions, but three of these were in the early days of the competition in the 1930s. During the same period they won the Balkan Cup more times than any of their neighbours. Since then, the biggest triumph for Romanian football was Steaua Bucharest winning the European Champions Cup for clubs in 1986.

Estonia, Latvia and Lithuania were minor players on the international football stage in the inter-war period and have remained so since their renewed independence in the 1990s. At present, Lithuania appears the strongest of a weak bunch in that they have won the Baltic Nations Cup twice in the new era.

The region has its share of traditional animosities in football history. Many of them are based on neighbourly rivalries in particular parts of Europe. For example, there is long-standing Central European rivalry between Czechoslovakia and Hungary (plus Austria), as well as a Balkan rivalry between Bulgaria and Romania (plus Yugoslavia as was) and the aforementioned Baltic rivalry.

Political history dictates some of the other enmities involving Eastern European countries. There remains a current of anti-Soviet/Russian feeling throughout the rest of Eastern Europe following the four decades of Soviet imperial dominance. Also, Hungarian minorities across the border in neighbouring countries have made for increased tension in Hungary's recent games with Romania and promise more in the future with Slovakia.

An unusual saga of violence on the football pitch surrounds matches between Eastern European countries and Brazil. In the 1938 World Cup finals Czechoslovakia clashed violently with Brazil in Bordeaux and in 1954 Hungary shared a hostile encounter in Berne against Brazil, again during World Cup Finals.

Spectator violence of the hooligan variety spread to Eastern Europe in the mid 1980s. However, thus far it has not been associated with matches involving the national teams. Rather it is supporters of the leading clubs who have attracted hooligan gangs, such as Sparta Prague in Czechoslovakia and Ferencvaros in Hungary.

Serious hooligan violence in Czechoslovakia began on the last day of the 1984–85 season, when Sparta fans broke train windows, slashed seats and threw bottles on the way to Banska Bystrica in Slovakia. Thirty fans were arrested and the authorities announced that they would not tolerate 'the manners of English fans' in our sport. So concerned were the authorities that they commissioned a documentary film on Sparta fans travelling to an away match entitled Proc (Why)? However, officials admitted that the film had resulted in more widespread copying of spectator violence, even among crowds leaving the cinema after watching the film.

The current state of Eastern European football is dominated by the legacy of communist rule and its distinctive organization of sport. The ongoing transition from state socialism to market capitalism is resulting in major economic, political and social changes which have inevitable repercussions for football in these countries. Most significant is the removal of large-scale state financial support, both from the national team and the leading clubs. The resultant financial crisis means that these countries are undergoing a transition period, while they learn to adapt to the new economic reality. One of the clearest effects is the strong economic pressure on leading players to move to the West. The increased political freedom to transfer abroad is likely to remain, although some countries (notably Romania) are seeking to reimpose some form of restriction.

It is only the leading Eastern European clubs with substantial Western sponsorship deals which have any chance of persuading leading players to remain in their home country. Even these clubs cannot compete with offers from Italy, Spain, Germany and France. The latter group of countries (especially Italy and Spain) stands at the apex of the new international division of labour in football, while Eastern Europe provides a new source of cheap labour.

From the point of view of the national teams, the migration of leading players abroad is a mixed blessing. On the one hand, these players are refining their skills in the best leagues and among the best players in the world (e.g. in Italy). But the main problem is then obtaining their release for international matches. Whereas FIFA can insist that players are released for World Cup matches, this is not the case for international friendly matches. Successful teams are built and team spirit forged in these friendly matches. What then of the future for the national teams of Eastern Europe? Although the current transition period is a difficult one, there are reasons for optimism. There is a long history of football success in the region and young players are still emerging with natural ball skills as well as high technical ability. Russia and the Ukraine are likely to be powerful football nations in the future in lieu of the former Soviet Union. It would be nice also to see the Czech Republic (more probably than Slovakia) and Hungary reclaim their leading role in world football. Alas neither qualified for USA 1994.

6

ON THE CONTINENT: FOOTBALL IN THE SOCIETIES OF NORTH WEST EUROPE

Stephen Wagg

If association football was produced in Great Britain, then the countries of North West Europe were its first and principal export market. The founder members of FIFA in 1904 – France, Belgium, Denmark, the Netherlands, Sweden and Switzerland, along with Spain – were nearly all from NW Europe and it has also, arguably, been from this region that, during the lifetime of football as an international game (roughly 1900 onwards), the game's most successful exponents have been drawn. England's claims to have the best national side were being confidently pressed well into the 1950s, but by that time England had already been defeated in a number of European capitals – Brussels, Zurich, Budapest and Prague among them – and other centres of excellence had emerged: notably, Austria and Germany. By the 1960s, the continent of Europe, with its apparently wider professional and commercial horizons, was the focus of aspirations for all the leading English (and some Scottish) clubs. British coaches admired, and tried to propagate, continental technique and, following the foundation of UEFA in 1955 and the establishment of intra-European competition, English managers, players and supporters spoke increasingly of the need to 'get into Europe'. In the period since, although other continents and regions – Southern Europe, Latin America . . . – have come to challenge the dominance of NW Europe in international football culture, the most accomplished football nation is nevertheless to be found here: West Germany (simply Germany since reunification in 1990) have won the World Cup three times since their readmission to FIFA in 1950 and only once (in Chile in 1962) have they failed to progress at least to the Semi-Finals of the competition. This chapter looks at football across the countries of this subcontinent, touching at different times on the societies of France, the Netherlands, Germany, Austria, Belgium, Luxembourg and Switzerland, as well as the Scandinavian countries: Sweden, Denmark, Norway, Iceland, Finland and the Faeroe Islands.

Stephen Wagg

BEGINNINGS: FOOTBALL COMES TO EUROPE

The arrival of football in Northern Europe is well documented (Meisl 1956, Mason 1986). In the main, it was carried by English and Scots who came to the continent as diplomats, migrant workers, students and in various other capacities and brought their footballs with them. Later, British club sides frequently undertook European tours, invariably with great success. The mode of assimilation of football to national culture and its subsequent social progress varied from country to country: the social class base of football was, for example different in different societies and so was the degree of willingness to embrace professionalism. Likewise, in some Northern European countries, football became the chief sport to bear the 'national interest'; in other, neighbouring societies – France, for instance, Belgium and Finland – this wasn't necessarily the case. In general though it can be assumed that, in each country, the growing power of an urban, industrial middle class was a factor in the spread of the game; indeed, the zeal of bourgeois figures to promote a rationalized, codified competitive game and their related concern to displace the political energies of their employees have become the conventions of sports history. Again, as the following case histories show, there were various national versions of this general theme.

The adoption of association football in **France** was, as the historian Richard Holt shows, attended by considerable ideological strife. The French upper and middle classes turned increasingly to 'English sports' in the wake of the military defeat by Germany in 1870. Association football was one of several sports linked to ideas of national revival, although, with its English associations, it was unacceptable to many members of the highly nationalistic gymnastics movement and too restrained for the Social Darwinists, who preferred rugby football (Holt 1981, 191–5). By the time of its importation to France, football was already popular among the British working classes and was therefore thought unsuitable for the French well-to-do actually to play (Holt 1981, 66). It was well established before the First World War, although initially rugby was more popular and several of the first association football clubs in France started as sections of rugby clubs. These tended to be in the industrialized north: Le Havre, for example, was founded in 1892 as part of a rugby club that was already 20 years old (Oliver 1992). Clubs devoted solely to football were founded the same year and British people, usually based for business reasons in the channel port towns, were often involved. The first all-French team – Club Francais – was also set up in 1892 (Murray 1994). The French football federation was founded in 1918, along with the French cup competition. By the 1930s, there were over 5,000 football clubs in France and professionalism was sanctioned during this decade (1932). Amateurism had, as in most countries, been a matter for political contention and, in 1907, the French, secular, state-sponsored sports body USFSA supported the (unavailing) bid by the English Amateur FA to affiliate separately to FIFA (Murray 1994).

France played international football from 1904, but were not among Europe's premier football nations in the pre-Second World War period.

Some of their defeats were spectacular: they lost 1–17 to Denmark in the Olympic Games of 1908, and 1–13 to Hungary in Budapest in 1927. One possible factor here is that association football, despite its popularity, was always challenged by other major sports in France: rugby prospered as in no other European country, especially in the south and west of France, and cycling likewise had built an impressive base by 1914 (Holt 1981, ch.5). France staged the World Cup in 1938, but made the least impression of any host.

Football is said to have come to the **Netherlands** via migrant cotton workers from Lancashire in England, where the industrial towns were an important early centre of football activity. They were playing football matches in the city of Enschede from the mid-1860s. As with most countries of the region, however, football clubs were not formed until the turn of the century: only Sparta Rotterdam remain of the first clubs; of the other major Dutch clubs, Ajax were set up in 1900, Feyenoord in 1908 and PSV Eindhoven in 1913 (Oliver 1992). The Dutch FA was founded in 1889 and the Dutch League in 1898. The comparative lateness in the founding of clubs between, say, the Netherlands and the Nordic countries on the one hand and Britain and France on the other, may have been related to the fact that the former countries became industrialized and urbanized later: in the mid-nineteenth century Dutch society, like the Scandinavian societies, was still predominantly rural (Gouldsblom 1967, 20; Morner 1989; Rojas 1991) and association football is an urban phenomenon.

Dutch society has been described as 'pillarized' – that is, divided into blocs. These blocs are religious (Calvinist, Roman Catholic), political (e.g. socialist) and general (i.e. secular, 'non-confessional'), each organizing activities in every sphere of social life. The first Dutch football clubs came from the latter sector, followed by clubs from the religious ones. All the founder members of the Dutch FA were drawn from the cities of North and South Holland, these provinces being the most powerful, economically and politically, and historically the bastions of the Protestant commercial class. Club members were drawn substantially from these 'burgher' classes. The Dutch imported a number of 'English' sports but none of them has approached football in its popularity (Gouldsblom 1967, 32; 113–15). The Netherlands excelled in early Olympiads and, like most of the more northerly European countries, it resisted professionalization until after the Second World War. Its international programme, again like that of its near neighbours, was limited.

As with France, the first area of football activity in **Germany** was the coastal ports to the north of the country, particularly Hamburg, where the first club devoted specifically to football was set up in 1887. (Rugby had been adopted earlier: some already established rugby clubs, such as TSV 1860 Munich, later took up association football). The German football association, the DFB, was founded in 1900 in Leipzig in eastern Germany and by 1904 it comprised 200 clubs and 10,000 members. The game's pioneers were young middle and lower middle class males, many of them beneficiaries of an amendment of trading regulations in 1891 which reduced working hours in offices and shops. Their conception of the game accorded closely with that of the English amateur: play was very individualistic and team spirit negligible. Players would often only join a club for one match and might even be moved to change sides at half-time if the game was too one-sided. This contrasted sharply with the military solidarity of the stronger and more influential gymnastics movement (Eisenberg 1991). Indeed, so ferocious was the antipathy to football in areas dominated by the gymnastics movement that steps were taken to suppress it: football was, for example, banned in Bavaria before 1913 (Murray 1994).

The game, however, flourished among the German working class during the inter-war years and crowds swelled as a consequence. One area of especially fervent enthusiasm for the game was the industrial heartland of the Ruhr where clubs such as Schalke 04, based in the town of Gelsenkirchen, became a deeply embedded part of the culture of working-class families, many of them migrants from eastern Germany attracted to the local pits and factories. Despite facing prejudice and discrimination as a 'Pole and Prole' club, Schalke were the premier German team of the 1930s and were known for their 'beautiful' football, based on teamwork. They also, to the consternation of the political left, affiliated to the nationalist WSV (West German Sports Association), rather than to comparable Social Democratic or communist organizations. This affiliation was based not so much on a lack of proletarian sympathy as on the now-familiar conviction that sport and ideological debate were not compatible: 'We wanted to play football', said a Schalke member. 'We wanted to have nothing to do with anything else. Politics and religion played no part whatever in our club' (Gehrmann 1989).

Football had, moreover, been 'a game of the national interest' since before the First World War – in 1911, for instance, the DFB became linked to the nationalist paramilitary organization, the *Jungdeutschlandbund*. After the war, Germany's admission to FIFA was delayed, principally by the opposition of the British FA, but Germany were good enough to win third place in the World Cup of 1934, beating the much admired Austrian 'Wunderteam' in the play-off for third place. And Hitler's hopes of celebrating victory over England in Berlin in 1938 to the greater glory of the Third Reich are well documented (Beck 1982). England, as it turned out, won 6–3, but, on FA advice, their players gave the Nazi salute before the match. (The English League side Aston Villa toured Germany at the same time and declined to perform the salute.) Germany annexed Austria during this year and the German national team appropriated Austrian international players. FK Austria, the team most closely associated with the Jewish liberal minded middle classes, was made to translate its name into German, becoming FK Osterreich; the Jewish team Hakoah was dissolved (Murray 1994).

Austrian football began in the capital city of Vienna among the colony of Britons working there for English firms. The first clubs, founded in the 1890s, were initially restricted to 'a noble minority' (Horak 1992a), but football soon had broad support across the social classes, both at local and national level. By 1914 there were 14,000 registered players, rising to 37,000 in 1921. By 1932 there were two leagues, comprising 25 teams; all of these were based on Vienna so that, even at club level, the keener rivalries were international as well as inter-city: with Berlin, Budapest, Prague and Bologne (Horak 1992b). This club rivalry was institutionalized in the Mitropa Cup, a smaller scale precursor of the European Cup which began in 1927 and concentrated on the countries of middle Europe. Austria became the acknowledged centre of football excellence and headquarters of the so-called 'Danubian school' during the inter-war years. From 1902, the national side played international matches against other European countries, chiefly Hungary: Austria's first ten internationals were all against Hungary. These international matches grew to be immensely popular: in 1923 85,000 people came to watch Austria play Italy in Vienna (a 0–0 draw).

Football had a particular place in Viennese culture. It thrived most strongly in the working-class districts of industrial suburbia. The club most closely associated with this sector of Viennese society was Rapid Vienna, its playing style being seen as a reflection of the harshness of life in the working-class districts. The Austrian international of the 1920s, Josef Uridil, a physically tough and combative player, is said to have represented this 'rapid spirit'. But football was also popular among the coffee houses of the liberal, largely Jewish intelligentsia; they too had their favoured style of play and their football heroes. Matthias Sindelar, of Wiener Austria, who played for Austria in the 1930s, was one such hero – another child of the industrial suburbs (in this case the son of a Moravian migrant worker), he nevertheless came to typify the delicate skills valued by Viennese intellectuals. Sindelar, a prominent anti-fascist with a half-Jewish mistress, disappeared during the Nazi occupation of the late 1930s (Horak and Maderthaner 1992). Uridil and Sindelar were among football's first celebrities and were extensively commercialised, being used to market a range of goods (Horak and Maderthaner 1992).

Football proved less compatible with the social democratic culture of 'Red Vienna', with its ideals of 'joy without purpose' (Horak 1992b).

Football came to **Belgium** via English students in the 1860s. The first football club, Royal Antwerp, was founded in 1880 and the Belgian league began in 1895. Among the founder members of FIFA in 1904, Belgium are said to have been the main instigators of the confederation (Murray 1994) – the initiative being taken by the football section of the country's sports federation, the Union Belge de Societes Athletiques. The Belgian FA split off from this union in 1912. Belgian sport was, as to some extent it remains, dominated by the ethnic divisions of Belgian society: from 1930 until after the Second World War there was a separate Flemish FA in Belgium, the official FA being perceived as exclusively Walloon (Colin and Muller 1982). Moreover, the power of the churches and the trade union movement led to a pillarization, similar to that of Dutch society.

Despite this, Belgian football administrators have been among the more internationally minded in Europe. Although most of their early international matches were against France or Holland, near neighbours with cultural affinities, they were strong supporters not only of FIFA but also of the World Cup: they were one of the few European nations represented at the inaugural tournament in Uruguay in 1930 and they also supplied the referee (Oliver 1992). Domestically, Belgian football was a bastion of amateurism and Belgium won the Olympic title, the country's only football trophy, in 1920 – a time when only Britain recognized professionalism (Oliver 1992).

The football league of **Luxembourg**, founded in 1908, has always been amateur: Luxembourg, a very small country with a population of under 400,000, could not support professional clubs. However, Luxembourg joined FIFA in 1910 and has entered every World Cup barring the first one. Football clubs are concentrated in the three main towns of Luxembourg, Differdange and Esch (Oliver 1992).

Switzerland is thought to be the first country on the continent of Europe where football was played. It was brought there, again by English students, in the 1850s and initially, as in Belgium, it was played in colleges. The first Swiss clubs date from the late 1870s and early 1880s; these were, as they remain, based on the major cities of Zurich, Geneva and Berne. As in other European societies such as Italy and England, there developed a pattern of strong rivalry between clubs within these cities – notably in Zurich, with Grasshoppers and FC Zurich. Regional championships were set up in 1898 but a national league did not emerge until 1934. By this time Switzerland were well established in European international competition, beginning with fixtures against France and Germany (Switzerland has substantial French and German speaking communities) in the period 1905–9. Switzerland won the silver medal in the Paris Olympics of 1924 and were World Cup quarter finalists in 1934 and 1938. Switzerland's greatest football heroes – the Abegglen brothers, Max and Andre, who are still the country's leading scorers – played during this period.

The principal Nordic countries – **Sweden**, **Denmark** and **Norway** – also imported British games in the latter decades of the nineteenth century. Like Germany, the Scandinavian societies had a strong gymnastics movement but here the militaristic model of gymnastics, although it had its adherents, was much less influential. In Scandinavia gymnastics, sports and physical education generally were seen as preparing young people for civic duty and promoting the spirit of cooperation among them (Meinander 1992) and games such as football and cricket were valued in this context. Football was taken up initially in Denmark, where the first club, KB Copenhagen, was founded in 1876. The development of football in Denmark closely paralleled its progress in Sweden in a number of respects. In both countries the game was largely confined in its early stages to a major city: the Danish League, when it was founded in 1913 was confined to teams from Copenhagen, while Gothenburg (where Orgryte IS, the nation's oldest club, was set up by Scots in 1887) was initially the centre of football in Sweden. Similarly, in both societies football clubs were often linked to social democratic parties, and rivalry between the two countries was a feature of their early football development. Sweden adopted a Danish version of football in the late nineteenth century, but in modified form: for example, they discarded the off-side rule – 'they could not understand it perhaps' observes an official history of Danish sport sourly (Det Danske Selskab 1978).

Football had been brought to Sweden by Scottish workmen employed in the shipyards along the Swedish coast. Indeed, the game developed in the major coastal cities of Gothenburg, Malmo, Stockholm and Helsingborg, flourishing in the big industrial workplaces of firms such as Eriksons. Football, according to the Swedish sociologist Tomas Peterson (interview with author), was promoted typically by activists in the Peoples Movements (trade unions, tenants' movements and the Social Democratic Party) but, as elsewhere in Europe, football was a site of struggle *within* these movements: the left of the Social Democratic Party (along, ironically, with the right of the gymnastics movement, led by educationalists such as Pehr Ling) were generally opposed to football because of its competitiveness. For left Social Democrats in Sweden, as for their counterparts in Austria and Germany, football was an unwanted displacement of political energy; for those on the right of the party it was the peoples' game.

A league began in Gothenburg in 1895 which four years later admitted clubs from Stockholm; the Swedish FA, based in Stockholm rather than Gothenburg, was constituted unofficially two years before the setting up of FIFA in 1904 and the two cities dominated Swedish football until well after the First World War: in 1921 IFK Eskiltuna were the first provincial club to win the Swedish championship and in the 1930s and 40s clubs from the other industrial cities, such as Helsingborg, Norrkoping and Malmo, were taking the title. Helsingborg IF won the championship four times between 1929 and 1934; IFK Norrkoping five times in six years (1943–8); and Malmo FF four years in five (1949–53).

In Denmark the supremacy of Copenhagen teams was not seriously challenged until the 1950s. Internationally, Denmark were the most progressive and accomplished of the Scandinavian countries. Denmark reached the Olympic Final in 1908, at which time they were coached by an Englishman – former Manchester City goalkeeper Charlie Williams. (Williams was one of a number of Englishmen coaching on the continent, latterly at the instigation of the British FA, before the Second World War.) Denmark were again in the final four years later in Stockholm, when they were beaten by England; their performance moved the English club Chelsea to sign one of the Danish team, Nils Middleboe, the following year. Women's football began in Denmark in 1918 – later than in England, where it was being played by the 1890s (Williams and Woodhouse 1991) and France where it was played a year or two earlier, but well before other countries in the immediate vicinity.

Sweden's first international match took place in Gothenburg in 1908, an unbalanced encounter in which they defeated Norway 11–3. As Olympic hosts in 1912, Sweden were eliminated in the first round by the Netherlands. They did not play Denmark in a full international until 1913; in this year the two countries met twice – in Copenhagen in May and in Stockholm the following October – and Sweden were overwhelmed on each occasion (0–8 and then 0–10). Sweden entered the Olympiad of 1924, in Antwerp, but engaged only in friendlies and local competition until the World Cup of 1934. Indeed, during the inter-war period the greater part of the international programme of the Nordic countries – that is, outside the Olympics – was taken up with playing each other in the Scandinavian Championship inaugurated in 1924. This once again confirmed Denmark as the leading football nation in the area (Winners 1924–9), with an emergent challenge from Norway (Winners 1930–32). Sweden didn't win the competition until 1933; they were known, nevertheless, as high scorers in this period – seven goals (and five conceded) against Finland in Helsinki in 1924, again seven the following year against Norway in Oslo, a further seven against Estonia at Talin in 1926, twelve against Latvia in Stockholm in 1927, and so on. This suggests a strong commitment on their part to the Scandinavian amateur ideal of teamwork above trophies. Many of these goals were scored by one of Sweden's football heroes, Sven Rydell, whose 49 goals in 43 games between 1923 and 1932 remain the national record.

Football had come to Norway, as to Belgium, via British students and was first played there in the early 1880s. The first club, Odd SK Skein, was founded in 1894 – Skein being a small town to the south of the country. Norway, it should be said, is a country of small towns, compared to its southern neighbours: the capital, Oslo, at under three-quarters of a million, has around half the population of Stockholm or Copenhagen. Clubs from towns such as Skein, Fredrikstad and Tromso have continued to prosper therefore in the Norwegian league, although, as elsewhere, the more successful clubs were, from the beginning, located in the industrial cities and larger towns. Despite the dominance of Fredrikstad in the early years of the country's championship, therefore, the Oslo clubs – SOFK Lyn Oslo, FK Skeid Oslo and Valerengens IF Oslo – along with SK Brann of Bergen, the Trondheim club Rosenborg BK and Viking FK Stavanger have generally been the principal contenders. Although the Norwegian FA, the Norges Fotballforbund, was established in 1902, roughly concurrent with a number of other national FAs in the region, Norway, more northerly and rural than Denmark or Sweden, did not have a national league until 1937. The league ran only for two years before a seven-year lapse (1940–47) owing to the Nazi occupation and its aftermath; for those two years, and for three of the first five years after resumption in 1948, the champions were Fredrikstad, from a town of around 50,000 inhabitants.

Despite their inauspicious international debut against Sweden in 1908, and the fact that most of their internationals up to the Second World War were against Scandinavian opposition, Norway were good enough to reach the Olympic Semi-Finals in 1936, beating the hosts Germany along the way in a hushed stadium in Berlin. Norway's only qualification for the World Cup, prior to 1994, was in 1938, when they were eliminated in the first round by Italy. As in Austria, Norwegian football had to contend with occupation and attempted Nazification during the period of the Third Reich; in this context, the country's team stood resolutely for nationhood and their coach, Halvorsen, was condemned to death by the occupying power for refusing to let his side play under the German flag.

In the case of **Finland** and **Iceland**, which is closer to Greenland than to mainland Europe, football has not approached the status of national sport that it has achieved elsewhere in Europe. Climate is a major factor here: the cold weather has meant that football has only been viable during the summer months (the season runs from April to October) and other sports more suited to the natural environment – skiing, ice hockey and, in the case of Finland, rally driving – have enjoyed greater popularity. Even in the summer months, athletics is as central as football to the sports culture of the area: this is perhaps part of the heritage of the gymnastics movement which was very strong in Finland.

Football reached Finland in the 1890s. The Finnish FA was formed in 1907 and the national side played its first match four years later in Helsinki against Sweden, who beat them 5–2. Their third match was in the Stockholm Olympics of 1912 against Italy, whom they beat 3–2. They also disposed of Tsarist Russia but lost heavily to England in the Semi-Final (0–4) and against the Netherlands in the play-off for third place (0–9). Their national league had begun in 1908, being based mostly on Helsinki, the capital, which houses roughly a fifth of Finland's 5 million people. The three main Helsinki clubs – HIFK, HJK and HPS – were founded in 1897, 1907 and 1917 respectively. Before the Second World War, the Finnish championship went almost always to one of these three clubs.

Finland participated in the Scandinavian Championships, in which Denmark, Norway, Sweden and Finland played each other four times and which lasted until the early 1970s. They mostly came last.

Domestically, a similar pattern can be observed in the football of **Iceland**, whence the game was taken, again by Scots, in the 1890s. Clubs were founded soon afterwards, all those of note being in the capital Reykjavik, where more than half the population of Iceland (around a quarter of a million) live. Five of the seven league clubs in Reykjavik were founded between 1899 and 1911. The Icelandic League began in 1912 and from that year until 1951 the champion and runner-up clubs were always drawn from Reykjavik. Outside the capital, Icelandic towns tend to be no larger than 14,000 or 15,000 in population. Several of these towns formed clubs in the 1920s, 30s and 40s, and those of more recent vintage – notably those from the towns of Akranes, Keflavik and Vestmannaeyjar – broke the metropolitan monopoly in the 1950s.

The Icelandic FA didn't form until 1929, the year of their affiliation to FIFA, and entry into international competition – with a defeat by Denmark in Reykjavik in 1946 – was late by Scandinavian standards. Iceland's first 11 international matches were against other Nordic countries. Iceland did not enter the World Cup before the mid-1950s and has never qualified for the finals, either of that competition or of the European Championships.

Football was brought to the **Faeroe Islands** by Danes. The islands have a population of less than 50,000 people and their economy is sustained by Danish money (Engel 1991). Their league began in 1948 and their cup in 1967. Their main club is in the town of Torshavn (pop. 14,000). In internationals, they have tended to play their near neighbours: Iceland, Greenland and the Shetland Islands.

We see, then, how the hitherto British pastime of association football was ingrained in the cultures of continental Europe by the early 1900s. It was a phenomenon, as in Britain, of urban industrial society and it flourished chiefly in the major cities. There it was embraced, again as in Britain, by people of different social classes, either as participants or as observers, and the game was often politically contentious – whether in *status* terms (as with the aversion to 'prole' teams in Germany) or in relation to *class* (as with the widespread fear of the political left in Germany, Austria and some Scandinavian countries that football was a digression from the class struggle). The game fed *religious* particularism (in France and in the Netherlands) and other *ethnic* rivalry (in Belgium), and almost everywhere in Europe it bulwarked feelings of nationhood and often became the extension of foreign policy. This was vividly so in times of war: after the First World War the British FA, a professed opponent of mixing politics with sport, nevertheless fought the readmission of Germany to FIFA; in the late 1930s and 1940s, the period of fascist ascendancy, football was used to rally both the despoilers (Nazi Germany, where the national team was regarded with suspicion by opponents of the regime) and the despoiled (Austria and Norway).

POST-WAR EUROPE: FOOTBALL, NATION AND MARKETS

The football world in North West Europe was not, of course, a free market although, naturally, it was more free in some regions than in others. In all European societies there was opposition to professional football and in general to the commercialization of the game, but this essential dispute had different political complexions in different countries and, similarly, was resolved far earlier in some countries than others. This final section discusses the influence of market forces and ideas of nation, and some of the tensions between them, in North West European societies in the post-war period.

It was in Britain, as we've seen, that professional football received its first formal legitimation. This was in the 1880s, although there remained a deep divide in status between amateur and professional players and the latter were subject to a maximum wage restriction until 1961. A number of European countries embraced professionalism in the inter-war period: Hungary and Austria in 1924 (although in Austria it was banned again after the Second World War), Czechoslovakia in 1925, Spain in 1926, France in 1932 and Switzerland in 1933 (Murray 1994). During this period, and indeed virtually ever since, the greatest commercialization and the freest football labour market was in Italy. In the Low Countries of Belgium and the Netherlands, and likewise in Scandinavian societies, resistance to professional football was stronger and more enduring.

The amateur spirit was especially strong in Belgium and the Belgian FA was strongly opposed to professionalism in the 1920s and 30s – although there was some sanction of the paying of money in 1934. In 1929 the Belgian international Raymond Braine was banned by the Belgian FA for running a cafe, which they deemed to be a commercial exploitation of his celebrity as a footballer. (Braine was signed by the English League club Clapton Orient, but refused a work permit by the British Ministry of Labour. He went instead to play for Sparta Prague.) Formalized professional football was not conceded in Belgium until the 1960s, and even then it was in practice only semi-professionalism.

In the Netherlands, professionalism was resisted until 1954 and in the Nordic countries this political wrangle was still more prolonged: for example, the Danish team which beat Sweden 2–1 in Copenhagen in 1965 was composed entirely of amateurs and the Danish FA did not relent on the matter of professionalism until 1976. Sweden has never adopted full professionalism – the top clubs are semi-pro – although amateur status was abolished there in 1967. Several interconnecting factors seem to have contributed to this uneven pattern of development towards professionalization.

All the societies involved here were capitalist societies, wherein the profit motive and the notion of organized competition were legitimated and well established. But, in some spheres and at some levels, they were nevertheless contested and this, as we've seen, could be either from the left or the right: indeed, professionalism might be kept at bay by a combination of the two. The balance of social forces varied from society to society. In Germany, for instance, professional football had been agreed in principle in 1933, but was vetoed by Hitler's National Socialists, who took power that year. In this instance, the restoration of amateurism was an ideological instrument – one way of demonstrating to the German working class that the nation and the state were more important than money – and it drew, naturally, on the militaristic tradition of the gymnastics movement. Elsewhere, the church was in the vanguard of opposition to professionalism. This was the case in Belgium, where the Catholic church fought the professionalizing of sport and received support from the union movement. Each, from their respective positions on the political spectrum, argued that there were higher ideals than the cash nexus to be pursued in sport: the church espoused the more militarist and national values that prevailed in Germany and France, while the workers' sports movement, with its notions of comradeship through sport, was strong in the Belgian unions.

In Scandinavian societies, decisive resistance to professionalism was more pervasive and related to important differences in social structure, as compared to countries to the south and west. Sweden is a good case in point: a society with a weak, state-oriented aristocracy, a capitalist middle class which, given the low rate of urbanization, had no great political presence, and an historically powerful peasant class, whose culture was characterized by 'the illegitimacy of luxury and a very sober relation to money'. The Swedish peasantry tended to disdain both 'aristocratic pomp' and 'individualistic bourgeois swagger' (Rojas 1991, 65–7). Such disdain strongly informed the campaigns of the various People's Movements, active in Sweden from the late nineteenth century, which fought to protect people from what they saw as the evils of the market. In the Nordic countries this social pattern, as I've suggested, promoted a more benign and cooperative idea both of nationhood in general and of sports in particular. The Swedish FA excluded professional footballers (mostly employed by Italian clubs) from its national side until the World Cup of 1958 – which they were to host. Even so, it is suggested that well into the 1970s matches between Sweden and Denmark were more in the nature of 'true folk festivals' (Det Danske Selskab 1978, 93). Indeed, it's even argued that, despite the popularity of association football, *rugby* football was given priority in Danish schools after the Second World War because it was felt to give more opportunity to the less gifted

(Det Danske Selskab 1978, 86). Opposition to professional football in this region – the Nordic and the Low Countries – was disarmed by several linked factors: the acceptance of commercialization in other European football leagues, which ultimately undermined football development at home; this came out of a new, more competitive sense of nationhood in relation to football which, in turn, was strengthened by the growth in the televising of the game; this growth of the game as television likewise fed the growth of domestic commercial lobbies against enduring amateurism.

For those international footballers in North Western Europe who were disgruntled with the amateur ethos of their home FA, the Italian and Spanish leagues had, since the 1920s, provided lucrative escape routes. After the Second World War these South European Leagues were recruiting as voraciously as ever on the north of the continent. For example, the three leading members of the Sweden team that won the gold medal in the London Olympics of 1948 – the 'Gre-No-Li'trio: Gunnar Gren, Gunnar Nordhal and Nils Liedholm – all signed for Milan the following year. Other players went abroad, immediately disqualifying themselves for the national side under Swedish FA rules. Sweden qualified for the World Cup Finals of 1950 despite retaining only two of the Olympic Championship team of only a couple of years earlier. They came third, having beaten Italy 3–2 in Sao Paulo in the first round, and after the tournament a further eight Swedish players moved to Italian clubs (Oliver 1992).

Similarly, Denmark, who had been third in the London Olympics, banned three of their leading players – Karl and John Hansen and Karl Praest – when they joined Juventus of Turin; the three became subject to a two-year 'quarantine' period. In the spring of 1947, Hungary had travelled to Turin to play Italy and the Hungarian player Ferenc Puskas had been offered the equivalent of £30,000 in cash to play in the Italian league (Puskas 1955, 37). He demurred, but moved to Real Madrid in the 1950s, during which time several Dutch players also travelled south – notably Fas Wilkes, who was engaged by the Spanish club Valencia. Several Austrian players also went abroad after their team came third in the World Cup Finals of 1954.

During this period, crucially, the broadcast media were beginning to become more involved in football in Europe. The relationship of the written media to the game was long established. Football magazines had replaced cycling ones as the most popular sporting journals in Europe and football was amply covered by the press in most countries: 275 reporters from 29 countries attended the World Cup Finals of 1934 in Italy (Murray 1994). Although only one nation (the Netherlands) took up the offer of radio broadcasting rights to the tournament, radio broadcasts of football matches – particularly international matches – were popular with national radio audiences in the 1930s; in Austria, for example, in December 1932, a crowd of several thousand gathered in the Heldenplatz, in the centre of Vienna, to listen to commentary of the England v. Austria match being broadcast from London and, on one occasion, a parliamentary debate was even suspended so that members could listen to an Austrian game on the radio (Horak 1992a, 5). Television entered the calculations of most European football adminis-trators in the mid-1950s; the World Cup of 1954 in Switzerland was, effectively, the first TV World Cup. From then on, European publics would think less about whether or not the members of their national side were paid professionals and more about that side's performance under the gaze of an international audience. Journalists, advertisers and business interests throughout the continent of Europe were in any event busy exploring the commercial possibilities of a new 'Euro consciousness' to accompany the emergent political and economic liaisons of the Common Market.

The foundation of UEFA in 1954 and the inauguration of the European Cup the following year can be seen in this light. The initiative for the competition was taken by the French newspaper *L'Equipe*, whose editor Gabriel Hanot took astute advantage of claims by the British press that Wolverhampton Wanderers, having beaten Moscow Spartak and the Budapest club Honved the previous year, were the best team in Europe. The trophy immediately went south, to Real Madrid, who beat Stade de Reims, the premier French club of the time, 4–3. In the Year of the first European Cup Final the award of European Footballer of the Year was also instituted and, in the first instance, was given to the veteran England player, Stanley Matthews. Over the period 1956 to 1991, however, this award has reflected both national football accomplishments – the winner has been West German on six occasions and Dutch on six – and financial power: the honoured player has mostly come from a Spanish club (six times), a German one (eight times) or an Italian (ten times – eight of them after 1982).

In the face of this commercial power, resistance to professionalism in the northern countries finally wilted. In the Netherlands, the issue was decided in 1953 by a classic carrot-and-stick assault on public opinion by the domestic pro-professionalism lobby. First it was arranged for a team of Dutch professionals, all with foreign clubs, to play France in Paris in aid of victims of the February floods; then, in the wake of a notable performance (the Dutch side won 2–1) a professional league was begun in the Netherlands, outside the jurisdiction of the official FA.

The Dutch national team had played 20 international matches between the beginning of 1950 and the end of 1953, losing sixteen of them and winning only two; the Dutch FA capitulated to professionalism the following year. The game continued to grow in the Netherlands: there were 4,000 football clubs there in 1960 (as against 1,000 in 1940) and a third of the male population over 12 attended a football match at least once a month (Gouldsblom 1967, 114). As elsewhere on the continent, no sport rivalled football in popularity.

But the consequences of commercialization for Dutch football are clear. First, as in other countries, championship success now falls only to the very few: only five clubs – Ajax, Feyenoord, PSV Eindhoven, DWS Amsterdam and AZ Alkmaar – have won the trophy since 1960. Of these, only the first three are now realistic contenders and DWS actually folded in 1982. Ajax and Feyenoord, the former with its roots in the Jewish middle class and the latter growing out of a working-class club in the Rotterdam docks, now draw support from all over the Netherlands. PSV's following is principally in the south of the country. Second, the clubs depend heavily on sponsorship: PSV are wholly owned by Philips, the electrical conglomerate, Feyenoord were sponsored until 1992 by HCS Computers, and so on. Third, since Dutch football cannot generate sufficient revenue to keep the best Dutch players in the domestic game, these players, when they return, exert considerable power on the Netherlands FA, the KNVB. For example, the players took 70 per cent of KNVB revenue from the World Cup in 1974, and a similar cut in 1988 meant that the KNVB actually made a loss on the European Championships, despite winning them. Similarly, the Dutch players in 1993 forced the removal of their coach, Dick Advocaat, and called for the appointment of Johan Cruyff, now resident in Spain (Dunne 1994).

In Denmark there was a similar tide of events. Important commercial interventions had already been made in Scandinavia, notably the introduction of football pools – in Sweden in 1934 and in Denmark in 1948. Danish football internationals had also begun to be shown on television in Denmark, beginning in 1956 with the second half of a 1–5 defeat by the Soviet Union relayed from Moscow. During the 1960s football became a fully national sport in Denmark in that provincial clubs came into their own and teams such as AGF Aarhus and Esbjerg FB began to win the national championship: the Danish team that played Wales at Wrexham in 1964 was composed entirely of players from the Danish provinces. Also, during the 1960s Danish advertisers began to press for access to shirts of sports players. This began with ice hockey but there was resistance from the Danish FA – and, indeed, from Danish TV, who refused until 1976 to broadcast games in which 'living billboards' were participating. By this time the Danish FA had relented on professionalism: the national side failed to win in nine internationals during 1970 and the following year professionals playing abroad were admitted. By the late 1970s Danish football was extensively commercialized: shirt advertising was permitted and the national team was being sponsored by the Carlsberg brewery. The Danish league became professional in 1978 (Det Danske Selskab 1978, 66, 88 and 92). However, in practice none of the Scandinavian countries can support more than a semi-professional arrangement; an increasing number of Danes and Swedes, as well as Norwegians, Finns and Icelanders, play professional football outside Scandinavia, mostly in Britain or in other European countries.

Elsewhere on the continent, Luxembourg cannot support professional football at all, although a number of its nationals play professionally in France and Belgium.

Since professionalism does not consist solely in the cash nexus, mention should also be made here of coaching. In English football culture, coaching historically infringed the prevailing code of both the amateur and the professional worlds. To the British amateur, in the early decades of this century, it tampered with the devil-may-care spontaneity of the game: for most amateurs, you should not, in the words of the famous Arsenal manager Herbert Chapman, 'organize victory'. And, for many British professionals, coaching was a pretentious and unhelpful interference in the people's game – a game which grew organically out of the life of working folk and, as such, needed no artificial sustenance. Either amateur or professional footballers might see coaching, whether for good or ill, as inherently defensive. On the continent of Europe, however, it was seldom seen as any of these things. Coaches were seen instead as enhancers of technique (a word only recently adopted in Britain in relation to football) and important assistants in the matter of building national identity through sport. Moreover, as I've already noted, they were often ex-League footballers brought over from Britain – prophets, apparently, without honour in their own country. From the continent, British football began increasingly, between the wars, to be seen as dull-witted, defensive and tactically backward (Meisl 1956).

Coaching was accepted early in Austria and Hungary, regions known for their football artistry and individualism in the period before the Second World War. The Scot Jimmy Robertson arrived in Hungary in 1911 to coach MTK of Budapest and was succeeded in the job by an Englishman, Jimmy Hogan. Hogan subsequently spent most of the 1920s and 30s coaching in Austria, in association with the eminent Austrian football administrator Hugo Meisl, and was regarded as the tactical inspiration behind the 'Wunderteam'. Denmark, as we've seen, had an English coach during their Olympic campaign of 1908. Similarly, Sweden were coached both for the Olympics of 1948 and at the Stockholm World Cup Finals in 1958 by another English ex-pro', George Raynor. Raynor, little known in England, observed that the 'development of the international team always got top priority in Sweden . . .' – an oblique reference to the historical feuding between the FA and the even more parochial Football League (Raynor 1960, 34). He too regarded British football as crude and tactically innocent by comparison with countries on the continent; he coached the English League club Coventry City for a while, and also Lazio in Italy (Raynor 1960, 28, 96 and 101). Coaching and strategic innovation were also a particular feature of Swiss football in the 1950s and 60s: the Swiss national team manager of that time, Karl Rappan, is said to have devised the 'sweeper system', now widely employed, which uses an extra defender patrolling behind the main defence. This became known as the 'Swiss Bolt' system; *catenaccio*, the word given to the defensive style of play adopted in Italy during the 1960s, also translates as 'bolt'.

Two further features of social and political life, which bear on the European football world, should be discussed here in relation to markets and nation: the ethnic rivalries, which fracture all European societies to some degree, and the globalization of economic activity – particularly in the field of mass media. On the first count, it is clear that ethnic-political divisions have a continuing importance in football cultures of North Western Europe. These divisions are expressed with varying measures of ferocity, according to the social context. In the Netherlands, for example, one of the major clubs, Ajax, with their historical associations with Jewry (Dunne 1994), have experienced anti-Semitic abuse from opposing supporters – particularly those of their main rival, Feyenoord. However, Ajax fans, be they skinheads or the drug-oriented 'violent eccentrics' of the 'F-Side' (Kuper 1991b), cheerfully acknowledge the Jewish link and usually hang the Israeli flag behind the goal. In Belgium the often sharp ethnic demarcations which inform political and social life have their ramifications in the football world. The French-speaking Walloons, who tend to predominate among the elite social groups and whose power base is in the industrial south of the country, have, as we've seen, generally controlled the Belgian FA. The Flemings, who speak a Dutch dialect, are more influential in the north of Belgium where the service industries and administrative centres (many of them to do with the European Community) are to be found. In Belgian football, Standard Liege are strongly associated with the Walloons and Bruges is the principal Fleming club. There is, predictably, an ongoing controversy over the respective numbers of Walloons and Flemings who are selected to play for the national side; this controversy is regularly stoked up by the newspapers that cater to each community.

It appears, though, that the fiercest expression of ethnic and racial hostility in this region in the time since the Second World War has been in the only area to experience a serious recasting of national boundaries: Germany. One of the manifold consequences of the social and political disintegration of the communist bloc in Eastern Europe was the reunification of Germany in 1990. The east of Germany, incorporating some of the least privileged and most heavily proleterianized parts of Germany (Tampke 1979, 90), had been the fount both of German socialism and German football. The German Democratic Republic, formed in 1949 but a *de facto* administrative reality from 1946 onwards, had had a football league of its own since 1948; it had entered the World Cup of 1958 and played its first friendly against a Western power (against England at Leipzig) in 1963. During the Cold War period, East German football, like most football in the Warsaw Pact countries, was disparaged as robotic and politicized in Western European football culture. Much was made of the involvement of the hated secret police, the Stasi, in the running of the Dynamo Berlin club; the political authorities of Eastern Europe, it was said, menaced their national side into doing well – it was 'Success or Siberia'. But the GDR were never a conspicuously successful football nation. Indeed, it has been argued that the country had a more authentically socialist culture than the West acknowledged, preferring to promote public participation in sport and building public gymnasia and swimming pools to facilitate this – an argument supported by the international prominence of East German athletes and swimmers (Tampke 1979, 90–91).

By contrast, West Germany, an increasingly vibrant capitalist economy after the Second World War, has, as we've seen, had a football team to match. The German squad, based on club sides from the thriving cities of Munich, Cologne and Dortmund, has dominated world football in the post-war era. No national side has been so successful during this period, their unexpected victory over the Hungarians in the World Cup Final of 1954 having been a major boost to national morale which in football terms has never visibly subsided. Moreover, West German football culture bears the hallmarks not only of modern capitalist efficiency, reflected in a thorough-going national coaching network set up in the 1950s, but also of a militaristic discipline, rooted in the traditions of the German gymnastics movement and of the Prussian landowners, the *Junkers*. This shows in the language of the West German football world and has done since the early decades of German football. The historian Christiane Eisenberg notes how during the late nineteenth and early twentieth century, in the cultural aftermath of the Franco-Prussian War, there was in the German game a

> strengthening of the team-spirit with militaristic language and imagery. Words such as *Angriff* [Attack], *Verteidigung* [Defence], *Flugel, Flanken* [both translate as Wing], *Deckung* [Protect] or *Schlachtenbummler* [Supporter] are primarily associated with football in the German language of today; about 1900, they were clearly associated with the army and war. (Eisenberg 1991, 212–13)

In more recent decades the national football team has been a major focus for nationalist sentiment and, when this sentiment has been expressed, it has like as not been in military terms. Witness the nicknames of West German popular football culture: among prominent West German footballers of the 1960s, 70s and 80s, Franz Beckenbauer was *Der Kaiser*, Gerd Muller *Der Bomber*, Karlheinz Rummenigge *Der Blonde Bomber*, and so on.

Not surprisingly, then, when the GDR's league, FA and national side were disbanded in 1990, only two East German clubs were invited to join the unified Bundesliga and very few players from the eastern region have since been selected for the national squad. And, perhaps predictably for a society in such economic and political disarray (unemployment was around 50 per cent in the early 1990s) football hooliganism in the east of Germany is said to be the worst in Europe. In the final season of the East German league several matches had to be abandoned because of serious disorder, a fan was shot dead by police in Leipzig and hooligans ransacked a number of city centres. Dynamo Dresden were also obliged to cancel a match because it fell on Hitler's birthday and local neo-Nazis had deemed it a desecration of their holy day (Kuper 1991a).

Black players (Bundesliga clubs began to recruit African players such as the Ghanian international Anthony Yeboah and Souleyman Sane from Senegal in the early 1990s) are sure of a grim reception, redolent with monkey noises, on some German football grounds, especially in the east. Likewise in France and Belgium, once both colonial powers in Africa, where a number of African players now play. Such racist manifestations are beginning to be seen on the terraces now in countries further north, such as Sweden, where populist parties of the far right are starting to make headway.

Finally, I want to say something about the mass media and globalization in regard to North West European football and national cultures. In the industrialized world, and indeed in many other parts of the globe besides, football is primarily a television show. The game is now experienced by hundreds of millions of people and the principal means of their experiencing it is via their TV sets: this factor alone, as I see it, can explain the award of the 1994 World Cup to the United States – a country with a negligible football tradition, but the world leader in the field of commercial TV and merchandising. In Europe, football was well established on TV in the late 1960s and the 1970s. The audiences, except for major football matches such as the European Cup Final, were national rather than international. During that period, the size of crowds was correspondingly in decline – an indication, no doubt, of the increased diversity of leisure time options – and clubs as a consequence have become more and more dependent upon TV revenue and sponsorship. There has, of course, been resistance and regret here – 'Soccer cannot live off sponsors. It needs spectators', insisted Dr Heinz Gero, President of the Austrian Football Federation in 1970 (Horak 1992a, 11) – but in no European country have football crowds recovered their pre- and immediate post-war level. In the Nordic societies spectators have never been plentiful, but in the more industrialized and urbanized societies to the south west contemporary attendances are also modest, compared to the 1950s. Dortmund and Bayern Munich average around 35,000 over a season, for example, and PSV Eindhoven, the biggest club in the Netherlands with its close links to the transnational electronics corporation Philips, draws less than 25,000. Crowds are lower in Belgium. No top European football club could now sustain its level of operations without the extraneous revenue that the mass media bring. Since the late 1980s, though, this revenue has come increasingly from media companies with an international compass – satellite companies, hungry both for profits and suitable events with which to fill the schedules of their specialist sports channels. This seems to me to have three important and related implications for national football cultures in Europe.

First, the social and economic base for the stewardship of what is undeniably the people's game in Europe has changed. The men (it is, of course, always men) who run the major clubs across north-west Europe are increasingly drawn from new-wealth, transnational elites in the media, media-related or service industries. In Italy, for example, the Agnelli family who have used the Fiat car fortune to fund Juventus of Turin since the 1930s, are now rivalled by the transnational media entrepreneur Silvio Berlusconi who runs the massive corporation Fininvest and owns AC Milan football club. Agnelli has always perceived his role as club proprietor in a semi-feudal way: the team is his gift to the local working class. For Berlusconi, the club is seen as a profit-making concern and as a means to promoting his other commercial and political ambitions (Portelli 1993). The same goes for Bernard Tapie, the flamboyant politician and entrepreneur, who, until corruption charges were brought against him in 1994, ran the Marseilles club in France; for Alan Sugar, who took over the London club Tottenham Hotspur in 1991 and whose international computer company Amstrad manufactures the satellite dishes now necessary to receive live TV transmission of Premiership League games in England; and so on.

Second, since the clubs are now run according to more unambiguously commercial criteria and since in many cases club moguls are also media moguls, access of the mass media to European football has been less and less restricted. But the access to the game of the ordinary supporter, especially if s/he doesn't have satellite TV, has been correspondingly threatened. In France, for example, live league football has since 1984 been broadcast, on subscription, exclusively by Canal Plus, a commercial channel part-owned by Berlusconi; the signal is scrambled before kick-off and can only be recovered through a decoder, activated by the subscription. In Germany, in 1992 the private SAT 1 cable channel bought exclusive rights to show live Bundesliga football for five years; around 75 per cent of German homes have the necessary cable – the lack is bound to be in the east (see Blain, Boyle and O'Donnell 1993; Goldberg and Wagg 1991; Williams forthcoming).

Third, we are now seeing, via the merging of television and football and the advent of satellite TV, the internationalization of football culture at the level of consumption. Although they were resisted in countries such as England until the 1930s, there were, as we've seen, trends towards the internationalizing of football at the level of production from the early part of this century. Coaches moved from country to country from the early 1900s and, latterly, so did club managers: by the 1960s they formed a continental technocracy, meeting on touchlines and in airport lounges across Europe. Football players in NW Europe have likewise taken work outside their own country for most of this century. Initially, as I said, the movement was mostly south – to Italy and Spain. But the commercialization of the 1960s began to change that: in Austria, for instance, League clubs, hitherto exporters of players but now faced with declining attendances, tried to revive public interest by signing players from Yugoslavia, Hungary, Germany, Turkey and Brazil (Horak 1992a).

There was, of course (as there remains), tension between national and international considerations – in Italy, for example, poor performances in the World Cups of 1962 and 1966 (when Italy were beaten by North Korea) led to moves to restrict the import of foreign players. But recent political developments, such as the collapse of the Soviet Union (see Duke 1991 and Chapter 5 in this volume) and the establishing of a single market in the European Community, have accelerated the movement of professional footballers across national boundaries. Most major club sides in Europe are now multi-national and, to safeguard indigenous football development, restrictions are now placed on the number of foreign players who may play for a club in European competition. This overall liberalization of the European football labour market, taken together with the introduction of transcontinental and global TV provision, has meant that now a person in, say, Belgium can turn on the television set and watch a match in the Italian league that features players from England, Denmark, Germany, France, Spain, Sweden . . . Here, European football participates in a postmodern culture of sorts, in which these disparate national elements mingle with others: class, gender, style and so on. An example from England illustrates this.

In England, the rights to show Italian league football live were bought in 1992 by Channel Four. Channel Four is a commercial channel, aimed principally at the liberal middle classes and cultural minorities. Italian football presents several audience possibilities for Channel Four, and the nature of their coverage reflects this. They have three basic paradigms: Italy as place of style and high culture where elegantly attired, attractive black-haired young males perform acts of physical grandeur in towering stadia before a host of passionate but discerning spectators; Italy, second, as the land of the quick temper and the extravagant gesture (a fast-talking young presenter sifts through a sheaf of Roman newspapers and translates apparent references to quirky Latin behaviour in the Italian football world); and, third, the Englishman abroad, wherein the Lazio player, Paul Gascoigne, an unreconstructed working-class male from the North of England celebrated in the British popular press for his 'couldn't-give-a-fuck-ness' (Williams and Taylor 1995) and spiritually at one with the English youths who visit Europe to drink lager and display their Union Jack boxer shorts (Williams et al. 1984), provides irreverent and semi-articulate reflections on football life in Southern Europe.

Thus, potentially – through television and globalization – European football in part severs its links with place and local cultures and enters the world of 'Eurovision'. Here, according to presentation and reception, it can be many things: national or international; high culture or low; earthy or chic; asexual or erotic. Football, as a television show, seeks and touches all of these markets. And it offers many stories: there will be periodic Clashes of Titans but, every so often, the tale will be of how Even a Cat Can Look at a King – as when in 1991 the Faeroe Islands, with their famously bobble-hatted goalkeeper, beat Austria. One thing is certain though: at top league level, truly national football in Europe, if it ever existed, has disappeared and national leagues, in any event, have different publics (via satellite) in different countries. Consumers can buy this country's league football or that, or all of them. Belgians can support Fiorentina, Swedes can follow Manchester United, Dutch can support Barcelona, and there will, of course, be no going back.

ACKNOWLEDGEMENTS

I'd like to thank Simon Kuper, who provided some of the material for this chapter, drawing principally on two texts: Francois Colin and Lex Muller, *Standard gouden voetbalgids* (Antwerp, Standaard, 1982) and Pierre Heijboer, *Kampioenen en krukken in kniebroek: Beelden en berichten uit de kinderjaren van de sport* (Bussum, Unieboek, 1978).

I have made extensive use of Guy Oliver's *The Guinness Record of World Soccer* (Guinness Publishing, Enfield, 1992). I made fewer references to these books than I might because I didn't want to interrupt the text unduly.

I also received a great deal of help from various friends and colleagues: at Leicester University, John Williams, James Fulcher, John Scott, Jonathan Osmond, Charlie Jeffery, Stephen Hopkins and Chris Hall gave me much valuable advice and information and so, from further afield, did Tomas Petersen (University of Lund), Richard Holt (University of Leuven), Pierre Lanfranchi (currently visiting De Montfort University in Leicester from the European Institute in Florence) and Roman Horak (Institute for the Study of Culture in Vienna).

REFERENCES

Beck, Peter J. (1982) 'England v. Germany 1938', *History Today*, June
Blain, Neil with Boyle, Raymond and O'Donnell, Hugh (1993) *Sport and National Identity in the European Media*, Leicester, Leicester University Press

Colin, Francois and Muller, Lex (1982) *Standaard gouden voetbalgids*, Antwerp, Standaard

Det Danske Selskab (1978) *Sport in Denmark*, Copenhagen

Duke, Vic (1991) 'The politics of football in the new Europe', in John Williams and Stephen Wagg (eds) *British Football and Social Change*, Leicester, Leicester University Press

Dunne, Donal (1994) 'Never, Netherlands', *The Absolute Game*, January/February, Edinburgh

Eisenberg, Christiane (1991) *The International Journal of the History of Sport*, vol.8, no.2, pp.205–220

Engel, Matthew (1991) 'Koyra Foroyar [Drive on Faroe Islands]', *Guardian*, 7–8 September

Gehrmann, Siegfried (1989) 'Football in an industrial region: the example of Schalke 04 Football Club', *The International Journal of the History of Sport*, pp.335–55

Goldberg, Adrian and Wagg, Stephen (1991) 'It's not a knockout: English football and globalisation', in Williams and Wagg, op. cit.

Gouldsblom, Johan (1967) *Dutch Society*, New York, Random House

Holt, Richard (1981) *Sport and Society in Modern France*, London, Macmillan

Horak, Roman (1992a) '"Austrification" as modernisation: changes in Viennese football culture', paper for conference on 'Soccer, Culture and Identity', University of Aberdeen, 1–4 April

Horak, Roman (1992b) 'The decline of Viennese football culture: Austrification, modernisation and the disappearance of the local club supporter', paper for conference on 'Professional Football', University of Nantes, 12–14 November

Horak, Roman and Maderthaner, Wolfgang (1992) 'Uridil and Sindelar: two interwar Viennese idols', paper for conference on 'Sporting Heroes in Contemporary Europe', European Institute, Florence, 19–21 March

Kuper, Simon (1991a) 'Football from a distance', *Ninety Minutes*, 3 July

Kuper, Simon (1991b) 'Flavour of the month', *Ninety Minutes*, 10 July

Mason, Tony (1986) 'Some Englishmen and Scotsmen abroad: the spread of world football', in Alan Tomlinson and Garry Whannel (eds) *Off the Ball*, London, Pluto Press

Meinander, Heinrik (1992) 'Towards a bourgeois manhood: Nordic views and visions of physical education for boys, 1860–1930', *The International Journal for the History of Sport*, vol.9, no.3, December pp.337–55

Meisl, Willy (1956) *Soccer Revolution*, London, Sportsman's Book Club

Morner, Magnus (1989) '"The Swedish model": historical perspectives', *Scandinavian Journal of History*, vol.14, no.3

Murray, Bill (1994) *Soccer: A History of the World Game*, Aldershot, Scolar Press

Oliver, Guy (1992) *The Guinness Record of World Soccer*, Enfield, Guinness Publishing

Portelli, Alessandro (1993) 'The rich and the poor in the culture of football', in Steve Redhead (ed.) *The Fashion and the Passion*, Aldershot, Avebury Press

Puskas, Ferenc (1955) *Captain of Hungary*, London, Cassell

Raynor, George (1960) *Football Ambassador at Large*, London, The Soccer Book Club

Rojas, Mauricio (1991) 'The "Swedish Model" in historical perspective', *Scandinavian Economic History Review*, vol.39, no.1

Tampke, Jurgen (1979) 'Politics only? Sport in the German Democratic Republic', in Richard Cashman and Michael McKernan (eds) *Sport in History*, University of Queensland Press.

Williams, John (forthcoming) 'The local and the global in English football and the rise of satellite television', *Sociology of Sport Journal*

Williams, John with Dunning, Eric and Murphy, Patrick (1984) *Hooligans Abroad*, London, Routledge and Kegan Paul

Williams, John and Taylor, Rogan (1995) 'Boys keep swinging: masculinity and football culture in England', in Tim Newburn and Elizabeth A. Stanko (eds) *Just Boys Doing Business*, London, Routledge

Williams, John and Woodhouse, Jackie (1991) 'Can play, will play? Women and football in Britain', in Williams and Wagg, op. cit.

7

CATHEDRALS IN CONCRETE: FOOTBALL IN SOUTHERN EUROPEAN SOCIETY

Pierre Lanfranchi, with Stephen Wagg

THE ORIGINS

The word *calcio* which defines soccer in Italian, is not, as in other European languages, a literal or phonetic translation of the English word 'football'. This term covered a variety of games played in the fifteenth, sixteenth and seventeenth centuries, all over Italy but especially in Florence.[1] This game was the Italian version of folk football and was very popular. Association football was introduced to Italy during the last 20 years of the nineteenth century, by Swiss and English students and by merchants in the textile industry. The contemporary reinvention of the *calcio fiorentino* did not compete with football, which was more popular.

The Italian aristocracy and business-bourgeoisie (*bourgeoisie d'affaires*) took to association football because it embodied their ideals – the values of the English industrial revolution and the myths of the English aristocracy. Football was part of an Anglophile cultural mode in this section of Italian society at the turn of the century: middle-class people wore English clothes and gave English first names to their sons. There was also a strong English influence on their discourse: they adopted terms like 'gentleman', 'fair play' and 'sporting', and, all over Southern Europe, chose English-style titles for their clubs like Milan Cricket and Football Club or Barcelona Football Club. But, fundamentally, the logic of football's promoters in Southern Europe was a mixture of an aversion to classical intellectual values and an allegory of liberalism.[2] More precisely, the English origins attributed to the football clubs which were founded across the whole Mediterranean area before the First World War, were different from the origins of the game in England itself. In the South of Europe it did not have the same strong links to working-class culture. Indeed, in Italy, the English culture of which football was a part was often imported not by English people themselves but by

Swiss, Austrians and Germans who had come to the country as engineers, technicians or merchants.[3]

In Catalonia, the Barcelona Football Club was set up in 1899 by Swiss and German technicians, who had learned a love of the game in their colleges. The rival club, Espanol, was established a few years later by engineers and students, who did not agree with the cosmopolitan recruitment policy of FC Barcelona and its president, the Swiss merchant Hans Gamper. Both teams, however, drew for their players on the same social sphere: the new urban elites.[4] The Italian club Genoa, which was founded in 1893 and is considered the oldest surviving Italian football club, is another good example. It is true that, initially, Genoa Cricket and Football Club was an exclusive club for British citizens and was mostly concerned with playing cricket. It is also the case that the founder of the club, Dr Spensley, had a British passport and was in charge of the health of the British community in Genoa. But, as Antonio Ghirelli pointed out: 'Genoa had an important British colony, made up of businessmen, consular officials and people in international trade who loved the city so much that they never moved out'.[5] In fact, the team developed from among a group of young businessmen, students and engineers, some of whom were English but who were more likely to be Swiss or Italians who had studied in Switzerland.

In Bologna, Bari, Naples, Milan and Irun in Spain, the first teams had English names like Sporting Club, Black Star, Football Club or Racing Club, but they did not have any particular relationship to Britain. In Italy, these English names were specifically opposed to those of the gymnastic clubs; these clubs, like their counterparts in France and Germany, were highly nationalistic and took Latin names like *Ars et Labor* or *Pro Patria*. So the common social characteristic of many founders of football clubs in the Mediterranean region was not to be British, nor to have learned the game there, but to be part of a modern urban society. James Walvin gives the example of Vittorio Pozzo, for many years coach of the Italian national side, who twice won the World Cup under his management. Pozzo learned English in the Northern English town of Bradford, but he learned his football earlier – at technical college in the Swiss town of Winterthur, 20 miles from Zurich and the birthplace of Hans Gamper.[6]

In 1909, the Italian Football Federation (Federazione Italiana Football) changed its name to Federazione Italiana Giuoco Calcio[7], now asserting a local tradition in the way it interpreted an international game. This symbolic purging of the British roots of the sport in Italy remained a feature of Italian football culture well into the twentieth century. Within this autonomous development, football as a spectacle, the crowd and the tactical and technical aspects of the game were intimately connected. From the 1930s onwards, Italian football was considered, both in Italy and generally on the continent of Europe, to be the antithesis of English football. In the prevailing style of play, in the players' labour market, in the attitudes of the crowd, in the press and media coverage and in the role of football in the life of Mediterranean societies, the mark of a Latin style was developing. In this short chapter, I would like to focus on this abstract idea of a Latin football, paying particular attention to Italy, but referring also to other Southern European countries like Spain, Greece, Portugal and Southern France.

There are some essential differences between Latin football in comparison to, say, the football of England or Germany. The English academic Lincoln Allison was impressed in Algeria, another Mediterranean country, by the fact that, for young people there, the English city of Manchester was associated only with the name of Bobby Charlton – the Manchester United and England footballer.[8] It is also surprising that the words used in Italian to describe being a football supporter are *La fede calcistica* – 'the football faith'. Throughout Catalonia, FC Barcelona is regarded as 'more than a club. It is the expression of an identity'.[9] In the face of a passion so firmly anchored in the culture and being of the Italian or the Spanish male, the games of calcio and football were never confined to the working class; instead they expressed local rivalries or regional oppositions.

Social scientists considered for a long time that football was lacking in cultural value: the old opposition between 'kultur' (high culture) and 'civilization' (a broader term embracing both high and popular culture) was transposed to the football scene. But recent research has shown clearly the place of football in the culture of Southern European societies, and how the fascination for a football team may represent some of the essential characteristics of industrial societies in the region.[10]

I will now observe four key aspects of the new Southern European football culture that has emerged and developed during this century: the crowd; the relationship between the game and the media; the players; and the styles of play.

THE CROWD

The stadium

Most of the major European stadia are to be found in Latin countries. Most of them were built during the periods of political dictatorship. The Olympic Stadium in Rome, for instance, was built for the World Cup Finals of 1934 and was authorized by Mussolini; the Santiago Bernabeu Stadium in Madrid, which holds 90,000 people and was constructed between 1944 and 1947, and the Nou Camp Stadium in Barcelona with its capacity of 115,000, are both symbols of the Franco period; similarly, the Estadio da Luz in the Portuguese capital of Lisbon, which can take 120,000 spectators, was erected in 1954 during the regime of Dr Salazar. For Mussolini, the big stadia were ideal places for the rallying of nationalist sentiment. Football matches in the thirties were moments in which mass culture and propaganda could go hand in hand. The new Italian stadia were built, not on the English model but in a neo-classical style, which, it was hoped, would 'give birth to new vigour worthy of the tradition of Rome'.[11] The stadia erected for the World Cup in 1934 – such as the Florence stadium, called Berta and designed by the futurist architect Nervi, or the Littoriale stadium in Bologna (now called

Stadio Dall'Ara) – expressed some of the modernist ideals of the Fascist regime and are now protected as patrimonial monuments.[12]

These stadia, in their structure and usage, were conceived in a way which was completely different from the British football grounds. They were located in non-industrial areas and designed to serve a variety of purposes. In Bologna, the stadium embraced a large sports complex, including tennis courts, a swimming pool and an athletics track, all dominated by a bronze statue of Mussolini on horseback. This multi-functional approach is remarkable in the case of the Barcelona stadium: at its heart the Nou Camp has a church and a museum.[13]

Latin stadia, unlike British ones, frequently display no obvious link to the working class or to the industrial development of the cities.

In Italy, two teams in the same town will often use the same stadium. The stadium is owned by the city; the clubs simply use opposite stands and terraces. This applies to all the big city clubs: Roma and Lazio, Milan and Inter, Juventus and Torino, Sampdoria and Genoa, and so on. In this sense, Italy differs from Portugal, Greece and Spain.

In Spain, the stadium is normally owned by the club and this marks the difference between the major clubs and the others: the big clubs have large numbers of *Socios* (members) – 99,000 at Barcelona, 65,000 for Real Madrid, 32,000 at Atletico Madrid and 30,000 for Atletico Bilbao. The stadiums of Benfica, Oporto and Sporting Lisbon have between them seen much of Portuguese football history being made: together the three clubs have won 57 Portuguese League championships. They also hold the greater part of the Portuguese football-going public.[14]

It is similar in the *cathedrales de beton* – concrete cathedrals – of Italy, where since before the Second World War many of the best footballers from other countries have been on view. Football still engages the passions of many thousands of Italians on a Sunday afternoon. In 1987–88, 65,100 season tickets were sold in Naples after the club signed the Argentinian captain, Diego Maradona, and 64,300 people bought seats for the same season to watch the two Netherlands players, Ruud Gullit and Marco Van Basten, turn out for AC Milan,[15] More than one million spectators came to Milan's 15 home matches during 1987–88 and three other teams – Inter, Roma and Juventus – had more than half a million. Even Ascoli, the club with the least financial resources, still had an average home attendance of 15,000.[16]

The supporters

The passion created by the big 'Latin' clubs reveals the football club as a central life interest for many people in the societies of Southern Europe. The sociologist Allessandro Dal Lago analysed the culture and rituals of Milan supporters.[17] The choreography of the terraces is well prepared, as are the slogans to be employed . Supporters generally arrive in the stadium at least two hours before the match; they will prepare the show that they will be putting on and they will chant against the other team. In the case of a 'derby' (a match between local rivals) these scenic aspects are visibly more important and more expansive. The social composition of the *ultras* who follow Milan does not necessarily reflect the composition of Milanese or Italian society.[18] Workers and the unemployed are a minority; their representation is less than in Italian society as a whole. The middle class remains the essence of Italian football support.[19]

In the Mediterranean region, supporting a football team may be seen both as an expression of local loyalty and as the concrete application of national rivalries. For example, in Spain, although Real Madrid was never really General Franco's team and the club survived the fascist regime, nevertheless in Barcelona or San Sebastian the match against Real – which is just called Madrid in Barcelona – is regarded as a symbolic battle against fascism and centralism.

The Franco regime had permitted the Spanish *liga* to resume immediately after the end of the Spanish Civil War and, perhaps concerned about the decline of traditional sports such as bullfighting, they attached increasing importance to football. In the 1950s and 60s, a period when they were still isolated politically in Europe, Franco and his ministers sought to identify with Real: the club were successful in European competition (European Cup Winners 1956–60) and, therefore, 'ambassadors' who could soften international attitudes towards a military dictatorship; and, being based in the capital Madrid, they were potentially a nationalist symbol. Likewise, in regions where the favoured political imagery was banned and political activity submerged, football icons served the purpose: every Spaniard knew, for example, that the red and blue of the CF Barcelona flag stood for the red and yellow of Catalonia and the red and white of Atletico Bilbao for the red, white and green of the Basque country.[20]

The same opposition was to be found in Greece with Panathinaikos, which was seen as the team of 'the Colonels' – the military group that overthrew the Greek government and monarchy in 1967 – and in Portugal, where Benfica were closely associated with the political faction of Salazar.

When the *ultras* of Roma are pitted against the Milan supporters, their favourite slogan is 'Milano in fiamme' (Milan's on fire) to which the Milan fans respond 'Milano capitale' (Milan's the capital). This opposition of centre versus periphery, Northern cities against Southern capitals, has been similarly transposed on to the football fields of other Mediterranean countries. In Greece, it appears in the rivalry between the Athenian clubs and Thessalonika; in Portugal in the feeling between the supporters of Sporting Lisbon and Oporto; and in Spain it is present in matches between Barcelona and the Madrid clubs. A common symbol has emerged in these confrontations in recent years and has been adopted by the supporters of such geographically disparate clubs as Naples, Marseilles, Seville and Benfica: they carry the flag of the Confederate army during the American Civil War, using it to assert their sense of difference, their Southern identity.

The French ethnologist, Christian Bromberger, showed in his work on Naples supporters some of the ironic humour present in their culture.[21] Answering the chant of the Juventus fans that 'Juve are magic' they wrote on the city's walls 'If Juve are magic, then Cicciolina is a virgin' (Cicciolina is a pornographic film star and member of the Italian parliament). And they responded to the anti-Southern and racist taunts of the Verona and Atalanta supporters with a large slogan saying 'Welcome to Africa'.

After Naples signed Maradona in the late 1980s, the pattern of the club's support changed. When Maradona, widely accepted to be the best footballer of his time in the world, arrived at the club the local supporters asked simply 'Allow us to dream'.[22] Two years later, when Naples had won the Italian championship for the first time, they shouted 'Naples are champions. Screw the nation'.

So the football publics of the Mediterranean often carry old political conflicts on to the football pitch, but, though it is present in Italy (the Italian parliament held a debate, and *Serie A* fixtures were suspended for a week, after the killing of a home supporter at a Genoa match in January 1995) and Spain, spectator violence seems a matter of greater concern in the Eastern Mediterranean societies of Greece and the former Yugoslavia. The hooligan phenomenon never seems to surface at international matches; support for national teams seems extremely pacific in the South of the continent. In the Spanish case, the team often plays in Southern cities like Seville where there is strong public support: Spain played all four home qualifying games for the 1990 World Cup at the Sanchez Pizjaun stadium in Seville. Admittedly, support might be less full-hearted in Catalonia or the Basque region, and to play too regularly in Madrid would lay the Spanish FA open to charges of centralism.

During the times of political dictatorship in Spain and Portugal, the election of the clubs' presidents at clubs such as Barcelona and Benfica were some of the few expressions of democracy in these countries. The election campaign among the *socios* of both clubs remains an important moment in the lives of their supporters and is one of the most fascinating aspects of South European football culture.

MEDIA COVERAGE

TV and radio

As elsewhere in Europe, the relationship between football and the media is, historically, a close one, both for the printed and the broadcast media: after Silvio Berlusconi became president of the Milan football club the game's relationship to television seemed to approach its ultimate. In 1989, the two best audiences for televised football games were attracted by Milan v. Steaua Bucharest (19,673,000 TV spectators) and Stuttgart v. Naples, which was seen by almost 18 million TV viewers.[23] On Sunday night in Italy six national channels have a football programme of at least one hour in length. During the 1993–4 season, a pay TV channel (Tele Plus 2) transmitted a match live every Sunday night at 8.30 pm. In 1986, the RAI (Italian public TV) showed over 500 hours football on its three channels.[24] The same year the national public service TV network paid more than 150 billion lire (£60 million) to the football federation.

But football in Italy also has a strong relationship to the radio. Walking in an Italian town or along an Italian seafront on a Sunday afternoon, you will certainly notice a lot of people with radios in their hands. You may be certain they are listening to a football commentary: 'Il calcio minuto per minuto'. Over eight million Italians – in their homes, in bars, in cars, at the stadium or any other possible place – perform this Sunday ritual,[25] which is closely bound up both with the gambling attractions of the football pools (the *Totocalcio*)[26] and the familiarity of the commentators' voices.

The press

During this century, Southern European countries have developed an autonomous sporting culture. It would be interesting to compare each European nation for the volume of work produced, respectively by its academic community and its sports press, on the subject of football. The result would very likely show an inverse relationship between learned books and popular papers. In Spain and Italy the sports press is particularly active. Three national daily newspapers provide exclusively sports news in Italy: *Gazetta dello sport* – founded in 1903, *Corriere dello sport* – *Stadio* and *Tuttosport*. *La Gazetta* is among the three leading papers at national level and sells over 300,000 copies a day. In Spain, two sports papers, *Marca* and *As*, are produced in Madrid; one – called *El mundo deportivo* – is printed in Barcelona and there are others at regional level. In Portugal *A Bola* has a fair circulation; it has its own special style of football coverage which incorporates a good deal of statistical and biographical information.

Through the sporting press, superlative words such as 'hero', 'wonderful' and 'magic' have become commonplace. The progress to an Americanization of football and the effective conversion of the game to a TV show has changed fundamentally the structure of football journalism. The recent period in the history of sports journalism in Mediterranean societies has witnessed 'the end of narration'. The sports press is becoming a user's guide for the TV viewer-spectator. Football reporters are now more like technicians, providing information about, and quotations of, the players; they are no longer concerned with the literary aspects of football writing. In Italy now the language of popular football culture is often the language of public life: just as British politicians talk of an 'own goal' or a 'political football', Italian economists refer to a 'second league Italy' or political commentators say that some politician has 'remained on the [substitutes'] bench'.

THE PLAYERS

In what is now a global labour market for professional footballers, a frontier between the two 'Europes' can be discerned: in the North lies an exporting, but poor, Europe; in the South are all the main football importers of the continent. Except for the Brazilians Pelé and Garrincha and the German Franz Beckenbauer, all the most famous European and South American footballers have played either in Spain or in Italy. Between the wars, as the chapter on North West Europe in this book makes clear, many of the best players went to Italy. From the 1950s, the Spanish clubs – particularly Real Madrid and Barcelona – tried to offer their supporters the best footballers in the world. In the late 1950s and early 60s the now legendary Real side of that period contained the Hungarian Ferenc Puskas and France's Raymond Kopa, as well as Alfredo di Stefano of Argentina: di Stefano was European Footballer of the Year in 1957 and 1959, Kopa taking it in the intervening year. In the 1970s Barcelona had Johan Cruyff of the Netherlands, European Footballer of the Year in successive years: 1973 and 1974. This star-system policy several times had negative consequences for the national team and, on different occasions, Spanish (and Italian) frontiers were closed to foreign footballers. But, each time, the economic power of the two big clubs and the political influence of the candidates for the club presidencies were sufficient to lift the ban and international stars reappeared in the Southern stadiums.

The case of Cruyff at Barcelona is interesting. Considered the best player in the world at the time, he arrived at Barcelona in 1973 and remained until 1978. During his five years, the club won the Spanish league and he became the most popular player in Catalonia. After a 10-year gap, spent mostly in the USA (where he played in the North American Soccer League, now defunct) and his home country of Holland, he came back to Barcelona in 1988 and is now considered a Catalan. His daughter has married a Catalan player in the Barcelona team. However, his 'Catalanity' has nothing to do with blood, marriage or race but with the fact that, on the football field, he defended Catalonia's honour and refused all offers from Madrid. The German player Bernard Schuster, who played for Madrid after leaving Barcelona, has been rejected by the fans for ignoring this fundamental rule.

The big Latin clubs prefer generally to use international stars, rather than young local talents. The large sums of money that these players cost are not considered either as an offence to talented young Spanish players or as a danger to the club's finances, but as an expensive and rare gift offered by the club to the public to defend the team's dignity. The success of Maradona in Naples, the French international captain Michel Platini at Juventus of Turin, Gullit and Van Basten at Milan and the Argentine Mario Kempes at Valencia is significant. They are not seen as mercenaries or foreigners, but adopted as local figures. In certain instances this integration developed into a kind of identification. This was the case for Maradona at Naples: the way he played, his attitude on the field and his style of life made him a real Neapolitan.[27] He helped Naples win the Italian League title by playing not an aggressive game but a subtle one; nowhere has the symbiosis between a club and a player been so strong. When they had Maradona, Naples, a city of the *Camorra* (Mafia), with its slums, its unemployment problems and its political crises – the city that was *losing* in life – was *winning* on the field.

There is only one exception to this general attitude to imported players: this is the Basque region of Spain, where separatist nationalist feeling is widespread and players must therefore be of local origin.

The styles

From the mid-1920s on, Spanish and Italian football began to develop an alternative way of playing. Having extensive contacts with Danubian clubs, and having recruited Hungarian and Austrian coaches, clubs like Bologna, Milan, Inter and Barcelona devised a style of football more adapted to the dry pitches of the Mediterranean area, based on short passing and intensive technical training. The 'Kick and Rush' approach – associated most closely, then as now, with British football – was replaced by the Austrian system. Trainers like Herman Felsner and Arpad Veisz, both of whom worked at Inter and Bologna, and the Hungarian Platko, at Barcelona, led the way in fashioning this distinctive, and successful, new style.

The style was based on a strong defensive trio, of which the best examples were Combi, Rosetta and Caligaris, who played both for Juventus and the Italian World Championship team of 1934, and Zamora, Quincoces and Samitier of Spain. Up to the 1930s, this trio – the goalkeeper and the two full backs – were the only specialist defenders; the centre half was a creative player, more in the manner of a modern midfielder. But, within the new formation, the centre half assumed a more destructive role. This tactical departure was first associated with the South Americans Luisito Monti, who played for Argentina in the World Cup Final of 1930, and Miguel Andreolo of Uruguay, the victors in that match. Both Monti and Andreolo were of Italian extraction and took Italian citizenship in the early 1930s, having come to Italy to play club football. Monti then played the new destructive centre half role for the Italian national side which won the World Cup in 1934. At club level, it was a particular feature of the style of Monti's team Juventus, and other Italian clubs brought it to the attention of Northern European football publics through the Mitropa Cup, founded in 1927 and contested by the leading clubs of Hungary, Czechoslovakia, Switzerland, Yugoslavia and Italy. The style was successfully deployed all over Europe by Italian and Spanish teams, both at club and at national level. The World Cup Semi-Final between Italy and Spain was one of the tensest matches of the inter-war period: it was played in Florence and it went to a replay, which Italy won 1–0, after a 1–1 draw in the first game.

After the Second World War, this evolution toward a more highly technical, tactical and defensive style continued and was personified by one man: Helenio Herrera. An Argentine by birth, Herrera had been a professional footballer, and subsequently a team manager in France during the 1930s. In 1949, he went to Atletico Madrid as their coach. Under him, Atletico won the Spanish championship twice. Later, with Barcelona in 1960, Herrera, despite the Real team of Kopa, Gento, Puskas and Di Stefano, was once again manager of the Spanish champions and they went on to the European Cup Final the following year, where they lost to another Latin team, Benfica of Portugal. Herrera's theory was decidedly not that of the Hungarians in the 1950s, for whom the objective was to score one more goal than the opposition. He chose instead to begin with a strong defence, reinforced by a fifth player – the *libero* or free defender – and to concede one goal less than the other side. Arriving at Inter Milan in 1961, he created one of the most consistently successful teams in the history of football. Inter frequently won 1–0 and Herrera's tactical approach, now called *catenaccio* or 'the lock', was stoutly defended by the Italian press: Gianni Brera, the best known of Italian sports journalists, called it *Il gioco all'Italiania* – 'the Italian game'. As a consequence, for decades Italy's first league, *Serie A*, had the lowest rates of goal scoring per match in Europe, but, at the same time, the highest attendance figures.

This style, originating with Juventus and Inter, was often – as it is still – expressed as The Three S's: Simplicity, Seriousness and Sobriety. Italian clubs concerned themselves more with the result than with the show offered to the public; they, after all, were likely to prefer a winning team that played badly than a losing one that played well.[28] But now, with the *condottiere* – tycoon – Berlusconi trying to establish an image of modernity for Italian football, there is an opposition in style between the traditional *catennacio* teams (Juventus, Torino, Inter, Lazio) and the modern *zona* or 'zonal' teams (Milan, Parma, Foggia, Roma). This often takes on the aspect of a religious war and it is not at all clear which school of thought will win it.

Spanish football, during the 1970s and early 80s developed this strategy toward an even harsher style – a *Futbol da muerte* – that married the passion for football to another element in the Spanish sporting tradition: the *corrida*, or bullfighting. The stadium at this time was often compared to the arena and the visiting team to the bull: the *toro*, who had to die. The European Cup Semi-Final of 1974, between Glasgow Celtic and Atletico Madrid, shocked international observers, as did the Final of the European Cup Winners Cup in 1982, in which Barcelona beat Standard Liege 2–1 at the Nou Camp. In both instances, Spanish defenders, with the apparent approval of the club's supporters who applauded enthusiastically, used all possible means to stop their opponents. In the Glasgow leg of the Atletico-Celtic match, three Atletico players were sent off for tackling which the British football public felt to be unprecedented in its savagery. Jock Stein, the Celtic manager, had to appeal for calm in the second leg, which Celtic lost. The treatment given to the Celtic winger Jimmy Johnstone in these games, though brutal and dangerous, perhaps lacked the elegance of the toreador, however.

The first affirmation of Portuguese football came in the 1960s and it centred on players from countries which were, or had been, colonies of Portugal. The style of Benfica, the premier Portuguese club side of the 1960s, was built around several key players, notably two Africans: Mario Coluna, born in Angola, and Eusebio, from Mozambique. Moreover, Benfica's coach, Otto Gloria, was from Brazil, a former Portuguese territory. In the 1960s, both Benfica and the Portuguese national side drew exclusively on these regions for players and the Portugal team came to be seen, from a stylistic point of view, as a Little Brazil in Europe, for whom technical ability was often more important than efficiency. This suited the Salazar dictatorship, anxious as it was to promote the notion of a Portuguese imperial family of nations, at one with itself.

CONCLUSION

In the Mediterranean societies, then, some of the oldest and most influential football cultures have flourished. In the international football world, Italy and Spain have led the way in the commercialisation and professionalisation of the game and in the importing of overseas players. It is in this region, moreover, that the majority of the most extravagant stadia in Europe are to be found and where the public fervour aroused by the major teams has often run highest. This fervour has grown out of, and has in turn fed, important political, regional and ethnic divisions in the respective societies of South Europe. The examples, as we've seen, are legion: the attempted identification of General Franco's fascist government with Real Madrid; the overt association of Barcelona with the cause of Catalan nationalism; the linking of Napoli to the resentments harboured by poor Southern Italians against the wealthier Northern and mid-Italian metropolitan centres; the perception that the Athenian team Panathinaikos stood for the military dictatorship that ruled Greece between 1967 and 1974; and, most recently, the ownership of AC Milan helped build the populist political platform from which Silvio Berlusconi launched his successful campaign for the Italian presidency in 1994.

However, political engagement with football has not always been the province of the right. In Yugoslavia, for example, as elsewhere in Eastern Europe after the Second World War, leading clubs were forged out of the success of the communist movement. Partisan and Red Star, the two major clubs in the Serbian capital Belgrade, were both founded in 1945, following the military victory of Tito's Partisan army. In the 1980s, however, older political and ethnic fissures re-emerged and were manifested in the Balkan football world in fierce fighting between supporters of Red Star and those of the Croatian team Dinamo Zagreb. Fighting among supporters has also been a major problem in Greece, where professional football has only been established since 1979.

The intensity of the emotional and political investment made in the game of football in many Mediterranean societies has, as this chapter has shown, led to a paradox. On the one hand, football's central cultural place in Southern European societies, its association with popular notions of art, physical beauty and technique, along with the acquisition of many of the world's best players, have conferred on Italy and Spain in particular a reputation for flair and sophistication among the football cultures of the world. But, on the other hand, the yoking of many Mediterranean teams (at the level both of club and of country) to the cause of various nationalisms, has at times produced some of the harshest and physically intimidating forms of association football in the modern era.

NOTES AND REFERENCES

1. cf S. Pivato (1991) *I terzini della borghesia, il gioco del palione nell 'Italia dell 'Ottocento*, Milan, Leonardo, pp.37–60. For a history of Calcio Fiorentino see L.

Artusi and S. Gabrielli (1986) *Calcio storico Fiorentino, Ieri e oggi*, Florence, Calcio Storico Fiorentino and L. Artusi and G. Sottani (1990) *Il calcio storico nella Firenze anni '30*, Florence, Calcio Storico Fiorentino.

2. E.J. Hobsbawm (1975) *The Age of Capital 1848–1875*, London, Weidenfeld and Nicolson, ch.9; G.A. Craig (1988) *Geld und Geist*, Munich, Beck, p.158.

   M. de Saint Martin (1989) 'La noblesse et les "sports" nobles', *Actes de la recherche en sciences sociales*, 80, pp.22–32 shows how the sporting ideal depends on social context in Fin de siecle France.

3. I have developed this point in two articles: 'Gli esordi di una practica sportiva. Il calcio nel bacino del Mediterraneo occidentale' (1990) in G. Panico and L. Giacomardo (eds) *Universita e sport*, Rome, FIGC, pp.41–5 and 'Calcio e progresso tecnologico' (1990) *Lancillotto e Nausica*, 7, 1–3, pp.58–65.

4. J. Garcia Castell (1968) *Historia del Futbol catala*, Barcelona, Ayma; E. Perez de Rozas and A. Reiano, 'Barca, Barca, Barca', *El periodico*, 11.5.89; G. Colome (1992) 'Il Barcelona e la Catalonia', in P. Lanfranchi (ed.) *Il calcio e suo pubblico*, Naples, ESI, pp.59–65.

5. A. Ghirelli (1990) *Storia del calcio in Italia* (4th edn) Turin, Einaudi, p.21f.

6. James Walvin (1975) *The People's Game*, London, Allen Lane, pp.94–5.

7. A. Girelli, op. cit. p.39.

8. Lincoln Allison (1978) 'Association Football and the Urban Ethos', *Stanford Journal of International Studies*, 13, pp.203–228.

9. G. Colome, op. cit.

10. C. Bromberger (1987) 'L'Olympique de Marseille, la Juve et le Torino. Variations ethnologiques sur l'engouement populaire pour les clubs et les matchs de football', *Esprit*, April, pp.174–195. In a conclusion to an article about Italian football, the French historian Pierre Milza wrote: 'Not only does Italian football remain a strong agent of social integration, it is the mirror of a society whose tensions have far from disappeared.' See P. Milza (1990) 'Le football italien, une histoire a l'echelle du siècle', *Vingtième Siècle Revue d'histoire*, 26, April–June, pp.49–58.

11. N.S. Onofri and V. Ottani (1990) *Dal Littoriale allo Stadio. Storia per immagini dell'impianto sportivo bolognese*, Bologna, CCC.

12. The Littoriale was erected in 1927, cf. Vera Ottani (1990) 'Lo stadio di Bologna. Quando un campo di calcio e monumento da tutellare' in *Azzuri 1990. Storia bibliographica emerographica iconographica della Nazionale Italiana di Calcio e del calcio a Bologna*, Rome, La Meridiana, pp.129–132; C.R. Guidotti (1990) 'Lo stadio comunale di Firenze', in *Azzuri 1990. Storia del calcio a Firenze*, Rome, La Meridiana, pp.109–118.

13. For this whole question see John Bale (1993) *Sport, Space and the City*, London, Routledge; A. Ehrenberg (1980) 'Aimez-vous les stades?', *Recherches*, 43, April, pp.25–54.

14. Porto's stadium Estadio das Antas has a capacity of 66,000 and Sporting Lisbon's Alvalade stadium accommodates 75,000. No other Portuguese club has more than 25,000 places.

15. As a comparison, Manchester United, in the season 1992–3, sold 700,000 tickets for 21 League matches and had an average of 33,429 spectators per match.

16. Official statistics of the Italian Football Federation, in *Almanacco illustrato del calcio* (1988), Modena, Panini, p.173.

17. A. Dal Lago (1990) *Descrizione di una battaglia. I rituali del calcio*, Bologna, Il Mulino; A. Dal Land and R. Moscati (1992) *Regalateci un sogno. Miti e realta del tifo calcistico in Italia*. Milan, Bompiani.

18. Dal Lago and Moscati, op. cit. p.38.

19. Another analysis in Bologna, made by Antonio Roversi, had the same results. See A. Roversi (1992) *Calcio, teppismo e violenza*, Bologna, Il Mulino.
20. See C. Fernandez Santander (1991) *El futbol durante la guerra civil y el franquismo*, Madrid, San Martin, p.154, and Duncan Shaw (1985) 'The Politics of *Futbol*', *History Today*, August.
21. C. Bromberger (1988) 'Sur les gradins on rit aussi . . . parfois. Faceties et moqueries dans les stades de football', *Le Monde Alpin et Rhodanien*, 3–4, pp.137–56; adem. 'Ciucco e fuocchi d'artificio. L'immaginario di Napoli attraverso il suo football' (1990) *Micromega*, 4, pp.171–181.
22. R. Ciuni (1985) *Il pallone di Napoli*, Milan, Shakespeare & Co, pp.75–91.
23. L. Minerva (1990) *Il pallone nella rete*, Rome, Nuova ERI, p.137.
24. ibid., p.118.
25. L. Minerva (1990) 'Radio – la Domencia del villaggio globale', in R. Grozio (ed.) *Catenaccio e contropiede*, Rome, Pellicani, pp.83–89.
26. In 1989, the Totocalcio, which finances all national sports federations had a turnover of 2,401 billion Lire (£9 billion). One third of this sum went to the Italian Olympic Committee (the CONI). Cf. P.L. Marzola (1990) *L'industria del calcio*, Rome, Nuova Italia, pp.127–40.
27. Cf. V. Dini and O. Nicolaus (eds) (1991) *Te Diegum*, Milan, Leonardo.
28. C. Bromberger (1991) 'The Passion for Football in Marseilles and Turin', Unit for Law and Popular Culture, Manchester Polytechnic [now Manchester Metropolitan University], England.

8

CULTURAL REVOLUTION? FOOTBALL IN THE SOCIETIES OF ASIA AND THE PACIFIC

Bill Murray

In the spread of soccer throughout the world, one of the least affected areas has been that large expanse of the globe that takes in Asia, outside the Middle East, and the Pacific region, with its innumerable islands, from Australia to the smallest atolls. And yet the Asia/Oceania group accounts for almost half of FIFA's registered players. Before the 1960s India was the major Asian power, without enjoying much success outside Asia. North Korea made its indelible impact in 1966, but since then Japan at the 1968 Olympics and South Korea in the 1980s are the only Asian countries to have performed well at international level. China was touted in the late 1970s as having a football future as bright as that of the United States, then going through its Pelé/Beckenbauer inspired boom, but neither giant of the football desert has emerged as a strong contender for world honours. Before the 1980s China's registered players were numbered in tens of thousands; today there are over 20 million, accounting for nearly half of the footballers registered by FIFA in the Asian zone. Like the figures for registered players in the United States – almost as many as the entire population of Australia – they tell us nothing about the strength of the game in these countries. All eyes are now on Japan, until a few years ago and despite their (minor) blaze of glory in the 1960s, a bit-part player. Now the world's leading industrial giant is on the verge of big things with the introduction of the J-League and full-time professionalism. In Oceania, Australia can hold its own with the best Asian countries, and dwarfs its neighbours in the Pacific, with only arch-rivals New Zealand to offer a serious challenge. Neither Australia nor the best of the Asian countries, however, have reached the class of the Europeans and the South Americans; even the Africans, whose spectacular success in recent years sets the modest accomplishments of the Asia/Pacific region in humble perspective.

For the peoples of Asia, international sporting fame has come through sports other than soccer: elitist games like cricket, squash and hockey in the

Indian sub-continent; specialist sports like wrestling and weightlifting in some regions; less physically strenuous games like table-tennis, volley ball and badminton in eastern Asia; and to a lesser degree in swimming and athletics, where Japan was outstanding in the 1930s, while more recently China has turned in some world class athletic performances. Soccer players are very seldom awarded the Asian sports personality of the year, but this is most likely a reflection of the social snobbery directed towards football from its early days. For while soccer is an essentially middle-class game in most of Asia, it is still not high on the register of sporting fashions. For example, when China hosted the eleventh Asian Games in 1990, it headed the medals table but failed to be placed in soccer after being eliminated by Thailand in the quarter-finals. Riot police had to be called out to quieten angry crowds yelling that they would sooner trade the 100 medals won in other sports for a single medal in soccer.

The fact is that the people's game has reached into every part of Asia, and in some countries and regions it has a fanatical hold, with crowds of well over 100,000 in India and as many as 150,000 in Korea and Indonesia. Games in Thailand and Malaysia are played before sell-out crowds, and one of the worst disasters in Asian sporting history was when at least 93 spectators were crushed to death at a packed football stadium in Nepal in 1988. A record 102,000 watched a soccer match in Australia, but this was for the last day of the Melbourne Olympics of 1956 and most of the crowd had come to watch the closing ceremony; the soccer final played between rival communist powers, Yugoslavia and the Soviet Union, was of little interest to them. Soccer in Australia has shared the same fate as that of the other former English-speaking colonies, where a local game or rugby is the passion of the people, and soccer dismissed as an alien activity. Both Australia and New Zealand have made it to the finals of the World Cup: Australia in 1974 and New Zealand in 1982, and neither was disgraced. Since then, Australia has become even more professional in its approach to the game, but historians of soccer can only be cautious about adding one more rosy prediction about the future of the game there. Nevertheless, there are strong grounds to believe that Australian soccer is on the threshold of its best ever era: it has more young players of international class than ever before, and they are home grown.

FOOTBALL IN ASIA

The British brought football to Asia as they did to most other parts of the world, but it was only after 1945 and the post-colonial period that soccer started to boom there. The Asian Football Confederation was formed in 1954, and in 1992 comprised 33 nations, the Middle-East countries included, with Bhutan and Mongolia waiting for admission, and Guam an associate member. The AFC presides over a host of regional competitions, as well as the Asian Nations' Cup (the Asian Cup), the Asian Champion Club's Cup, interrupted in 1971 to reappear in 1985 as the Asian Club Championship, and the football section of the Asian Games. The Asian Youth Cup was played annually from 1959 to 1978, when it became biennial, and has enjoyed great success. The first international football competition in Asia was held in the Philippines back in 1913, with only two participants: the host nation and China. Japan entered later competitions. Football in the Philippines, with its large American influence, never caught hold, but both China and Japan went to Berlin for the Olympics of 1936. Japan, before being eliminated in the second round, astonished all observers with their thrilling recovery to defeat Sweden 3–2, but China were beaten 2–0 by a disorganized UK team in their only game.

From the late 1950s many regional competitions were introduced in Asia, the most important of which was the Merdeka (independence) tournament started in Malaysia in 1957 to celebrate the country's freedom from colonial rule. Various other competitions followed, the most notable of which are the King's Cup in Bangkok from 1968, the President's Cup in South Korea from 1971, the Kirin Cup, which began as the Japan Cup in 1978, and the Nehru Gold Cup in India, founded in 1982 in honour of India's great nationalist leader. Pakistan, Bangladesh and China also have their tournaments.

Most of these are invitational competitions, and teams from all around the world are invited. As a result, a second-rate team from Argentina might find itself billed as 'Argentina', although more likely a team from, say, Brazil or Germany would be announced as 'a Brazilian XI' or 'a German XI'. Club competitions are played throughout Asia, but they have not caught on the way games involving national teams have: England or Scotland team managers can only dream of the power held by national team bosses in some Asian countries, where national glory is prized above the triumphs of mere clubs. Sometimes an Olympic or national selection is included in the domestic league to give them regular practice. Professionalism has had a chequered career: Hong Kong inaugurated a professional league in 1969, a minuscule version of the North American Soccer League, with all its faults and none of its star attractions – its major imports were usually Europeans past their prime, or young hopefuls on the way up. Professionalism was introduced in Malaysia in 1990 to try to offset the craze for gambling that runs like a fever throughout the region, and which was blamed for several fixed games. Corruption and violence are part of the game in Asia. In India, riots are as common in football as they are in cricket, and referees have gone on strike in protest at their lack of protection; North Korea were banned for two years from 1983 for attacks on a referee. Administration is often of a low standard; less so in the areas (outside mainland China) where the Chinese are politically dominant – but in Singapore, which has one of the best run competitions in Asia, the tiny population is never going to produce a national team of any strength.

Television has played an ambiguous role in the region. The acquisition of TV sets by formerly impoverished peoples has brought the world game to tens of millions of Asians, and so encouraged some interest in football, but playing highlights from the best leagues in the world, most notably Italy's Serie A, has shown up the local product to be somewhat woeful by comparison. There have been attempts to promote the local game by banning expatriates from playing for their country; on the other hand, China recently allowed players over 28 to go abroad, in part in the hope that they would return with new skills to teach the young. When the Hong Kong league introduced a three foreigner limit in 1984, runners-up in the 1983–84 season, Bulova, withdrew in protest. South China, founded in 1904 and the most successful team in the Hong Kong league, played only Chinese players and remained amateur even when the league went professional. Eleven years later they adopted professionalism, employed a German coach and in the 1981 season signed on non-Chinese players.

The failure of soccer in Asia is most obvious in the paucity of Asian players who have reached the highest international standards; only a few have made the grade in the top teams in the European leagues, where the highest standard of football is regularly maintained (some of the best football is still being played in South America). The success of this handful has only underlined the failure of Asia to produce world-class footballers. Among the best, and none of whom played outside Asia, were Kunishige Kamamoto of the Japan national teams of the 1960s, Jarnail Singh of the same epoch, a Punjabi star who played his best years with Mohan Bagan in Calcutta, and Rong Zhihang of China, praised by Pelé as a 'superstar' after a game between Cosmos and China in 1978. Inder Singh was another Punjabi of great skill, who refused offers from Bengali clubs, the Malaysian government and Khalso Sporting Club of Vancouver, preferring to stay in his native Punjab. Another gifted player who stayed in his own country despite overseas offers, was 'Supermok' Mokhtar Dahari, star striker for Malaysia in the 1970s and 1980s. He declined an offer from Réal Madrid, but was well compensated by the government for his patriotism, with the offer of a well-paid and not very strenuous job in a government department.

Cheung Che Doy was one of the first Asian players to try his luck abroad, but he did not enjoy great success. Born in mainland China in 1942, and a regular for the Taiwan national team, although he played in the Hong Kong league, Cheung was also a regular in the Asian All Star teams of the mid-1960s. He played for Blackpool in 1960, although he couldn't adjust to the British weather, and for Vancouver Royals in 1969, but neither he nor the team did well so he returned to the new professional league in Hong Kong, where he was one of the highest paid players. The greatest of the Asians to play abroad is Cha Boom Kun of South Korea, who starred in the Bundesliga from the late 1970s. Another Asian success in Germany was Yashuhiko Okudera of Japan, but thereafter the Asians from Thailand, China, South Korea and Singapore who have played in Europe have failed to raise much excitement.

Size and physique, related to dietary practices, account in part for the comparative lack of success of Asians, but more so the geographical and above all cultural, distance from Europe. Asian players, too, can make a handsome living out of the game without going abroad, unlike African players who have to emigrate if they want to cash in on their talents. Some clubs in Asia are the sporting hobby of multi-millionaires, while governments have also been happy to intervene to keep local talent in the domestic league. At national level Korea has threatened to reach world class, but in the foreseeable future the only country other than a united Korea that seems likely to challenge the leading nations in Europe and South America is Japan. The Japanese have shown themselves to be immensely successful in anything they take up seriously, and they have beaten Europeans and Americans in many of their non-sporting activities, so there is reason to believe, now that they are taking football seriously, that they might do the same there. Creating a world-beating football team, however, is likely to prove a more formidable task than producing a best-selling car or television set. There is, too, the lesson of baseball, which the Japanese took up with great determination, but which barely achieved a standard higher than low-grade American games. Already, however, soccer is proving to be more popular than baseball with young Japanese, and early indications are that the J-League will not be a one-season wonder.

ASIA IN WORLD COMPETITION

Qualification for the Olympic Games and the World Cup has helped inspire a new interest in the game at club and national level, and given a boost to the many regional competitions. Victories in top international competition outside Asia, however, have been sparse. After the success of Japan at the 1936 Olympics, Asian progress was somewhat painful. Four Asian teams took part in the 1948 Olympics in London, with only Korea enjoying any success – they beat Mexico 3–0 in the first round – before being thrashed 12–0 by Sweden. France eliminated India 2–1, and Turkey beat China 4–0, while Luxembourg disposed of Afghanistan by 6–0 in a preliminary round.

At the Helsinki Olympics of 1952, India was the only Asian entrant, and they were beaten by the state amateurs from Yugoslavia (10–1) in the first round. These were the first Cold War games; China turned up to play belatedly, and then refused to take part in the competition when a place was made for them. In 1956 the Hungarian Revolution and the Anglo/French invasion of the Suez, with Israel taking advantage of the conflict to secure its own interests, ensured that politics could not be kept out of the Melbourne Games. By this time there was a need for qualification games to decide who should go to Australia: China withdrew before kicking a ball, and Vietnam after defeating Cambodia in two elimination matches. Iran and Afghanistan pulled out before they were due to play each other and so Thailand, Japan, Indonesia and India went on to Melbourne. Thailand and Japan were eliminated in the preliminary rounds: Thailand lost to Great Britain by 9–0, (Great Britain were in turn beaten 6–1 by Bulgaria); Japan lost to a poor Australian team, which was then beaten by India, who advanced to the semifinal, where they lost to Yugoslavia (4–1) and Bulgaria (3–0) in the play-off for third place. Although Indonesia were eliminated in the first round, their 0–0 draw with eventual winners, the Soviet Union, who won the replay 4–0, is still regarded with great pride by Indonesians.

For Rome in 1960, the unequal nature of the teams and the increasing number wanting to take part in the Games, introduced the need for area play-offs. Of the eight Asian teams (including Australia, who did not play their game against Indonesia), Taiwan and India went on to Rome, with India's 1–1 draw with France their only bright spot. In 1964 Japan hosted the first Olympic Games to be held in Asia. Soccer was then low in Japanese sporting priorities, but success, and above all the playing skills of Kamamoto, brought a hitherto uninterested Japanese public to follow the fortunes of their team. North Korea won several games in the preliminary rounds, but withdrew before the finals to avoid playing South Korea, who joined Japan as Asian representatives. South Korea lost 10–0 to Egypt and did not win a game in their group of four, but Japan beat Argentina 3–2 in their smaller group and went on to the quarter finals. There they lost 4–2 to Czechoslovakia, and by an even bigger margin (6–1) to Yugoslavia in a somewhat pointless play-off for 5th to 8th place.

Japan's moment of glory came in the 1968 Olympics when they became the first team from Africa or Asia to gain a soccer medal, inspired by the maturing skills of Kamamoto. Japan won through to the finals by coming top in a preliminary tournament held in Japan, ahead of South Korea, who also qualified, and Lebanon, South Vietnam, Taiwan and the Philippines. Burma, India, Iran and North Korea all withdrew rather than play Israel, and so in the Final Tournament, Japan and Thailand represented Asia. Thailand failed to pick up a point, but Japan beat Nigeria and drew with Spain and Brazil to go through to the elimination rounds. There they beat France 3–1, but lost their semi-final against the Hungarian state amateurs (5–0). In the play-off for the bronze medal they beat Mexico 2–0 before 120,000 delirious if disappointed home fans.

Malaysia and Burma made it to Munich in 1972, and won a game each. Burma were then at the peak of their golden age before withdrawing to political isolation. Thereafter the oil-rich Middle-eastern powers dominated the Asian region. Politics in 1976, 1980 and 1984 resulted in large-scale boycotts by Asian and African countries. North Korea were the most successful Asian team in Montreal, while in Moscow in 1980 and Los Angeles in 1984 all the Asian representatives came from the Middle-East. Soon it would be the African teams who would leave their Asian colleagues in the shade. At Seoul in 1988, Kalusha Bwalya inspired the Zambian team, to its good win over Italy: neither of the two Asian finalists, China and South Korea, won a game. At the Seoul Games, China headed Japan, Thailand and Nepal in the East Asia qualifying league, to join the hosts in the finals. China managed a scoreless draw with Tunisia, and South Korea drew with Argentina and the United States. At Barcelona in 1992 Australia made it to the last four, showing that soccer there seemed to be advancing faster than in Asia. The best performance by an Asian team at Barcelona was South Korea, who drew with each of their opponents in their group of four, but were eliminated by Paraguay on goal difference.

In 1978 FIFA tried to encourage Third World participation in the Olympics at the same time as it struck at the anomaly of state amateurs from the communist countries and full-time professionals from some European and Latin American countries playing in the amateur competition. This they did by decreeing that any player from Europe or Latin America (but not Africa or Asia) who had played for his country in the World Cup was ineligible for the Olympics. Nevertheless, it was still the World Cup that the Asians saw as the pinnacle of achievement. Before 1966 most Asian teams entered this competition as lambs to the slaughter. The Dutch East Indies were the first, when they went to France in 1938 – the colonials taking the place of Japan who were playing more deadly games with China. They played a few friendlies in the Netherlands, before being rudely eliminated by Hungary (6–0) in the first round. India and Burma were among the many withdrawals from the 1950 World Cup, India enjoying some unwonted publicity for FIFA's refusal to allow them to play in bare feet. Taiwan withdrew in 1954, and Asia was represented by South Korea who eliminated Japan. In Switzerland they conceded 16 goals in their games against Hungary and Turkey. Asia and Africa were combined for the preliminaries for the 1958 World Cup, but several Islamic countries withdrew rather than play against Israel. One of these was Indonesia, who had beaten China by the narrowest of margins, in a play-off in neutral Rangoon, after winning 2–0 at home and losing 4–3 in Beijing: after a scoreless draw Indonesia was awarded the qualification on goal difference. There were no Asian representatives in Chile four years later, but this time because of the organization that had Asian teams playing against European opposition in the preliminaries. They were all outclassed.

Asians absented themselves voluntarily from the 1966 World Cup, in solidarity with the Africans who were objecting to FIFA's refusal to grant more than one place between the two continents. North Korea, however, did not take part in the boycott, and after two convincing wins against Australia, went on to enthral the English crowds and humiliate the Italians with their ball skills and teamwork. The Korean team that won the hearts of English supporters as they disposed of Italy (1–0) and drew with Chile to go on to the elimination rounds, were the Asian equivalent of the great Hungarian national team of the early 1950s, albeit without the Golden Team's superb skills. They trained as a unit for years before the event, away from the eyes of western observers, and their right to go to England was won somewhat cheaply, having to beat only Australia. A pre-competition loss to a Hungarian XI (7–0) further confirmed them in the eyes of the experts as a team whose best hopes would be to escape being disgraced. Instead, it was they who administered the disgrace, and even looked like going on to greater things when they took an early 3–0 lead against Portugal in the first elimination game. Unfortunately for them they met one of the stars of the tournament in scintillating form, and Eusebio, the African from Mozambique, inspired a Portuguese revival that saw them run out eventual winners by 5–3.

North Korea in 1966 and Japan at the Olympics in 1968 were the high-water marks of Asian soccer achievement in world competition. Thereafter they played in the shade of the Middle-East countries and then the Africans. Israel represented Asia in 1970, Australia in 1974 and Iran in 1978. Thereafter two places were granted, shared by New Zealand and Kuwait in 1982, Iraq and South Korea in 1986. The South Koreans, recently turned professional, also lifted their ban on expatriates playing for the national team, and so allowed Cha Boom Kun to play in Mexico in 1986. They were the first Asian country to make the finals since North Korea in 1966, and like them withdrew the national team for special training, upsetting the recently formed professional league. Although they managed no more than a draw, 1–1 with Bulgaria, and tried to put Maradona out of their game with Argentina before settling down to play football, they performed heroics in a 2–3 loss to World Cup holders Italy. South Korea also dominated Asian tournaments at both club and national level during this period. Korean football was clearly the best in Asia, but it was still a long way short of international class: in Italia 1990, South Korea failed to win or even draw – the other Asian qualifier, the United Arab Emirates, fared no better.

Since 1974 and the election of Havelange as president of FIFA, the world body has sought to encourage football in the Third World soccer countries through the provision of coaching and other facilities, but above all by a series of age competitions, the most successful of which has been the FIFA Under-20 World Youth Tournament. Another world trophy, for under-17s, has also been a great success – although it is the Africans who have fared best, Nigeria and Ghana contesting the 1993 final in Japan. FIFA also decided that from the 1992 Barcelona Olympics teams would be made up of players under 23 years. The Europeans tended to downplay these under-age competitions, providing full facilities for their young hopefuls at club level, and preferring competitions that involved less travel. This has allowed the underdeveloped soccer countries a better chance to progress, although, apart from the Africans, it is Australia that has taken most advantage of these competitions.

In the under-20 competition, the best Asian performances have been by South Korea. In Mexico in 1983 they went through to the semi-finals, when they were beaten for third place by Poland. A united Korea team made their way to the quarter-finals in Portugal in 1991, and in Australia in 1993 Korea drew with England, Turkey and the US before being eliminated on goal difference. The only other Asian team to qualify for the finals of the World Youth Cup is China, who have usually distinguished themselves by failing at the last hurdle. At the Soviet Union in 1985 they were eliminated by the hosts in the quarter-finals. In the under-17 competition only South Korea, in Canada in 1987, had gone through to the quarter-finals, but in Japan in 1993 the most successful Asian countries were the hosts, who lost to Nigeria, the eventual winners, in the quarter-final and China, who came bottom of the qualifiers. At the inaugural Women's World Cup, held in China in 1991, the host nation and Taiwan went as far as the quarter-finals, with Japan coming bottom of their group. Nine Asian teams took part in that competition.

POLITICAL FOOTBALL

The world game cannot avoid world politics, and in Asia the problem of Taiwan has been at the heart of many disputes, while that of Israel has been visited upon it. Taiwan has never been a serious soccer power, in part because of the American influence, and its national team has usually been made up of players from Hong Kong. The problem of Israel was the discord between certain Muslim countries and the Jewish state, and for a while FIFA tried to unload both problems on Oceania.

Israel now seems to have found a permanent home in UEFA, but since its inception, and above all since the rise of the Middle-Eastern powers and the influence wielded by their oil money, Israel has been ostracized both in their own immediate region and elsewhere. Thus when the Asian nations rejected them they had to play in the Oceania section, which meant vast travel for them and their opponents, at the same time as it set up something of a long-distance local derby with Australia. The problem of Taiwan was simply related to the power politics of the tiny island propped up by the Americans to represent China against the mainland regime turned communist from October 1949; the anti-American forces supported the People's Republic. Both countries claiming to represent China refused to take part in a competition in which one or the other was invited. A similar, though less grotesque, situation existed with the two Koreas, each claiming to represent Korea and refusing to participate in a competition where the other took part. Other countries have refused to set foot in enemy territory: Pakistan, for example, refused to take part in the first soccer tournament in the Asian Games in 1951 because they were held in India.

Havelange's accession to power in 1974 was a welcome change for the enemies of Israel and Taiwan. He was committed to having communist China brought into FIFA, and in this he had the support of Hong Kong millionaire Henry Fok, who wanted to open up the mainland to football and trade, and who in turn won the backing of the Middle-East countries by supporting them against Israel. The result was that when the AFC – Asian Football Confederation – expelled Taiwan in 1976 in order to admit the People's Republic of China, this was tacitly accepted by FIFA. China finally joined the world body in 1980, and Taiwan was forced to play in Oceania. The spectacular increase in registered players in China might give a rosy glow in FIFA headquarters about the progress of the game throughout the world, but it has not resulted in China making any serious impact on the world game. They were within an ace of qualification for Spain in 1982, but a poor performance by Saudi Arabia against New Zealand allowed the New Zealanders to force a play-off in Singapore. Against the Saudis in Saudi Arabia, New Zealand had to win by 5–0 to draw level with China, and this is exactly what they did. In political terms the Saudi government had no love of the communist regime, which it refused to recognize; in footballing terms the Saudis had been demoralized by previous defeats and their Brazilian coach had just resigned. Three star players were also rested for the game, but overriding all these factors was the commitment of a New Zealand team that was playing above itself. In the deciding game in Singapore they again played like a team inspired and despite late pressure from China held on to a 2–1 lead.

In addition to the problem of politics, Asian competitions have suffered from that of vast distances, but also from corruption and maladministration, with gambling almost a way of life in some countries. Perhaps the best example of the failure of soccer to capitalize on grass-roots support is in

Indonesia, where badminton and soccer share the popular passion. International success has won badminton a special place in the hearts of Indonesians, but soccer is played before crowds of well over 100,000 in Jakarta: 150,000 are said to have been packed into the Stadion Utama Senayan Pintu VII for the big games – a stadium restricted for safety reasons to well below that figure. None of this commitment has been converted into international success. Government inquiries into bribery in football have been no more successful than those set up to uncover or prevent corruption at other levels of public life. India is another case in point. Calcutta has been a veritable cauldron of football fever for most of this century, with crowds of over 100,000 to watch the local derbies between the big three – Mohan Bagan, Mohammedan Sporting and East Bengal. Teams from Kerala, Bombay and Goa have at times challenged the Bengal supremacy, but none of this enthusiasm has been transformed into a strong national team. Mohan Bagan, the oldest team, won undying gratitude among Indians in 1911 when they won the India FA Shield against British regimental teams. They played in the national colours and carried the hopes of Indian nationalists thereafter, and this and their many victories saw them being honoured as the national team of India in 1989 – this was despite their having been involved in recent unsavoury scandals in regard to bribery and corruption.

FROM COLONIES TO NATIONHOOD

The British and the French were the main agents spreading football in Asia: above all the British, whose empire stretched over large parts of south Asia, and whose commercial influence spread out even further. The popularity of soccer came despite vast differences in climate and terrain. In parts of south Asia the game was played over 60 minutes because of the intense heat, but soccer is also played in the most remote and inhospitable mountainous regions: in Afghanistan, Tibet, Mongolia and Nepal. Mongolia was one of the latest teams seeking admission to FIFA: wrestling and equestrian sports are the most firmly entrenched, but soccer is played by 35,000 players in 20 annual tournaments.

After they gained independence, most of the former colonies continued to play the game. In the Indian sub-continent outside India, the rivalry of Abahani Chakra and Mohammedan Sporting in Bangladesh has developed into one of the most intense local derbies in the game: in Pakistan, on the other hand, and in Sri Lanka soccer is a minor sport. Myanmar (formerly Burma), Malaysia and Hong Kong established successful local competitions, the latter two importing players from other Asian countries, especially Thailand.

In the former French colonies the legacy of war and division was much worse than that left by the British, and while football was played in Indochina, especially in Saigon, it was never a major leisure activity. Nevertheless, throughout the war in the region football has continued to be played, and Cambodia, Laos and South and North Vietnam have all formed their own associations. The unified Vietnam has staged the SKDA

Tournament since 1979, a competition open to communist countries throughout the world, usually the army teams.

Colonial India had the best soccer teams in Asia, and just as the English language was the only tongue that could be understood by all members of the nationalist Indian National Congress in their denunciation of the colonial overlords, so visiting British football teams could unite otherwise warring factions in their desire to see the intruders defeated. This first reached fanatical proportions with the victory of Mohan Bagan in 1911, a victory that was likened by some to the recent victory of Japan over Russia in the war of 1904–5. The touring British amateur team, Islington Corinthians, played several games in Asia in their world tour of 1937, and found that the spirit of 1911 had not died. They reported a cabinet minister in Congress as saying on the eve of the All-India game:

> I want to give the I.C.'s a friendly warning. Tomorrow something is going to happen which we politicians have been trying to achieve for years. Hindus, Moslems, Anglo-Indians, Parsees, the Bangals [sic] and the Bengalees, Indian and European, all the communities of India will be united for the first time. All their one common object will be that our local All-India team will lower the colours of the I.C.'s. Whether we win or lose we hope to watch a first-class match. (Alaway, 106)

The English amateurs were impressed by the sportsmanship of the players, but less so by that of the crowds, who would attend in their tens of thousands, but leave as soon as it became obvious that the home team was not going to win. When the locals scored or came close, a sort of vocal Mexican wave broke out, as news passed from those who could actually see the game to those further back who knew what was going on only from what they were told by those in front of them.

The stiffest opposition faced by the touring amateurs was in Burma (now Mynamar), where they claim to have lost the only game of the tour on merit. In Malaya (now Malaysia) they came across the involvement in football of the witchdoctor, or 'pawang'. At a Sultan's Cup game between Malays and Eurasians, a riot nearly broke out when the Eurasians wiped out the efforts of the pawang by rubbing lard over the goalposts where he had exercised his powers. It was just as clear that more potent forces to ensure a win were at work that day, and one familiar elsewhere, when it became apparent that the referee had been encouraged to help the Malay team: the first goal was about twenty yards offside, the Malay linesman performed cartwheels of joy and the Malay manager rushed on the field to congratulate the referee. After ten minutes the Eurasians refused to continue, whereupon the Malays ran a series of goals in from the centre spot to win 12–0.

FOOTBALL AND THE CHINESE

India was the continent that once promised to be the giant of Asian football, but in the late 1970s that mantle fell on the People's Republic of China. More than a decade on that hope seems to be fading, but the influence of the

Chinese on Asian football has been paramount from its earliest days, mainly through British trading and missionary connections with China, and the cultural and commercial bases it set up in places like Shanghai, Hong Kong and Singapore. Games organized by expatriates were eventually taken up by the locals, especially students who had been abroad, and who from early in the century wanted to modernize China. By the 1930s the Chinese had begun to play in earnest, with South China Athletic Association carrying the banner of the locals against the missionaries and other 'foreign devils'. Many games ended in riots and attacks on the referee, but this did not stop the crowds turning up, and as many as 90,000 came to see a cup final in Shanghai in 1935. Throughout this time the Chinese had to cope with domestic problems as well as getting rid of the Europeans, one revolution in 1912 disposing of the effete Manchu dynasty, another battling against the war lords and the exploiters in what became the Long March to communism in 1949.

Neighbouring Japan proved to be a much more vicious enemy than the Europeans, and from the invasion of Manchuria in 1931 to the full-scale war that opened in 1937 and lasted until 1945, China found its attentions centred on matters other than sport. Despite all this, football was played, and not just in the 'treaty ports' that were saved some of the worst atrocities of the Japanese. It was the peasants, most of whom lived in dire poverty, who made up the vast bulk of the population, and who carried the brunt of the civil and foreign wars, and so football was played mainly by middle-class clerks and students for teams that were often owned by millionaire businessmen. When Mao Zedong came to power in 1949 many of the mainland's best players fled to safer havens, but some stayed on, and as the great leader had written a treatise on the need for physical education early in his revolutionary career, the new regime set about creating the healthy bodies for politically healthy minds.

The European intruders in China had set up their elite sports in Shanghai as early as 1843, but by 1879 football matches were being played, under the encouragement of an expatriate Scot – in this case John Prentice from Glasgow, who became president of the Engineers team. In November 1887 a football section set itself up separately from the Shanghai Athletic club, and became known as Shanghai FC. Four years later Prentice donated a trophy that resulted in the derby matches between Engineers and Shanghai FC. Many further trophies would be put up for competition in the region, including the Interport, between Hong Kong and Shanghai, and the International Cup (1907) where Scotland dominated other nations and ethnic groups that included in addition to England and Ireland, Germans, French, White Russians, Jews and above all Portuguese. A Shanghai FA was founded in 1910.

Hong Kong FC were founded in 1886, and in September 1896 a Hong Kong Shield was set up for competition between Navy, military and civilian teams. Games were played in Singapore in 1889 and an FA was founded there in 1892. In northern China a Tientsin football club was founded in 1884, and the game flourished for a while before falling into abeyance. Football was strong in Beijing in the early years of the century, and although the British were dominant, the French, Austrians and even Americans took part. By this time the railways were being driven into the mainland and the ships of European commerce and war patrolled the seas, while Christian missionaries, particularly through the Young Men's Christian Association, used sport to win converts for Christianity.

When Japan defeated Russia in the war of 1904–5, the need for European industrial know-how was driven home, and five years later one of the major obstacles in the way of progress was removed with the overthrow of the Manchus.

In 1904, in one part of the modernizing process, the South China Athletic Association was founded, with soccer included among other sports: it would become the flag-bearer for Chinese pride in the decades to come. In 1910 the first National Athletic Games were held in Nanking, with soccer included alongside athletics, tennis, basketball and baseball. The competitors were mainly the products of the elite schools, those involved in trade and those under the influence of the YMCA. In 1911 the Singapore Chinese FA was founded, and in 1913 South China AA represented China in the inaugural Far East Asian Olympic Games. They were defeated by the Philippines, who included, however, against the rules, British, Spanish and American players. Thereafter China (through South China AA) would dominate this competition, which lasted until 1934. The last Far Eastern Games were held in Manila, with 15,000 packed into the José Rizal stadium to see China play the Netherlands East Indies (Java), having defeated the Philippines in a game that was accompanied by a riot. China went on to beat Japan in the final to win the gold medal. For the next competition, Japan demanded that Manchukuo/Manchuria be admitted and, when China protested, left to found with the Philippines the Orient Athletic Association.

This was the era that belonged to the South China AA, and although the best Europeans, with their more physical game, could usually win against the speedier and more skilful Chinese, in 1929 SCAA won the Hong Kong Shield, defeating Kowloon, made up of non-Chinese and appearing for their seventh final in a row, 5–0. The China National Athletic Association was set up in Nanking in 1924, and in that year the 'Hongs' (businessmen) established the Hongs Chinese Football League in Shanghai for teams representing their companies: 'ethnics' were not allowed to play. The Shanghai League had to bow to the need to play Chinese, and from the 1926–7 season the Three Cultures team was admitted. The reluctance of the Shanghai team to include ethnic Chinese was said to be because of the trouble they caused, blaming them for the riots and attacks on referees, and certainly the unwillingness to accept the referee's decisions was inflamed by nationalist agitation. Games where no Europeans were involved were just as likely to end in riots, however.

By the 1930s Chinese were starring in formerly all-European teams, and Chinese were involved in administration, especially in Hong Kong. Then the Kuomintang advised all Chinese clubs to withdraw from foreign competition for what it saw as bias in the suspension of two Canton players by the Hong Kong FA for professionalism. There is little doubt that the two players had accepted money – the Chinese were no different in this regard from players elsewhere in the world. The Chinese, however, were asserting themselves not just in the field, but in the administration of the game, and in the cause of their own independence.

In 1931 the China National Amateur Athletic Federation, run by Chinese, was accepted into FIFA. The European-controlled FAs of Shanghai, Singapore, Hong Kong and later Tientsin were affiliated with the London FA. After the National Games of 1935, which saw 90,000 at the final to see Hong Kong beat Canton, a national team was formed in preparation for the Olympic Games to be held in Berlin the following year. It was made up mainly of players from South China AA, but also included six Malayan Chinese, an indication of the growth of the game away from the more traditional centres. The team that went on to Berlin was eliminated by the UK team, but they played many games against European opposition both before and after the Games. Whatever experience they gained, however, was lost when the country became engulfed in war with Japan. Mao Zedong came to power four years after the end of this conflict.

Under the communists, soccer in China has fluctuated in rhythm to the politics of the day. In the early years games were played against varied opposition, but usually fellow communist regimes. In 1960, after the Big Split between Beijing and Moscow, China severed relations with the Warsaw Pact countries. Then came the Cultural Revolution from 1966, with the fanatical anti-elitism of the leaders sending intellectuals to plough fields and sports stars to clean streets. From 1971 Ping Pong diplomacy (the encouragement of international table tennis matches, for state political reasons) brought sport back into favour, and Henry Fok set about having China admitted into FIFA. Before this was realized China was allowed to play against member countries of FIFA, and in the late 1970s competed in an incredible number of matches with foreign opposition: according to Ken Knight (Knight, 1991), 158 games were played against opponents from 36 countries in 1975, and four years later 29 countries visited China, while China toured 47. These were the circumstances that led many acute observers to believe that China was a sleeping giant, which by the turn of the century would be a leading soccer power. In fact, as it turned out, the Asian country of the 1980s was South Korea.

THE ROAD TO 2002

The success of soccer in North Korea came with the communist government's attempts to create a showpiece team for the 1966 World Cup; since then it has been South Korea that has risen to be the top Asian footballing nation, a success based on the Hallelujah team from the late 1970s. Before then football in South Korea was strictly amateur, played mainly by the military, tertiary institutions and commercial enterprises. As a result, some of the best players went elsewhere to play professionally, losing their right to represent their country as a consequence. In the 1970s, too, baseball became more popular than soccer as a spectator sport, and it was this that prompted the

Korean FA to introduce partial professionalism in 1980. Hallelujah, founded by evangelical Christians, were the first to turn professional, and four years later they were joined by five others in a fully professional Superleague. Six professional and two amateur teams made up this league, which sported names that reflected the political and economic realities of the time: Lucky Gold Star Bulls, Yukong Elephants, Hyundai Tigers, Pohang Iron and Steel Dolphins and Daewoo Royals, while the two amateur teams were called Hanil Bank Carnations and Citizens' National Bank Magpies.

It was a league obviously backed financially by the industrial giants who had been transforming the Korean economy; there is a large American presence. American, rather than European, influence was apparent in the points system and various awards. Three points were given for a win, two for a score draw, and one for a non-score draw, while players were given awards such as the 'golden shoe' (not 'boot'), for the greatest number of 'assists' and the best 'fighting spirit'. Managers could aspire to being named 'Most Meritorious'. There were no 'home and away' games; instead teams played in various parts of the country like a travelling troupe, with two rounds determining who would play off for the championship.

The industrial magnates behind these teams could not prevent the state removing their best players in preparation for the 1986 World Cup, and as a result attendances at games in the Superleague fell drastically in the 1985 season. The Christian team, now called Hallelujah Eagles, were particularly hard hit by the fall in gates, and found themselves with serious financial problems before turning amateur and playing in lower grade competition. The successful holding of the 1988 Olympic Games, the continued dominance of Asian competition, and the possibility of reunification, make Korea a front runner to host the 2002 World Cup.

It is Japan, however, ahead of Korea and China, which must be favourite to be the first Asian nation to host the World Cup in 2002. Not only is Japan backed by such soccer luminaries as Franz Beckenbauer, Pelé and Bobby Charlton, but local governments and multi-national giants have poured money into the new league which kicked off on 15 May 1993. The investors do not expect to see any return on their money for a few years, and some clubs are expanding from a more typical 15,000 all-seater stadium to one that will seat 100,000. Support for the game is unevenly spread, but the significant figures are those that show how soccer is now more popular than baseball among children and young adults. Teams, no longer the social arm of an industrial concern but usually still sponsored by one, are allowed three foreigners; as has been the case for many years; most of these are Brazilians, although the signing of the Englishman Gary Lineker by Grampus Eight attracted much publicity. Most of the coaches are foreign, but among the Japanese managers is Kamamoto, head of Gamba Osaka, based on the old Matsushita team. An American influence can be seen in the marketing: anything that can be worn, watched, eaten or drunk has the J-League imprimatur attached to it, most teams have flamboyant names, drawn games have been eliminated. The honourable draw has been replaced with a sudden-death shoot-out in extra-time and penalties if no goals are scored after 30 minutes. It is a punishing schedule for players who have to play twice a week in a competition that sees each of the 10 teams play each other four times. The success of the game in Japan will depend on the continuing interest at local level.

SOCCER 'DOWN UNDER'

Australia, though not very significant in the world scene, is a giant in the Oceania area, with only New Zealand to offer serious opposition. New Caledonia and Tahiti have supplied players to the French leagues, but the islands and atolls of the Pacific are too small and scattered to make a serious impact. New Zealand's influence in the area has been important, but this has resulted in the spread of rugby union, which is popular in many of the islands in the region, most particularly Fiji. Even there, however, soccer has the edge: the Indians, who are in a majority, have little interest in rugby, while the indigenous Fijians play both codes with equal relish.

Rugby had established itself as the national sport of New Zealand by the turn of the century, despite the efforts of some Victorians to export the Australian game: although it had a promising beginning, 'Victorian Rules' never took root. Soccer barely managed a promising beginning. In Australia and New Zealand, the Scottish were to the fore in founding teams and organizing administrations, but the game has done little more than meet the needs of a few enthusiasts. A Football Association was founded in Auckland, New Zealand's largest city, in 1886, and three years later in the south island province of Otago. The first national FA was formed in the capital, Wellington, in 1891, and the following year competition began for the Brown Shield, put up by a Scottish whisky merchant from Glasgow. This remained the main national competition until the Football Association donated a trophy for competition in 1925. The trophy that was to have the longest life, however, was the Chatham Cup, donated by the crew of HMS Chatham in appreciation of the hospitality they had received during their stay in 1922: beginning in 1923 it was run along the lines of the FA Challenge Cup. A national league was founded in 1970, but despite some success in the early 1980s, culminating in qualification for the World Cup Finals of 1982, soccer is still very much a minor sport in New Zealand.

New Zealand's first contact with international soccer came with the visit of a New South Wales team from Australia in 1904, a visit that was returned the following year. Official international competition had to wait until 1922, when an Australian national team, made up mainly of players from New South Wales, toured New Zealand. The following year the New Zealanders returned the compliment. They won both 'test' series, but it was the last time New Zealanders were to enjoy such success. Although they have taken great pleasure in acting as Australia's nemesis on important occasions, the fierce rivalry built up over many tours – in 1933, 1936, 1948 and many times thereafter – has usually come out in Australia's favour. New Zealand's day in the sun came when they qualified for Spain in 1982, defeating Australia and some tough opposition from the Middle-East and Asia on the way: in all they had to play 15 matches and travel 55,000 miles to qualify. For the first and only time the All Whites (named in opposition to the rugby team called the All Blacks) won the attention of the media and the hearts of the New Zealand public. In Spain their scores against Brazil (0–4) and the USSR (0–3) were respectable, and they gave Scotland a fright when they came back from 0–3 to 2–3 before finally losing 2–5. Their rising star was 17-year-old Wynton Rufer, born of a Maori mother and a Swiss father, even then perfecting his skills in England in trials with Norwich City. Unable to get a work permit he moved on to Switzerland to play for FC Zurich and later to Germany with Werder Bremen. Notably absent from New Zealand soccer has been the 'ethnic' influence. Unlike other former British colonies the migrants were overwhelmingly British and this is reflected in the names of the teams and the vast bulk of the players. In Australia the game was virtually taken over by non-British migrants from the late 1950s.

Soccer administrations were formed in Australia in the early 1880s, and in 1882 the New South Wales FA was the first to be formed, along with Natal, outside the United Kingdom. By then Victoria had founded and developed its own local code of football which swept all before it from the late 1860s, not only in Victoria but in all other states except New South Wales and Queensland. There rugby took root, with league the dominant code after the split of 1907. Soccer became what it would remain, the second most popular sport in every Australian state, the only national football code, but the game for non-Australians – 'Poms' and other 'Brits' before the 1950s, 'Wogs' and whatever other insulting epithet for 'continentals' thereafter.

The migrants have been the strength and weakness of the game from the beginning; they are the ones who have kept it going, but they have given it an un-Australian image which resulted in an almost paranoid hatred on the part of some native Australians, especially in the assimilationist days of the 1950s. It was not until Australia reached the finals of the World Cup in 1974 that the game enjoyed any favour with the media. Until then press, radio and television more typically preferred to highlight the riots and attacks on referees that were a frequent accompaniment to games played by 'New Australians', blaming the disturbances on old world hatreds which they did not want to see brought to Australia. A National League was formed in 1977, capitalizing on the euphoria that came with Australia's qualification for West Germany, but this evaporated with a lacklustre World Cup campaign for Argentina in 1978 and then Australia's elimination by New Zealand in the 1982 World Cup. In the meantime the National League struggled along with its problems of distance, semi-professionalism and ethnic discord.

SOCCER'S TYRANNY OF DISTANCE

From the earliest days there were plans for teams to visit Britain – the Old Country – but it was not until the 1920s that Australian teams engaged in serious international competition. New Zealand had been Australia's main opponents, and it was against them, in Wellington in 1936, that Australia recorded its record win: 10–0. A team of Chinese university students played before large crowds in 1923, including more than 47,500 in Sydney, but failed to attract the same interest on a return visit in 1927. Canada played before impressive crowds in 1924 and in 1927 Bohemians of Prague toured the continent, playing several closely fought games and attracting crowds of up to 18,000. They returned to Czechoslovakia with a nickname – the Roos – and a new emblem which they retained: a golden kangaroo. The big attraction of the 1920s, however, was a professional England team that played to capacity crowds wherever they went in 1925: nearly 50,000 came to the game in Sydney and 25,000 in Brisbane. They won all their games comfortably.

These tours showed that there was an immense interest in the game if the standard of play was high enough, but they also showed that thousands were refusing to follow the local game. Most of the new arrivals in Australia found the standard of play so far below what they had left behind that unless they became actively involved, they lost interest. Another lesson was that the Australians were no match for professional opposition. The touring teams did give the local game a boost, however, and in New South Wales, always the dominant state in Australian soccer, a more professional group of teams challenged the established administration in what led to the split of 1929. The damage this caused was further exacerbated by the Depression, which wiped out the progress of the game in the coal and other industrial regions around Newcastle and Wollongong.

At this time Australia received many invitations to tour in Europe but the cost and distance were prohibitive: the best they could manage were the trips to New Zealand and neighbouring Asia: in 1928 and 1931 Australian teams toured what was then the Dutch East Indies. In 1938 a visiting Indian team was unable to match the Australians, who lost only one match, winning three and drawing one. In the previous year an amateur English team lost two of its three games: in New Zealand the English amateurs had runaway victories. At this time the Australian team included many players born in Britain, and there were only a few teams of non-British/Australian origin, consisting of Italian, Maltese and Jewish migrant players. After the Second World War, the face of soccer in Australia changed completely. In the early 1950s the administration of the game in New South Wales was mainly in the hands of Australian-born officials, and many of the players were also Australian born. However, by the end of the 1950s it was the non-British migrants whose clubs dominated the competitions, and who in turn sought to take over the administration. This they succeeded in doing in the Big Split of the late 1950s.

THE 'NEW AUSTRALIANS'

Soccer in Australia was transformed in the years after the Second World War with the arrival of over a million migrants, mainly from Britain and Ireland, but also from other parts of Europe. Italians outnumbered all other non-British migrant groups, and Marconi in Sydney and teams called Juventus in Melbourne and Adelaide rose to national prominence. Behind the Italians in number came Greeks, Yugoslavs, Dutch, Germans and Poles. After the suppression of the Hungarian uprising in late 1956, enough Hungarians arrived for rival Hungarian teams to be formed in some state capitals. From the mid-1960s Greeks and Yugoslavs came in proportionately higher numbers than Italians, and throughout Australia games between Greek and Italian teams became highly charged local derbies. Turks came in increasing numbers in the 1970s, and later in that decade the Boat People and other Asians arrived in significant numbers. So far the Asians have been the only immigrant group not to form soccer teams.

Many of the 'New Australians' brought with them their great love for the game. They came to an environment often both suspicious and hostile, which was encouraged by a policy of assimilation at official level, and at the grass roots, by racism in some areas. For those who arrived in Australia unable to speak English, and subjected to the distrust or even contempt of those who could, it was natural to seek solace in clubs where language was no problem and which provided a cultural cushion in an otherwise alien environment. The public face of these ethnic clubs was often their soccer teams, which carried the burden of being the flag-bearer for their particular society. Riots were frequent, especially attacks on referees, usually by spectators, occasionally by players, and all-in brawls between players with spectators joining in. At times this violence had an ethnic edge, but most frequently it was sparked by an unwillingness to accept bad decisions or defeat. Above all it was not the sort of macho violence sanctioned by sections of Australian society, and the media denounced it as un-Australian activity.

There was another culture clash, familiar enough to British teams from their first visits to the continent but becoming a regular event in the 1950s: the conflicting styles of the British game, based on brawn, and the continental, based on ball skills. The Australian game was essentially a variation of the British, with emphasis on hard tackling, courage and stamina; the 'New Australians' delighted in individual artistry, ball work and display. Such culture clashes were cause enough for dispute, and occasionally ended in brawls. Nevertheless, most of the 'ethnic' teams in the early days relied on British players: some were even composed entirely of British-born players, or perhaps with a 'token' member of the country that the team represented – as elsewhere and in other times (with the exception of Glasgow Rangers and some Basque clubs), it was the club committee and the supporters who gave the club its political, religious or ethnic affiliation; the religion, private beliefs or national origins of the players were irrelevant.

Soccer in Australia was a microcosm of the changes affecting the game in Britain at this time, with conservative British officials treating the players as servants, while the new continental clubs treated them as stars. For players whose footballing talent would have been lucky to get them into a high-grade amateur team in Britain, the financial rewards offered to play for south or central European teams was too much to refuse. In addition to the money they received, they were the object of much popular adulation.

This difference in outlook was behind the Big Split which led to the breakaway from the Australian Soccer Football Association to form the 'ethnic' dominated Australian Soccer Federation in 1961. By the mid-1950s the non-British ethnic teams were attracting the largest crowds, and in the spirit of Super League enthusiasts of any time or place, wanted to keep the money to themselves. The British/Australian administrators of the game, on the other hand, thought that the money received at the gate should benefit the game as a whole, and wanted to use it to encourage junior soccer and improve grounds. This they did, only to see the best juniors brought up through the ranks of local clubs snapped up by the free-spending continentals. Some of the grounds built up by the Australian clubs would in turn be taken over by the 'ethnic' clubs.

The issue came to a head in New South Wales, prompted by the peculiarly Australian organization of games into 'districts', which meant – in rugby and Rules as well as soccer – that the top teams had a monopoly on players from 'their' district. In soccer, the district system was a reality in name only, but there was no automatic promotion and relegation. When ethnic teams starting from scratch won their way through to the premier division – the district league – they had to rely on the incumbents allowing them to join. In 1955 Prague and Sydney Austral gained promotion to the top league in New South Wales, but then Sydney's Hakoah were refused acceptance. This brought the simmering discontent to a head, and in 1957 the major 'migrant' clubs formed a break-away federation. Other states eventually followed the NSW lead, although in South Australia and Victoria there had been no discrimination against ethnic clubs. By 1961 the best teams, nearly all ethnic, were playing in leagues controlled by the Federation and not the Association. A few of the old Association officials stayed on, and many more would re-join the Federation, but the game was no longer a monopoly of the British/Australians.

In the meantime Australia was banned by FIFA. In 1958 the NSW Federation had allowed its leading club, Prague, to poach quality Australian and Dutch players, without paying any fees to the clubs to which they were contracted. The ban did not come in until 1960, thus cutting Australia off from international competition. After some negotiations, however, in which the value of the players poached was reduced considerably from the £46,000 claimed (not unrealistically) and a smaller sum repaid, Australia rejoined the world body in 1963.

AUSTRALIA AND THE WORLD GAME

For many migrants, British or continental, the big event of the year was the visit of one of the leading European teams. Hajduk Split came in 1949, Rapid Vienna in 1955 and in 1957 Ferencvaros and FK Austria. It was still the British teams that aroused the greatest interest, however. In 1951 an England team angered at the poor hospitality offered them, took it out on the locals with a 17–0 drubbing that was the most devastating in a series of defeats inflicted on their luckless opponents. By the late 1950s the game had improved considerably, and although Blackpool, featuring Stanley Matthews in 1958 and Hearts in 1959 won all their games, the margins were narrower. Blackpool played before record crowds, but these were broken when Everton toured Australia in 1964, with crowds of 51,566 in Sydney and 32,500 in

Melbourne. In the local game record crowds were also being set, and reached a peak with the 30,158 who came to see the 1963 Grand Final in Sydney between APIA and South Coast United.

From this time visits by class overseas opposition was an annual event: AS Roma played before delighted Italians and their Australian-born children in 1966, while a Greek national team played before slightly less ecstatic Greeks in 1969, for it was during this tour that Australia recorded its first international victory against European opposition. Others would follow, against Uruguay, in some acrimony, in 1974 and Argentina and Yugoslavia in 1988: in the Australian Bicentennial Cup in the one case, the Seoul Olympics in the other. Before the 1980s Australia was often in the uncomfortable position of playing all its home games against crowds who supported the visitors and jeered the mistakes of the home team. In official world competition, however, especially against Asians, the crowds did get behind the Australians. In this context, the geographical proximity of Asian societies, their perceived 'racial' difference, their rising prosperity and the increased numbers of Asian people migrating to Australia, are all factors.

Australia first entered the Olympic Games soccer competition in Melbourne in 1956, and although they defeated Japan 2–0 before being eliminated by India, the standard of play was very poor. For a long time thereafter Australia did not take the Olympic soccer competition seriously. Australia first entered the World Cup in 1965, when they played North Korea in a two-match competition in neutral Phnom Phen, Cambodia. Before what for them were record crowds of 60,000 and 55,000, they were beaten 6–1 and 3–1. Australia then went on to tour other parts of Asia, the first of many tours in which they generally established a supremacy over their often more skilled but less physical opponents. In 1967 they won all their games, and when the Japanese team that would go on to win bronze in Mexico played three internationals in Australia in 1968, honours were even with a win, loss and draw apiece. The Australians had to suffer the indignity of seeing the Japanese star, Kamamoto, carried off in triumph by local supporters after Japan's 1–3 win in Melbourne. Johnny Warren was made captain of the Australian team during the 1967 Asian tour, following in the footsteps of other Australian-born captains of British backgrounds, like 'Judy' Masters in the 1920s and Joe Marston in the 1950s. Marston had played the best part of his career as a professional with Preston North End from 1950 to 1955, winning in the process a League cap for England and a runners-up medal in the FA Cup. Future Australian-born captains would just as likely come from a 'continental' background.

In subsequent World Cup competitions Australia had to embark on marathon runs, with extra hurdles placed in their way because of FIFA dumping its political problems on the region. The first example of this came in 1969, when Australia beat Japan and South Korea to head their sub-group, but then had to face Rhodesia (now Zimbabwe) in Mozambique because South Korea had refused Rhodesia entry for the qualifying tournament. Thailand refused to have the Rhodesians on their soil for the extra game, so Australia had to play three energy-sapping games in Africa to break a deadlock that took them on to play Israel, who beat an exhausted and injury-stricken Australia by the only goal in Tel Aviv. A draw in Sydney saw Israel qualify. Since Mexico would not have allowed the Rhodesians to enter their country for the 1970 World Cup in any case, the whole exercise was somewhat futile.

Australia, now dubbed the 'Socceroos', reached Germany in 1974 after 11 games, which included New Zealand, Iraq, Indonesia, Iran and South Korea. For Argentina in 1978, Taiwan played in the Oceania region, but after winning their group against them and New Zealand, Australia came second bottom in a group that was led by Iran, South Korea and Kuwait, while only Hong Kong finished below them. For the game in Kuwait, 12 Australian players had to be issued with new passports, as Kuwait refused entry to anyone with an Israeli visa on their passports. In the 1982 World Cup, Australia lost to New Zealand who had the joy of beating their old rivals and going on to acquit themselves well in Spain. In 1985, Scotland was the extra hurdle placed in the path of the Socceroos. Having lost 2–0 in Glasgow, Australia put on one of their most exciting performances in the return in Melbourne, and were unlucky not to fare better than a 0–0 draw against a Scottish team comfortable on its two-goal cushion. Israel went through ahead of Australia in 1990, but it was New Zealand who proved to be their downfall, inflicting a 2–0 defeat in New Zealand against their much more fancied opponents, and so leaving Israel with the odds on their side for the deciding game in Sydney. Israel won by a narrow margin, and then had to go and play the consolation losers in the South American section. The same barrier existed for the 1994 games, with Australia having eliminated Canada, second in the North and Central American group, then having to play Argentina, who finished second in their South American group. It is true that the Asia/Oceania representatives are not as strong as many of the teams eliminated in Europe and South America, but soccer has thrived on the romanticism of the small teams occasionally beating the financial giants. To eliminate this might make more fiscal sense, but it would help extinguish the romance that has played as important a role as money in the progress of the people's game.

MULTICULTURAL FUTURE

By the 1970s many of the young Australians who were making names for themselves as soccer players had obviously non-Anglo names: Eddie Krncevic went on to star in Europe in the early 1980s, the first of a steady flow that would include Jimmy Patikas, Frank Farina and the three current stars of international class: Marc Bosnich, Paul Okon and Ned Zelich. These young stars made their names in the various youth competitions, in which Australia has performed brilliantly in recent years, winning a bronze medal in Portugal in 1991 at the FIFA World Youth Cup, coming fourth in the Barcelona Olympics in 1992 after a sensational qualifying victory over the Netherlands in Utrecht, and faring well as host country in the FIFA Youth Cup in 1993 against fully professional opposition. Notably absent from these youth squads are young aborigines, who are more likely to star in Australian Rules, or even rugby. Charles Perkins, Australia's best known black football player, helped pay his way through university in the 1960s on the money he earned playing soccer, the first step on a political career in which he has promoted the cause of his people. He found in soccer an acceptance that he was refused in Australian football and cricket, but while a few have followed in his soccer footsteps, most notably Harry Williams who played for the national team in the 1970s, other football codes have claimed the best aboriginal sporting talent in recent times.

Since 1974 Australians have not been as hostile to soccer as they once were, while the game is less plagued than it was in the 1950s by crowd and player violence. This may in part reflect the apparently successful integration of newcomers to the continent – in which soccer has certainly played a role. Since 1980, too, soccer has been granted the positive media coverage so long denied the code, with the advent of the Special Broadcasting Service, a government-sponsored television channel devoted to multiculturalism. The channel gives a genuinely international sports coverage, but makes no secret of its support for soccer. Now soccer has not only a friendly media outlet, but the world class expertise provided by Les Murray and his team. Murray left his native Hungary as a youngster, and is backed up by Australian-born Andy Paschalidis and former Australian captain, Johnny Warren.

One of the ironies of the new multiculturalism encouraged by the government and supported across party lines, is that while this is generally accepted in society at large, ethnic names have been banned for soccer clubs, some of which have had names like 'sharks' and 'zebras' foisted on them. Some people see this as essential if more Australians are to be won over to soccer, others see it as a futile attempt to hide an inescapable reality: Hellas, Juventus and Croatia will remain the teams of the Greeks, Italians and Croatians no matter what you call them. Many Australians are understandably put off by presumed allegiances to foreign countries, but to the extent to which Greeks, Italians and Croatians (to name merely the most successful soccer communities) have become Australians, and Australians don't necessarily see their identity as Anglo-Celtic, this is not a serious problem. In fact, it appears that the sponsors were the main group objecting to ethnic identities.

Perhaps the way to the future can be seen in the case of young Zelic, who has been the subject of fan mail and media attention, the sort of hero worship that has generally been absent from the Australian soccer scene. He is just one, albeit the most exceptional, of the three or four dozen Australians now playing overseas. Herein lies the problem that has been the fate of all underdeveloped soccer countries, where players leave not just to earn more money, but to play with the best. When they retain a loyalty to the country that gave them their start, are proud to return to play for it in the big internationals, and ultimately return with the skills learned overseas, they improve the local game. With a combination of continental class and Australian resolve, together with European technique, a new brand of soccer is developing in Australia. The new heroes also speak with broad Australian accents, endearing them to a wider national public. A successful qualification for some future World Cup Finals could do wonders for the game in Australia. FIFA rules have militated against this, however, since the winner of the Oceania group was not guaranteed a place in the Finals: in 1986, 1990 and 1994 the winner was required to play-off against teams from other groups.

CONCLUSION

The irony of the world game today is that all the best players are playing in Europe. The reality is that only in regular competition with Europeans or European teams, can the players and teams of Asia and Oceania improve. Since regular contests with European opposition are hampered by distance and expense, the hope is that expatriates starring overseas come back to enhance the game at home. Australia lost Craig Johnston and Tony Dorigo because they chose to take out English nationality, and it was only by a narrow margin that Wynton Rufer played for New Zealand instead of Switzerland. On the other hand, it was the South Korean football authorities who barred players such as Cha Boom Kun from playing for South Korea before 1986, when the restrictions against expatriates were lifted. Air travel has eased the problem of distance from Europe (and South America), but it is still a difficulty. But the main problem remains: how to keep a star player happy to strut his stuff on his local turf after he has played before thousands in the great stadiums of Europe.

ACKNOWLEDGEMENTS

For corrections, comments and suggestions I would like to thank Paul Moon, Philip Mosely and Pat Woods. Thanks also to Julie Forey of the Sir Norman Chester Centre for research assistance.

REFERENCES

Alaway, R.B. (1948) *Football All Round the World*, London, Newservice
Hilton, Tony (1991) *An Association with Soccer. The NZFA Celebrates its First 100 years*, Auckland, NZFA
Knight, Ken (1991) 'Soccer in China', a desktop publication
Mason, Tony (1990) 'Football on the Maidan. Cultural imperialism in Calcutta', *The International Journal of Sports History*, vol.7, no.1, May, pp.86–96.
Moon, Paul and Burns, Peter (1985) *The Asia-Oceania Soccer Handbook*, New Zealand, Oamaru
Moon, Paul and Burns, Peter (undated [1986]) *Asia-Oceania Soccer Yearbook. 1986– 87*, New Zealand, Oamaru
Mosely, Philip (1987) 'A social history of soccer in New South Wales. 1880–1957', unpublished PhD thesis, University of Sydney
Mosely, Philip (1992) 'The game: early soccer scenery in New South Wales', *Sporting Traditions*, vol.8, no.2, May

Mosely, Philip (forthcoming) 'European immigrants and soccer violence in New South Wales. 1949–1959', *Journal of Australian Studies*, 40 March, 1994, pp.14–26

Moseley, Philip (forthcoming) 'The Depression and football patronage: a regional study, Newcastle district, 1929–1939', *Australian Journal of Politics and History*

Mosely, Philip and Murray, Bill (1994) 'Soccer', in Wray Vamplew and Brian Stoddart (eds) *Cambridge History of Australian Sport*, Cambridge, CUP

Murray, Bill (1994) 'Football. A History of the World Game', Aldershot, Scolar Press

O'Hara, J. (ed.) 1994 *Ethnicity and Soccer in Australia, ASSH Studies in Sport History*, no. 10. See in particular the article by Roy Hay, 'British football, wogball or the world game? Towards a social history of Victorian soccer.'

9

MR DRAINS, GO HOME: FOOTBALL IN THE SOCIETIES OF THE MIDDLE EAST

Stephen Wagg

The term 'Middle East' ordinarily refers to the countries of North Africa, the Western shores of the Mediterranean and the Persian Gulf. From the early nineteenth century, there was a strong European presence in this region designed to protect trade routes or, as in the British case, colonial interests in India. In more recent times, the preserving of oil supplies has been the principal consideration. Most Middle Eastern nation-states were, from the late nineteenth century to the mid-twentieth, part either of the British or the French Empire. Virtually all the societies of the Middle East, with the obvious exception of Israel, are either officially or predominantly Muslim; for the most part, therefore, their football is an exclusively male affair. Sexual division aside, however, association football now prospers in the Middle East, although the climate, terrain and cultural experience of most Middle Eastern countries have been less conducive than those in other areas to the game's development. Commentators agree that it is the premier sport among these nations and that it is probably more popular than all their other sports put together. This applies most especially to the societies of the Arab peninsula, where football only began to thrive in the 1960s: it was actually illegal in Saudi Arabia, for instance, until 1959. As in all other parts of the world, people have, to adapt Marx's well-known adage, made their own football, but not in circumstances of their own choosing. Football has been an important factor, throughout this part of the world, in attempts to define, assert or resist national identities. Thus, the vexed politics of the region – oil-rich oligarchies, Islamic theocracies, sporadic pan-Arabism, the embattled Israeli state, the Palestinian diaspora, the plight of the Kurds in Northern Iraq – have been variously reflected in its football cultures. These cultures have been forged, as I'll show, in collaboration with the football communities of other countries, notably Britain and Brazil.

FOOTBALL IN NORTH AFRICA

The first football nation to emerge in the Middle East was **Egypt**, which at 53 million people has the largest population in the region. Egypt was occupied by the British in 1882 and the game of association football, which came with them, has been one of their most enduring cultural legacies. Partial independence was granted in 1922, although the British maintained a strong military and political presence (Hargreaves 1988, 6), and the founding of the Egyptian football authorities dates from that time: the Egyptian FA formed the previous year and it affiliated to FIFA the year after. The organization of domestic Egyptian football was shaped by, and gave focus to, political opposition to the British presence. As in other parts of the world, nearly all the major football teams in Egypt bear the English title 'Sporting Club'. One – Al Zamalek – was founded by the British, while its principal rival, Al Ahli ('National Club') was started by leading figures in the nationalist independence movement. Both clubs are based in the capital and when they meet in Cairo's National stadium they always attract 100,000 spectators. In fact, although there are other major clubs, particularly the other two Cairo clubs Al Makaouloum ('Arab Contractors') and Al Tersana ('Arsenal') and Olympic Sporting Club of Alexandria, Al Ahli and Al Zamalek dominate domestic competition rather as Rangers and Celtic have done in Scotland. One or other has usually won the Farouk Cup, inaugurated in 1922 and renamed The Cup of Egypt in 1949. Each of the two clubs has its own newspaper and magazines and most Egyptians take sides when the teams meet. Al Ahli, moreover, have supporters in all Arab countries; each of those Arab countries has its *own* club of that name as well. The Egyptian Al Ahli won the African Cup Winners Cup in 1993, for a record fourth time, beating Africa Sport of the Ivory Coast in the final. Al Zamalek, for their part, won the African Champions Cup, defeating the Ghanaian side Ashanti Cotoco in the final.

Egypt were the first nation from the Middle East to enter international competition; they participated in the Olympic Games of 1920 and also the World Cup of 1934. They have periodically qualified for the Olympic Finals, and were semi-finalists in 1928. They also reached their second World Cup Final Tournament, in Italy in 1990.

Egypt came very late, however, to professionalism. It was only adopted after the World Cup success in 1990 and is not yet established, principally because of the 12 premier league clubs, only Al Ahli and Al Zamalek can cope financially with the new system. There have been some calls for a return to semi-professionalism. This is symptomatic of the broader situation in Egyptian football, which is familiar in other African countries (see Ossie Stuart's chapter in this book) and, indeed, in Europe, wherein the leading clubs have a great deal more financial power than the governing body.

Football in **Algeria**, which was a French colony until 1962, was also importantly inscribed by the struggle against colonial domination. The Algerian existentialist writer Albert Camus, a lover of football, lent intellectual and political weight to the game by referring to it in his work (for example, in his novel *La Peste*, written in 1948). For this, he drew on his experience as a goalkeeper for RUA (Racing Universitaire d'Alger) juniors from 1928 to 1930, and subsequently as a devoted supporter both of RUA and the Paris club Racing (McCarthy 1982, 17–18). As with other colonial relationships – for example, between Portugal and Angola or Mozambique (see Pierre Lanfranchi's chapter in this book) – France promoted the notion of the imperial family, and football was one means to this promotion. Algerian footballers came to play for French League sides – Ben Bella, later to become President of an independent Algeria, played for Marseilles in the 1940s – and they were, of course, eligible to play for France. Likewise, Algerian clubs played in the French cup competition.

Football in Algeria in general facilitated a coming together of Muslims and Europeans. The French talked often of *assimilation* between French and Algerian society (around 12 per cent of Algerian society were of French origin) and even left thinkers like Camus, who as a journalist in 1939 covered the famine in the mountainous Kabylia region of Algeria that supplied many migrant workers to the French economy, argued that Algeria could not survive economically as an independent nation (Thody 1961, 11). The political mood hardened in favour of independence during the early 1950s, however, and a war of liberation began in 1954. In 1958, 12 Algerian footballers contracted to French clubs deserted to form an FLN (Front National Liberation) team, based in Tunis. Two of these – Zitouni, a defender, and Mekhloufi, a midfield player – were members of the French international squad. The FLN team was banned by FIFA, but welcomed by the communist regimes of Eastern Europe, who turned out unofficial national sides to play them.

Mekhloufi subsequently came back into the French league, with St Etienne, and in 1968 became the first Algerian to captain a French cup-winning side; he received the cup from General de Gaulle. In the early 1970s, when an all-Africa team was still in operation, Mekhloufi was its trainer; he went on to manage the Algerian national side in 1982, when they beat West Germany in a World Cup match in Gijon (Algeria also beat West Germany in 1964, in Algiers) and, in 1986, he became president of the Algerian Football Federation. More than a million white Algerians, meanwhile, though born in Algeria moved to France at independence in 1962. Known as the *pieds noir*, they have failed substantially to integrate into French society and form a cultural enclave in the south of the country: this includes running their own football league (Whitaker 1993).

Algeria qualified for the World Cup Finals in both 1982 and 1986, although they did not progress beyond the first round on either occasion. Neither **Libya** nor **Morocco** has ever qualified for the Finals, but **Tunisia** were in Argentina for the 1978 tournament, beating Mexico impressively and losing narrowly to Poland.

Algerian football is arguably more diverse than Egyptian football. Until 1950, it had regional leagues, based in Algiers, Oran and Constantine and, along with two other neighbouring former French territories, Morocco and Tunisia, Algerian teams have participated in North African club and international competitions (Oliver 1992). As in other parts of the world, regional feeling is strong in North Africa. The town of Tizi-Ouzou, where Algeria's leading club side JS Kabylie play, is in the aforementioned Kabylia region. This region is dominated by the Saharan warrior group, the Berbers, and the club has sometimes provided a focus for local patriotism. When this happened in the 1980s the club was obliged to change its name to JE [Jeunesse Electrique] Tizi-Ouzu. Similarly, in Western Sahara, the Polisario liberation movement, which is seeking independence from Morocco, has formed its own national football team in waiting. The team was invited to play a series of fixtures in Italy during the summer of 1993, thus helping Polisario to publicize its national aspirations.

But the most eminent case of an aspirant national identity being preserved through sport is that of **Palestine**, which still maintains a national side, in exile. Here, once again, football provides a political metaphor – in this instance, for the Palestinian diaspora. The Palestine team has no nation and its players are not selected from clubs. Squad members come from a variety of countries: in 1992, there were, for example, 750,000 Palestinians in Israel, one and a half million across the Gaza Strip, Jordan and the East Bank and 80,000 in Chile. The team is not internationally recognized: the Palestinian Football Federation had its membership rejected by FIFA in 1946, prior to the establishment of the Israeli state in Palestine in 1948. Two years later, the Palestinian Olympic Committee similarly lost recognition because it had no country to represent. The sports politics of the Palestinians rallied in 1964 with the founding of the Palestine Liberation Organization. The forming of a Palestinian Sports Association was part of this political renewal and the following year Palestinian teams were granted international acceptance in a number of sports – table tennis, for example – but football was not one of them. The Palestine football team, which is trained in Tunisia by Ali Miloud, an ex-Tunisian international, plays only intermittently: it played in France in 1982 and in Algeria in 1986. Naturally, it never has a home match; moreover, few of its players have ever seen Palestine (*El Pais*, Madrid, 2 February 1992, 39–43).

In September 1994, following the recent readmission of the Palestinians to the Occupied Territories, the Palestine football team played an unofficial international match there to mark the occasion. Among an exuberant crowd that saw Palestine beat Qatar 4–1 was PLO leader Yasser Arafat, aware perhaps that many of those present would soon be looking to him for more tangible benefits from the agreement with Israel to add to this sealing of renascent national identity.

There was also, briefly, an Arab football team in the mid-1950s (Williams 1993), which stemmed from Nasserism: the resurgence of pan-Arabist and anti-imperialist feeling inspired by the charismatic Egyptian president Gamal Abdul Nasser.

Other political problems have manifested themselves in North African football. In post-independence Algeria, for example, football stadia became typical contexts for the expression of opposition to the government. This opposition was often led by the young, who were campaigning for more Westernization, more French television and so on; in 1976, in an attempt to staunch this criticism, the government moved to close down the Algerian football championship (Halliday 1974, 21–5).

WHERE IS THE OPPOSITION? THE CASE OF ISRAELI FOOTBALL

With the Balfour Declaration of 1917, the British government asserted that Palestine should be the 'national home' of the Jewish people. Jewish migration to Palestine began in the early 1920s and the Palestine FA was established in 1928 in Tel Aviv. The Palestinian Cup began that year, followed by a championship competition in 1932. Major clubs, such as Hapoel and Maccabi Tel Aviv (both based in the capital), date from then. Although there was no cup final in 1931 or 1936, Palestinian football seems to have developed without too much political difficulty in the 1930s. Palestine took part in the World Cup of 1934, during the course of which they played Egypt both in Cairo and in Tel Aviv. This raised no diplomatic problem, although the Palestine team was composed entirely of Jews. There were apparently no objections either when they entered the World Cup of 1938 or when they played a friendly against **Lebanon** in Tel Aviv in 1940.

However, the Israeli state was formed in 1948 and it has, of course, never gained the acceptance of its Arab and Muslim neighbours. This lack of acceptance, and the ascription of pariah status to the Israelis, has understandably been reflected in the subsequent progress of the nation's football. There was a temporary halt to football in Israel in 1948, when there was an Arab invasion, and the Israeli cup competition did not resume until 1952. There were further disruptions in 1953, 1956 (the time of Nasser's blockading of the Suez canal and the resulting invasion by British and French troops) and 1961. More importantly, in a post-war world which has witnessed the growth to international football status of so many Third World countries – many of them in the Middle East region – and the resultant globalization of FIFA, it has become a politically more complex task to accommodate Israel.

In the World Cup of 1958, Israel technically won their group when all their designated opponents in the Asia-Africa section withdrew, but, since FIFA rules stated that no nation other than the hosts and the holders could qualify for the Final tournament without playing a match, Israel were obliged to play off against wild-card opponents. These opponents turned out to be Wales, who won both the qualifying games and progressed to their only World Cup Finals.

In 1962, the Asian Cup tournament was awarded to Indonesia who, mindful of its large Muslim community, declined to invite Israel. Israel, however, was given the tournament in 1964 and won it, beating South Vietnam, India and South Korea to do so. Since then, the tournament has been won by a Gulf country. Israel made the World Cup Finals of 1970 in Mexico, having performed well in the Olympics there two years earlier. They were in a strong group which included Italy and Sweden, along with Australia. They did not progress beyond the first round. The Israeli player that caught the eye in the tournament was the Russian born midfielder Mordecai Spiegler (Glanville 1980, 167): the Jews, of course, have had their own diaspora and many Israeli players – indeed many Israelis – have been migrants, born elsewhere.

In 1974 Israel lost to Iran in the Asian Cup Final in Tehran, their passage to the final having been eased by the refusal of both North Korea and Kuwait to take to the field against them. Two years later, after sustained lobbying by the Arab countries, the Asian Football Federation expelled Israel, who were now admitted to UEFA: improbably, for the purposes of international football administration, Israel now 'went into Europe'. They subsequently moved into the Oceanic Federation, as associate members, but returned to UEFA in 1991.

As members of such a competitive grouping as UEFA, Israel will find it hard to qualify for World Cup Finals. They were close to qualification for Italy in 1990 but lost a play-off match to Colombia. They didn't qualify for the USA in 1994 either, although they did beat France 3–2 at the Parc des Princes stadium in Paris and thus prevented the French from going.

Football is extremely popular in Israel, where there are 45,000 registered players and nearly 550 clubs. There is some crowd violence at Israeli football matches, especially at matches involving clubs based in Arab communities (Semyonov and Farbstein 1989). Given the strong sense of expropriation felt by Palestinians, both in Israel and beyond, this might not be thought surprising.

MONEY NO OBJECT: FOOTBALL AROUND THE PERSIAN GULF

Politically, the Arab world – an estimated 150 million people, most of them in the Middle East – now revolves around **Saudi Arabia**. Saudi Arabia has been constituted as a nation only since 1932. It has a population of 9.5 million, about three-quarters of the total population of the Arab peninsula, which is bounded by the Red Sea, the Indian Ocean and the Persian Gulf, and it covers 80 per cent of the land area of the peninsula. Only 0.2 per cent of the land in Saudi Arabia is cultivatable; most of the rest is stony rather than sandy. In the late 1970s, Saudi Arabia, like the other wealthy Gulf States of **Oman**, the **United Arab Emirates**, **Qatar**, **Bahrain** (which consists of 35 islands in the Persian Gulf itself) and **Kuwait** began importing astroturf pitches for their football clubs. These six countries, which are all monarchies ruled by royal decree, form the Gulf Cooperation Council (Rosandich 1991).

Arabia was transformed in the period 1950 to 1970 by the discovery of oil. This brought a strong American presence in the 1950s and 60s: the Americans drilled for the oil in collaboration with local elites through ARAMCO – the Arabian American oil company.

Saudi Arabia by the mid-1970s was known to hold a quarter of the world's known oil reserves. It is an Islamic state whose ruling royal family are members of the Wahhabi sect. The influence of the royal family is tentacular and, through one or other of its 5,000 princes, it extends to all facets of society. This certainly includes football, which has been accorded a high priority in Saudi society in the last 25 years, as in all the countries of the Arab peninsula.

Table 9.1 Table collated from: Guy Oliver *The Guinness Record of World Soccer* Enfield. Guinness Publishing 1992

State	Local FA founded	Affiliated to FIFA
Algeria	1962	1963
Egypt	1921	1923
Libya	1962	1963
Morocco	1955	1956
Tunisia	1956	1960
Bahrain	1951	1966
Iran	1920	1948
Iraq	1948	1951
Israel (as Palestine)	1928	1929
Jordan	1949	1958
Kuwait	1952	1962
Oman	1978	1980
Qatar	1960	1970
Saudi Arabia	1959	1959
Syria	1936	1937
Turkey	1923	1923
United Arab Emirates	1971	1972
Yemen (North)	1976	1980
Yemen (South)	1940	1967

Source: Guy Oliver (1992) *The Guinness Record of World Soccer*

Historically, the people of the peninsula engaged in equestrian and blood sports, as well as archery, swimming, fishing and a game known as *Saba'a Toobat*, which resembles cricket or baseball. The first peninsula society to sample Western sports was Bahrain, a maritime nation where the British brought football and cricket in the 1920s; the first football club was established there in 1936. Similarly, Western sports took root first in the coastal towns of Saudi Arabia: Dhahran, where a lot of oil company personnel were based, and Jeddah, which was the largest port on the peninsula and gave access to the holy cities of Mecca and Medina. Football began to be played here in the mid-1940s, and spread slowly inland. In the early years it was played mostly by Sudanese migrants (Rosandich 1991). (All the Gulf states, incidentally, have high proportions of migrant workers – both unskilled and highly skilled – in their populations: this may be because labour is scarce, as has been the case in Qatar, or because the local population can assume a parasitic position – as in Saudi Arabia and Kuwait, where a minority of the population are actually Kuwaiti nationals and there is a large Palestinian community [Halliday 1974, 422].) As can be seen from Table 9.1, all the national FAs on the Arab peninsula, with the exception of South Yemen, were formed after the Second World War and the earliest affiliation to FIFA was Saudi Arabia's in 1959. Serious attempts to develop football in the Gulf states were made in the 1970s; in all cases these measures were taken by the 'free standing ministries or quasi-ministerial organisations' that have responsibility for sports: the Supreme Council for Youth and Sports, in Qatar and the United Arab Emirates, the General Organization for Youth and Sports, in Bahrain, and so on (Rosandich 1991). The most significant steps were taken in Saudi Arabia.

Saudi Arabia, as I've observed, only legalised football in 1959, the same year that the national FA was formed and affiliated to FIFA. Football had been banned until then, not only because the royal family 'disapproved of Saudi youths desporting themselves with their thighs naked, but because soccer clubs were suspected of being a cover for subversive political activity' (Holden and Johns 1981, 169–70). This official view was abandoned by the Saudi ruler of the time, Prince Feisal, and his motive is a matter for speculation. Some variant of the 'bread and circuses' thesis is tempting, however: Saudi society is replete with bread but affords relatively few circuses – 'bonanza and repression', to borrow Fred Halliday's apt phrase (Halliday 1974, 47). There had, for example, been serious working-class unrest in the Damman oilfields in the 1950s – a strike involving 13,000 workers was called there in 1953; trades unions were banned and trades union membership made punishable by imprisonment; there was a demonstration against King Saud in 1956; and migrant workers were frequently deported, particularly those from neighbouring Yemen, where left-wing ideas and movements were strong: there was a revolution there in 1962 (Halliday 1974, 66–7). Both the Yemeni states are republics.

Football rapidly moved nearer to centre-stage in the political deliberations of the Gulf states. This was reflected in the founding of the Gulf Cup in 1970, the inaugural tournament being held in Bahrain. Royal elites were anxious now to use their oil wealth to boost national credibility both in the region and further afield, while strengthening national identity at home. These countries, especially Saudi Arabia, were industrializing fast and cities were growing at a comparable rate – for instance, the industrial cities of Yanbu and Jubail in Saudi Arabia have been built from scratch since the early 1970s and they now accommodate over 100,000 people between then (Rosandich 1991). This has brought many migrants – from nearby countries, from Europe and, not least, from the desert, where the Bedouin way of life has prevailed. Regionalism and tribal loyalties have been strong in many areas and the urban workforce is, as I have suggested, ethnically very diverse. In the Mercedes car plant in Jeddah in the 1970s, for example, there were no Saudis except the chairman: instead German managers supervised Turkish manual workers (Halliday 1974, 592). Elsewhere in Saudi were unskilled workers from Sudan, Palestine, Egypt, Yemen, Korea and numerous other countries: around two-thirds of the Saudi workforce was migrant. This remains the case. Today there are large contingents of Pakistani and Filipino workers in Saudi Arabia; they, and all other migrant workers, are known pointedly as 'TWNs' – Third World Nationals'. In a society where the prevailing interpretations of Islam placed severe restrictions on popular culture, football must have been seen as having great importance in the forging of national identity and the diversion and integration of the multicultural workforce: football is, after all, *the* international sport, comprehensible now in virtually all cultures. However, this takes place only at a certain social class level in Saudi Arabia. Saudi Arabian football is the province of the middle classes, Saudi and expatriate; it is not a game for the proletariat, almost none of whom are Saudi nationals. Migrant Pakistani workers may be at the match but, as an English expatriate in Riyadh told me, 'they're selling the Pepsi'.

Islam and football are both manifestly important elements in national identity and culture, but this remains a contested area. The royal family support the limited Westernization, of which football is a part, and, of course, they run the game, as they run everything else in the kingdom. Football is also available on satellite TV, which is formally illegal, but widely received nevertheless: the Italian League is the most popular with Saudis, who like most Arab football publics prefer the passing game. Stricter Muslims among the priesthood of the Wahhabi sect, however, are opposed to football on the ground that it distracts the nation's youth from Islam. At present, though, in Saudi Arabia Islam and football are reconciled: matches begin with mid-afternoon prayers and end with sunset prayers.

For the purposes of FIFA, the Gulf countries have been assigned to the Asian grouping and those with substantial oil wealth have dominated this section since the mid-1970s. During the early part of that decade, most of the Gulf states started to buy in football expertise, principally from Britain and Brazil. In Saudi Arabia, there was concern that, despite Saudi political and economic power, the country had come bottom in the Gulf League Tournament between 1974 and 1976. The General Presidency of Youth Welfare, the body presiding over Saudi sport and run by Faisal Bin Fahd, the king's son, engaged World Sports Academy, a British sports consultancy, to run Saudi international football at full, under-19 and under-16 levels. World Sports Academy was run by Jimmy Hill, a leading figure (as players' union official, club manager and broadcaster) in the post-war football world in England and prime mover in the commercialization of the English game; Hill's reputation as an entrepreneur was balanced by the engagement of Sir Stanley Rous, representative of the now declining public service tradition in British football, as President of the company. World Sports Academy brought in club managers from the English Football League.

There is some history of Britons coaching in the Middle East and the relationship between teachers and taught has had its difficulties. One has clearly been racial stereotyping. For example, George Raynor, later coach to the Swedish national side, was a PT instructor and football coach in Iraq during the Second World War. Later, he recalled 'the laziness and lack of will-power of a great number of Arab soldiers' and observed that 'Indians, who were more used to the conditions, had nothing like the same perseverance' as the British: 'The British lads could take it', he concluded (Raynor 1960, 17–18). It is likely that these residual notions of the Arab carried over into the British presence of the 1970s and that they were expressed both in a view of Arab players as undisciplined – a common complaint among British coaches in the Middle East – and in differences over how the game should be played. In Britain a more physical and aggressive style has generally been favoured and it is a long-standing prejudice of the English football world that players from hotter climates (or simply darker skinned players) lack 'bottle' – courage or staying power. A British coach who was in Saudi Arabia at this time told me: 'The Saudi middle classes loved football. But they didn't like us much. They preferred the Brazilians. They identified with them.' The perceived British strategy of 'kick and rush' is neither popular, nor very apt, in the Middle East. As a British journalist noticed, while covering the World Cup play-offs in Doha (the capital of Qatar) in the autumn of 1993 which involved Saudi Arabia, Japan, North and South Korea, Iran and Iraq: 'the skill factor of all six countries is impressive. They kill the ball dead, run with it comfortably at their feet, pass and move. Glenn Hoddle [a British club manager favouring the passing game] would enjoy it. Dave Bassett [a manager known for the more physical style] might not' (Palmer 1993).

In the late 1970s the Saudi Arabian side was coached by Bill McGarry, former manager of Wolverhampton Wanderers in England. Bahrain were managed by the former Reading manager Jack Mansell and Oman by another Briton, Jim Smith. Similarly, former Manchester United manager Frank O'Farrell managed Iran for two years in the mid-1970s. One thing about the job that these men found to be no different from the British experience was the impatience with which employers and local publics longed for success. McGarry, as successive England managers have done, fell foul of the national press. In Saudi Arabia, the press is subject to strict government control, but there appeared to be little restriction on criticism of that highly paid migrant worker, the national football team manager. A contemporary recalls: 'They abbreviated his name anyway to *Mkrry*. When the team started to do badly they altered it to *Mjrry*, which in Arabic means "the drains" or "sewage"'. Likewise, O'Farrell, under whose management Iran won the Asian Games cup final of 1974, told the *Yorkshire Evening Post* in 1977:

> No matter how much money you get, you simply can't buy the sort of success they want. To them, football is not a sport as such, it is a game of political one-upmanship and the chances of success are extremely small because the paymasters are impatient. They want instant success. If you don't begin to give them what they want then they can make your life very unhappy. (14 July 1977)

The most celebrated instance of the importation of British football expertise was the appointment of former Leeds United and England manager Don Revie to coach the United Arab Emirates in 1977. Revie was another apostle of the harsher British mode of playing the game and his sojourn in the Gulf was predicted to be brief but, although he lost the national team managership in 1980 on the appointment of an Arabic speaker, he went on to manage Al Nasr ('Victory') in the Emirates' 12-club league, returning to England only in 1983.

It is the attraction, though, of a large number of Brazilian football people to Saudi Arabia in the late 1970s that is likely to have had the greater effect in developing Saudi football, both at club and at international level. If the West Germans were the most successful international side in the post-war world, then the Brazilians were the most charismatic, especially for emergent nations. World Cup winners in 1958, 1962 and 1970, Brazil's international football standing began to wane during the 1970s, but, for the heroes of the 1970 World Cup winning side there were some big pay days during that decade: Pelé came out of retirement to sign for New York Cosmos, although he played a number of lucrative friendlies in the Middle East while still with Santos in the early 1970s, and a number of his team-mates came to play in Saudi Arabia. The Brazilian winger Rivelino, for instance, signed for the Riyadh club Al Hilal ('Crescent') and Mario Zagalo, Tele Santana and Carlos Alberto Parreira all spent time with Saudi clubs, while the Brazilian coach Jose Kandino for a time had charge of the Saudi national side. If, as seems probable, the Saudi side are eliminated from the 1994 World Cup Finals early on, then popular support in Saudi Arabia will switch to Brazil.

Saudi Arabian league sides now dominate Gulf competition. There are 54 clubs and 9,600 registered players. Each of the two main cities – Riyadh, the capital, and Jeddah – have two major established clubs: Al Hilal and Al Nasr play in Riyadh, and Al Ahli and Al Ittihad ('The Union') play in Jeddah. As in all the kingdoms of the Gulf region, each club is supported financially by a member of the royal family. Each of the four leading clubs has had its share of domestic, Gulf and Arab honours in recent years and a third Riyadh club, Al Shahab ('Youth'), has emerged in the early 1990s and won the Saudi league in three consecutive years – 1991–3. Although smaller than the other two Riyadh clubs, Al Shahab has gone on to win the Arab Champions Cup, the Gulf Club Champions Cup (twice) and has been runner-up in the Asian club champions cup. It also supplied a number of players to the national squad which qualified for the World Cup Finals in the USA in 1994, including Said Al-Ouiran, Fahd Al-Muhallal and Fouad Anwar.

The Saudi FA has recently decided to adopt full professionalism in the league and placed a limit on imported labour: they permit three foreign players per club, who are now recruited mostly from Egypt, Tunisia and Ghana.

Saudi Arabia are also a growing force, on and off the field, in international football: aside from qualifying for the USA, they won the Under 16 World Cup in Scotland in 1989 and the Asian Cup in 1986 and 1988. Saudi Arabia also organized and staged the Continents Cup competition in 1992, contested by themselves, Argentina, the USA and the Ivory Coast (and won by Argentina). FIFA are now likely to take over the running of the tournament. England came to play a friendly in Riyadh in 1988 and were held to a 1–1 draw. The British popular press, oblivious to football developments in the Gulf region, were indignant; one newspaper, the *Daily Mirror*, mocked both the England team's opposition and its manager Bobby Robson with the back page headline 'IN THE NAME OF ALLAH GO!'

The other Gulf countries, although they have thriving football cultures, have been unable to match Saudi Arabia's achievements; they lack not the financial wealth but the playing resources. Qatar, for example, is a tiny country of only half a million people but it is rich enough to provide education, electricity and a health service free to all of them (Williams 1993). It has 12 clubs and 830 registered players. Qatar reached the Olympic Finals in both 1984, in Los Angeles, and 1992, in Barcelona. They were also runners-up to West Germany in the Under 21 World Cup of 1981 in

Australia and their Under 16 team came fourth in the World Cup of 1991 in Italy. Moreover, the Qatari club Al-Sadd were the Asian champions in 1988 and the full national side won the Gulf Nations Cup in 1992.

The United Arab Emirates, only a nation since 1971, has a population of around two million. It supports 25 clubs and well over 3,000 players, and has one of the best climates for football in the region: although football isn't possible in the summer months of June, July and August, for the rest of the year the temperature hovers in the 80s and thus permits a reasonably energetic game. UAE qualified for the World Cup Finals of 1990. Kuwait were the first Arab Gulf country to quality for a World Cup Final tournament: they were in Spain in 1982. Kuwait is similarly a small country, with around two million people. It has a 14-club league, of which Al-Qadissia, Al-Arabi and Al-Yarmouk are the most prominent members.

Iran and **Iraq**, historic enemies over several centuries, met in Qatar in October 1993 as part of the regional World Cup play-offs for the USA in 1994. The game was billed, paraphrasing Saddam Hussein's words at the outset of the Gulf War of 1991, as 'the mother of all football matches' (Williams 1993). Iraq won 2–1, but neither side made the Finals. Both countries, as we've seen, have employed European football assistance in the past but are unlikely to do so now, neither government enjoying good relations with the West.

In Iran, since the overthrow of the Shah's regime in 1979 and the setting up of an Islamic state, football has had a reduced priority and there has been a close vetting of the import of Western popular culture. Football has survived this. It is widely played – there are 6,300 clubs and 300,000 players – and watched; as elsewhere in the Gulf area, it is available on TV. There are big audiences for football matches on the Sunday sports programme, for which only women's sports are censored, and the government in 1994 bowed to widespread cultural resistance (Sreberny-Mohammadi and Mohammadi 1991) by legalizing satellite TV. (This trend is not universal, however. Satellite TV was recently banned in Syria.) Iran won the Asian Champions Cup in 1993, but in general their standard of football has declined since the Islamic revolution. However, the Irani government felt sufficiently strongly, either about qualification for the USA or the prospect of beating Iraq, to fly a mullah to Qatar with an offer to the Iran players of free pilgrimages to Mecca, as well as cash, a car and an apartment each, if they won (Williams 1993; Bose 1993). Iran did qualify for the World Cup Finals in Argentina in 1978 and drew, 1–1, with Scotland. This was viewed as an unpardonable humiliation by the British press and the Scotland manager Alistair McLeod was much abused throughout the British sports media as a consequence (Wagg 1987).

Iraq were the second team from the Middle East to reach the World Cup Finals: they qualified for Mexico in 1986. They also qualified for all the Olympic Finals in the 1980s – 1980, '84 and '88. Iraq too clearly attached considerable importance to the Qatar match. The team was managed by Udai Hussein, son of the country's ruler Saddam and former deputy head of Iraqi intelligence, and coached by Ammu Baba, a veteran of the Arab national side of the 1950s. Baba told reporters in Qatar of a vibrant football culture back in Iraq:

He remembered with special fondness a match in Baghdad during the second Gulf war, between the Air Force team and the al-Zorah club, in front of a crowd of 30,000. 'The stadium was full when the aircraft started to come and the rockets went, and still the people inside were happy and cheering. They never thought of going into the shelters. The game was continuing and not a single person ran away.' (Williams 1993)

Football, then, is plainly a strong element in the defining of Iraqi national identity and the appointment of his son to run the national side reflects the political importance attached to the game by Saddam Hussein. Football was actually part of Iraqi calculations in the invasion of Kuwait in 1991: Udai Hussein flew several Kuwaiti players to Baghdad in an unsuccessful effort to persuade them to play for Iraq (Smyth 1993). Moreover, the Hussein regime knows that, as elsewhere in the region, and beyond, football can provide an arena for political dissent: in May 1992, when a Baghdad football crowd were chanting anti-Saddam slogans, Udai ordered guards to open fire and three spectators were killed (Smyth 1993). Likewise, to have reached the USA in 1994 would have brought not only a measure of rehabilitation abroad in the wake of the second Gulf war, but a distracting national euphoria at home that might temper social discontent. This discontent is strongest and most explicit in Kurdistan, in northern Iraq on the mountainous border with Turkey; the Kurds have been fighting Iraqi rule since the 1970s and have, so far without success, declared independence. Tens of thousands of Kurds died in the late 1980s and an uprising in 1991 was savagely put down. Since then, an uneasy armed truce has obtained, supervised by Western military observers. The area is in a state of economic siege and Iraqi troops hover nearby. Football is a vital part of Kurdish popular culture; historically it has been a vehicle for Kurdish nationalist aspirations for independence and it has expressed the hostility of Kurds towards the Iraqi state and metropolitan Baghdad. The unofficial capital of 'free Kurdistan' is Arbil, home of the leading football club in the area. In 1986 the Arbil midfield player Kamiran Mohammed was dropped without apparent reason from the Iraqi national squad; Kurdish football supporters were convinced that this was because he was a Kurd, and not an Arab. The following year, there was a near-riot when Arbil had a goal disallowed in an away match against the Baghdad side Zaura.

Outside Arbil's ground the mandatory portrait of Saddam Hussein is defaced by bullet holes, while a painting of the 'Football Martyr', a former player and Kurdish guerrilla called Mursil Hussain Mursil killed fighting the Iraqi army in the mountains in 1978, has pride of place (Smyth 1993).

Arbil have been successful in recent years and in 1988 were promoted to the Iraqi premier division of 24 clubs. Since the uprising, however, the Baghdad government has forbidden opposing teams to travel to Arbil. The club must now travel 70 miles to the city of Mosul to play its home matches and its regular crowds of 20,000, with their nationalist fervour, have been dissipated. This has imposed an important cultural and political deprivation to go with the physical suffering of the Kurds. To intense local disappointment, Arbil finished 17th in the premier division in 1992.

When the journalist Gareth Smyth visited Kurdistan in the autumn of 1993, he was struck by the depth of feeling in Kurdish football culture. 'Football is fever here', he wrote. As in most other football worlds in the Middle East, the Brazilians of the 1970s are revered – the Brazilian Romereo managed the Iraqi national side in the mid-1980s – and Smyth met a Kurdish football reporter who waxed lyrical in conversation about Brazil's World Cup winning side of 1970. Late in 1993 there was a petition to the Kurdish parliament to revive football in the province, so that morale might be raised. And Smyth was approached by a football administrator, who 'points out matter-of-factly that Western aid (which prevented starvation last winter, if not the one before) has not included help for football' (Smyth 1993).

Probably the strongest football nation in the north of the Middle East region is **Turkey**. Turkey is one of the larger countries in the area; like Egypt and Iran, it has over 50 million people. Once again, the British were responsible for introducing the game – in the 1890s – and the leading Turkish clubs of today were founded in the early 1900s. The Turkish Football Federation was formed in 1923 and a system of regional leagues became established; from 1937 a play-off was held between the winners of these leagues to establish a national champion. Professionalism was adopted in 1951.

There are two major teams in the capital Ankara and two in Izmir, and towns such as Trabzon, Bolu, Deizli and Adapazari have developed strong teams since the 1960s, but Turkish football history has been dominated by the Istanbul clubs: until a national league was set up in 1959, winners of the Istanbul league were regarded as national champions. There are three leading club sides based in Istanbul: Besiktas (founded in 1903), Galatasaray (1905) and Fenerbahce (1907). The football culture of Istanbul is similar to that of Vienna in the inter-war period, in that it draws in all social classes and the pattern of club support is along class lines: Besiktas is known as the working-class club, Fenerbahce are associated with the rich of the city and Galatasaray have the support of the intellectuals.

Turkish clubs have employed football people from Western Europe in the 1980s – the former England international and Leicester City manager Gordon Milne managed Besiktas for a number of seasons – but they are more likely to recruit from Muslim communities in Eastern Europe, such as Bosnia. Turkish clubs play in European competition and are not disgraced: Galatasaray disposed quite easily of a strong Manchester United side in the European Cup of 1993–4.

Turkey played their first international match in 1923, against Romania, and they entered several Olympic competitions in the 1920s and 30s, without success. Their strongest side to date was probably in the years immediately following the Second World War. This side made the quarter finals of the London Olympics in 1948 and qualified for the World Cup Finals of both 1950 and 1954. In one of the qualifying matches for 1950, they scored seven goals against Syria, but then withdrew from the finals on grounds of expense; in Switzerland in 1954 they scored another seven goals, against South Korea. Turkey's main football heroes played at this time: Metin Otkay, Burhan Sargin and, in particular, Lefter Kucukandonyadis, who made his debut in

1948. Kucukandonyadis was born of Greek parents in Istanbul, and is still resident and widely remembered there.

IN SUMMARY: WHITHER ARAB FOOTBALL?

As we've seen, football history in the Middle East over the last 25 years has been dominated by the Arab states, particularly those of the Gulf. In recognition of the progress of these football nations, FIFA have indicated that three places, rather than the present two, will be given to the Asian group in future World Cup competitions. This will be at the expense either of Europe or of South America.

The modern Middle East offers piquant contradictions to liberal cultural and political observers. Modernization has been achieved in several societies, but mostly with Western capital and expertise and in the context of repressive and undemocratic social structures. There is material and sexual inequality virtually unmatched in the West. Football has had its place in all this: the football teams that have raised the international status of this part of the Third World are owned and ordered by rich and unaccountable males. Few would doubt either that the massive poverty that exists across large tracts of the Middle East has helped to breed Islamic fundamentalism. In the streets of many cities in the region, therefore – Algiers, Cairo, Tehran, Ankara, Baghdad – we have seen angry and violent expressions of an explicitly anti-Western creed that could once again threaten football as an activity; upstairs in many of the decrepit residential blocks, however, and in many of the more salubrious dwellings across the Persian Gulf, people are watching football on satellite TV and dreaming perhaps of one day seeing an Arab Pelé in their country's colours.

ACKNOWLEDGEMENTS

I want to thank a number of people for their help in the preparation of this chapter. Once again, I have drawn more heavily than I acknowledge in the text on Guy Oliver's *The Guinness Record of World Soccer*, particularly for information on Turkish football. A great deal of material was provided by Tony El-Hage of the Arab newspaper *Al Hayat*, and I was given much help by John Harding (School of Oriental and African Studies, London University), Pierre Lanfranchi (De Montfort University, Leicester), Steve Hewitt (Birmingham University Library, Centre for Sports Science and History), Ali Mohammadi (Nottingham Trent University), Jan Melisson and Stephen Hopkins (both in the Department of Politics, Leicester University), Isabel Ferrer Gil of *El Pais* magazine, Zed Books, Francesca Ryan at *GQ* magazine, the library staff of the *Yorkshire Evening Post*, Tim Dawson, Zafer Cirhinlioglu (Sociology Department, Leicester University) and Janet Tiernan of the Sir Norman Chester Centre for Football Research, Leicester University.

REFERENCES

Bose, Mihir (1993) 'Desert storm? No, a wind of change blows', *The Sunday Times*, 24 October

Glanville, Brian (1980) *The History of the World Cup*, London, Faber and Faber

Halliday, Fred (1974) *Arabia Without Sultans*, Harmondsworth, Penguin

Hargreaves, J.D. (1988) *Decolonisation in Africa*, London, Longman

Holden, David and Johns, Richard (1981) *The House of Saud*, London, Sidgwick and Jackson

McCarthy, Patrick (1982) *Camus: A Critical Study of his Life and Work*, London, Hamish Hamilton

Oliver, Guy (1992) *The Guinness Record of World Soccer*, Enfield, Guinness Publishing

Palmer, Mark (1993) 'Fertile talent flourishes in the desert', *The Sunday Telegraph*, 24 October

Raynor, George (1960) *Football Ambassador at Large*, London, The Soccer Book Club

Rosandich, T.J. (1991) 'Sports in society: The Persian Gulf countries', *Journal of the International Council for Health, Physical Education and Recreation*, vol.XXVII, no.3, Spring, pp.26–31

Semyonov, Moshe and Farbstein, Mira (1989) 'Ecology of sports violence: the case of Israeli soccer', *Sociology of Sport Journal*, vol.6, pp.50–59

Smyth, Gareth (1993) 'Kurds United', *GQ*, November, pp.158–161

Sreberny-Mohammadi, Annabelle and Mohammadi, Ali (1991) 'Hegemony and resistance: media politics in the Islamic Republic of Iran', *Quarterly Review of Film and Video*, vol.12, no.4, pp.33–59

Thody, Philip (1961) *Albert Camus 1913–1960*, London, Hamish Hamilton

Wagg, Stephen (1986) 'Naming the guilty men: managers and the Media' in Alan Tomlinson and Garry Whannel (eds) *Off the Ball*, London, Pluto Press

Whitaker, Mark (1993) 'Empire of sand', *Guardian*, 20 March

Williams, Richard (1993) 'Desert storms and American dreams', *Independent on Sunday*, 24 October

10

THE BUSINESS OF AMERICA: REFLECTIONS ON
WORLD CUP '94

Stephen Wagg

During the American presidential campaign of 1924, Calvin Coolidge, the incumbent and candidate for the Republican Party, made the memorable declaration that: 'The business of America is business'. Sixty years later, the playwright Arthur Miller recalled in his memoirs seeing the singer Frank Sinatra comport himself like royalty at the inauguration ball of President John Kennedy in 1961.

> Could this signify that the business of America was not business, as an innocent Calvin Coolidge had said, but show business, symbolic display, the triumph at last of metaphor over reality . . .? (Miller 1988, 510)

These observations come inevitably to mind in considering the World Cup Finals of 1994, because, in so much of what was written and said about this tournament, America and the whole paradoxical being-held-in-America-ness of the tournament was the recurrent theme. And the apparently universal assumption was that the United States, the only major country in the world without a national football league, had been awarded the World Cup because its business was business, especially show business.

This, then – and the related matters of the globalization of football culture; the competing discourses of the modern international football world; and the ever narrowing convergence of the social worlds of football, television and consumption – form the body of this final chapter.

COMING TO AMERICA

The World Cup Finals of 1994 were the 15th tournament in the history of the competition and the first to be staged outside of Europe or Latin America. Nominating the US was also significant because, in doing so, FIFA demonstrated that a thriving national association football culture is no longer a prerequisite for hosting the World Cup. A thriving *commercial* culture, however, is.

As I suggested earlier in this book, the accession of the Brazilian businessman Joao Havelange to the presidency of FIFA in 1974 marks an important turning point in the cultural history of international football. While his predecessor, the English schoolmaster Sir Stanley Rous, saw FIFA as exercising an essentially *public service* role in promoting football as a worthwhile activity, Havelange, skilfully employing the rhetoric of enfranchisement in the Third World and of decentring European football, opened the way for a massive commercializing of the game internationally. Coming to America can be seen as a consummation of Havelange's 20-year project and is worth considering in some detail.

In the context of the award of the World Cup Finals to the United States, some observers pursued the theme of not discounting the US as a football nation. This might take the form of talking optimistically about the prospects of the US team: some hope was vested in the US coach, Bora Milutinovic, a Serb, who had managed the hosts Mexico to the Quarter Finals of the 1986 World Cup and coached Costa Rica with some success in Italia '90. 'He's from the old Yugoslavia. He's always played football', said one of his players, confident that Milutinovic's grounding in Mediterranean football culture would ensure the continued prescription of a passing game for the Americans (Hayward 1993). Other early commentaries mused on the possibility that the Finals could prove a significant boost to football in the US (Davies 1993). Indeed, at the outset of the tournament, the President of the United States Soccer Federation, Alan Rothenberg announced plans for Major League Soccer in the States, beginning in 1995 (Engel 1994).

But, as I suggested earlier, most of the discourse on World Cup '94 in advance of the actual matches themselves, and much of it during the actual competition, was essentially about markets. Under Havelange, FIFA, like the International Olympic Committee and, indeed, all sports administrative bodies of any size, has become primarily a franchising body, licensing entrepreneurs to trade on its own activities (for example, to broadcast the matches under its jurisdiction) and commodifying its own authority – as, for instance, in designating its sponsors the 'official World Cup airline', 'the official World Cup soft drink', 'the official World Cup chocolate bar', and so on. As a consequence, the financial power of FIFA, as stewards of the world's most popular spectator sport, is now enormous.

Havelange has continued to speak the romantic language of enfranchise-ment, styling himself 'the democratically elected head of one of the most powerful states on earth, football' (*Observer Magazine*, 1992) but, on other occasions, a commercial *sang froid* is evident. He has said: 'FIFA is the biggest multinational in the world. It has to run without passion' (Frankel and Margolis 1994). The interplay between these political and commercial strategies has been crucial during the time of the Havelange regime, and there is little doubt that, in determining the course that international football culture has taken, commercial factors now greatly outweigh considerations of the 'passion' for the game that may be felt among the people of poorer nations. The last 10 years of FIFA history demonstrate this.

The consummation of Havelange's campaign promises to expand the number of World Cup finalists from 16 to 24 and to stage FIFA tournaments in non-Anglo-Saxon Third World countries was funded in large part by the multinational soft drinks company Coca Cola. This deal was brokered by Horst Dassler, whose sportswear company adidas, in return, received Havelange's undertaking that all players in FIFA tournaments would wear adidas kit. Dassler's company, International Sport and Leisure, has exclusive control over the marketing of FIFA events (as well as the Olympics) (*Observer Magazine*, 14 June 1992). FIFA's concern to maximize its profits dictates that any country hoping to host a World Cup Final tournament must offer the necessary infrastructure and access to markets. This means, among other things: modern stadia, equipped to hold large crowds and, more importantly, the massive international media contingent that now attends any finals tournament; a television service providing exportable coverage – for example, for the World Cup Finals of 1978, Argentine broadcasters were persuaded to change their camera angles by the European Broadcasting Union (Whannel 1992, 166); suitable geographical location in relation to time zones and their vital bearing on television audiences; and facilities – hotels, transport and so on – for visitors, many of whom will provide a market for tournament memorabilia.

This has opened out a clear contradiction between Havelange's rhetoric of enfranchising neglected members of the world's football family on the one hand, and the commercial imperatives of the modern FIFA operation on the other. Havelange has continued to expand participation in FIFA: 12 new nations were admitted in 1994, bringing the membership to 191. And, in 1994, he countered opposition to his presidency by promising an even bigger finals tournament in 1998, with 32 teams and a greater representation for Asia, Africa and the Caribbean. However, none of the recently enfranchised FIFA countries has a realistic prospect of being awarded a World Cup Finals tournament unless it can meet the exacting commercial criteria which are now decisive. Indeed, Brazil, widely celebrated as the most passionate football culture on earth, dropped out of the race for the 1986 finals and Colombia, a long-established football nation but one of the poorest countries in Latin America, likewise lacked commercial and political credibility in contending for recent tournaments. Furthermore, despite the growing strength of African football cultures and the excitement that African sides have created in recent World Cups, the likelihood that the Finals will go to Africa in the foreseeable future is slim; the tournament goes back to Europe in 1998, when France are hosts for the second time, and the front runners for 2002 are Japan and South Korea (McCarthy 1994). Both have thriving capitalist economies and, especially in the case of Japan, negligible football traditions.

Thus, the United States, a founder member of FIFA but nevertheless a nation with no national association football league, whose social and cultural elites have, as we've seen, set their face most firmly and enduringly against 'soccer' and sought instead to promote distinctly 'American' sports, becomes, paradoxically, the ideal venue for a modern World Cup. As Rothenberg proclaimed at the award in 1991:

> FIFA were geniuses. They took the greatest sport in the world, looked at the most important nation in the world, if you'll excuse the jingoism, and decided they had to break into that market.

The market which the US offered FIFA was conceived roughly as follows.

Association football, as is by now well known through the publicity generated by the tournament itself, *does* have a following in the United States. This following divides roughly into two social groups: white, often college-educated, middle classes and ethnic minorities. These two groups account for most of the States' 16 million amateur footballers.

On the first count, 'soccer' appeals to liberal and/or Democratic families concerned to promote equal opportunities but deterred by the aggressive masculinity with which many mainstream 'all American' sports are bound up (Allison, 1976): 37 per cent of players in the US are female (Katz 1993) and, at the time of the Finals of 1994, the United States were already women's world champions. This group could reasonably be expected to provide a market for match tickets and tournament souvenirs, as well as promising a sizeable audience to ABC television, who were showing the weekend games of World Cup '94. (The sports cable network, ESPN, mostly owned by ABC, took the mid-week games.)

On the second count, the US, as shown in a previous chapter, has a huge number of migrant and migrant-descended ethnic communities, most of whose cultures mingle a love of football with a sense of national identity-in-exile. These communities, in some cases, sustain regional football leagues: there is, for example, an Italian American League in New Jersey (Katz 1993) and some 40 Latino leagues around Los Angeles (McGuire 1994). Colombian Americans turned out in huge numbers to see Colombia play a pre-tournament friendly in Boston, as did Mexican Americans in LA, and so on (Engel 1994). These communities, then, constituted a further market for match tickets and merchandise and, more importantly, for the more specialist TV stations.

In this latter context, the most important social grouping was the Hispanic communities. These communities are large, many of their members are of recent migration and they maintain a high level of cultural distinctness from Anglo-Saxon American society. An estimated 30 million Spanish-speaking households regularly watch football on TV in the States, be it on ESPN, via satellite, or through the Miami-based, Spanish language TV channel Univision which took all 52 matches of World Cup '94. (The importance of this market was already long since clear to Havelange and was a big factor in the siting of the Mexico finals of 1986, which Univision's proprietor helped to organize.)

To these well-defined markets, and the numerous other football publics around the world, the US could be expected to provide a television service of the required quality. As a time zone, the States could offer compatible viewing hours to the vitally important European audiences and ABC, whose pictures would be relayed to other countries, had pioneered the spectacularization of sport through television (Whannel 1992, 167–8).

The prospect of a smooth global TV operation, orchestrated from the US, attracted a range of multinational companies as sponsors: regular patrons Coca Cola were joined by General Motors, JVC, Canon (previous sponsors of the English Football League), McDonalds, Gillette, Fuji Film, Philips . . . in all 11 companies paid up to 19 million dollars each. For this they were titled 'official World Cup partners' and given advertising boards at each game in the tournament. 'They're in this for Europe, Asia, Africa and South America, where the ratings are Super Bowl scale', said a US television consultant, adding that any real enthusiasm for the competition in the US itself would be 'gravy' (McGinn 1994). As it turned out, domestic viewing figures were modestly good for the tournament: for example, the United States' game against Romania was seen on ABC television in 6.5 million homes – a US TV record for a football match, although only a third of the regular audience for basketball or American football (Freedland 1994). But the worldwide TV audience promised by the tournament was estimated at 30 billion people – drily summarized as 'an awful lot of eyeballs' by an American advertising executive (McGinn 1994). This priority, ironically, was said to have worked against the organizers, who had been hoping to publicize the Finals in the US via some of their already famous sponsors.

> Sponsorship deals with Coca Cola and Mastercard were meant to raise the tournament's profile – but the corporate giants spent their promotional budgets in the football heartlands of Europe and South America, not in the US where they were needed. (Freedland 1994)

Finally, there are the factors of the size, infrastructure and dominant culture of America itself.

America is, of course, a vast country. It has a population of around 250 million people and numerous major cities. These cities, importantly, had hotel and stadium accommodation adequate to the needs of the tournament, so that, unlike for other World Cup Finals, no financial contribution from government would be required; World Cup '94 was financed solely by private capital. The lure of this capital persuaded FIFA to make significant concessions. For example, Simon Inglis, a leading writer on football stadia, suggested that

> had FIFA insisted on bringing California's two venues, the Rose Bowl [in Pasadena and designated venue for the World Cup Final] and Stanford Stadium, up to the standards which are now commonly required in Europe, USA '94's projected profits of 20 million dollars would have sunk without trace in a vat full of concrete. (Inglis 1994)

Moreover, in contrast to other countries that cover a comparable geographical area, such as Russia or Brazil, air travel between one part of the United States and another is a routine part of life for people of a certain income. This would be advantageous not only to travelling national sides, their official entourages and accredited media personnel, but also to travel agents bringing over parties of the more affluent football enthusiasts. But flights to, from and around the States, hotel rooms and match tickets (offered initially in packages of ten – two for each of five separate matches – at 525 dollars a package) would be beyond the financial compass of European 'football hooligans', about whose activities there was now a considerable literature (see particularly Williams, Dunning and Murphy 1984, 1989). And, according to available academic research and argument, FIFA had every right to expect no intervention from American street gangs either. Sporting events, on the whole, did not provide a context for gang violence: the gangs, mostly drawn from America's underclass, based on ethnic minorities, usually rejected 'American' sports; besides, they couldn't afford to go to matches; and they would, in any event, be unlikely, because of the big travelling distances involved, to encounter a suitable 'outsider' group of away supporters whom they could fight (Murphy, Williams and Dunning 1990, 208–9).

The low expectation of public disorder must have been important to FIFA. The likelihood of any mayhem first and foremost discourages sponsors and, in a culture where association football was not fully accepted, it could have deterred paying customers too. The political root of the definition of 'football hooliganism' as a social problem in European societies is its disruption of vital commercial activity: it pollutes modern football, and the nexus of business activities (advertising, sponsorship and so on) of which it is a part, with bad publicity.

Safely removed from these malign influences, FIFA, Havelange hoped, could look forward to unprecedented financial returns, as the world's most entrepreneurial culture merchandized the world's most popular game. Rothenberg had taken control of the US Soccer Federation in August 1990, with overt backing from Havelange and other FIFA officials who had observed his success as Commissioner for Soccer at the Los Angeles Olympics of 1984 (McIlvanney 1991). He now promised four billion dollars' worth of business (Freedland 1994).

In addition to the revenue generated by TV and sponsorship, ordinary ticket sales, accommodation, transport and so on, there would be other important commodifications. Prestigious access to the championships would be sold, principally in the form of VIP packages, priced at 2,500 dollars for each match, and via a 'Gold Club' offering tickets both to games and to elite parties where business people could meet potential clients. A British TV reporter, roaming one such lavish function, confirmed that guests' knowledge of football culture was minimal. 'Does the name "Maradona" mean anything to you?' 'Pardon me?' (David Smith, *Channel Four News*, 21 June 1994). There was also some discussion of developing virtual reality technologies which would 'fly' wealthy football fans to one or other of the World Cup stadia and show them the view from their seat (Bannister 1994).

And then there would be merchandising, an activity more zealously pursued in the US than in most other cultures. This was expected by Time-Warner Sports Marketing (generous entertainers of FIFA officials during their deliberations on the placing of World Cup '94) to generate over one billion dollars. It would entail principally trinkets and football apparel, but would also include such devices as World Cup temporary tattoos, soccer-style pinball and World Cup Hot Wheels cars for children (McGinn 1994). At the World Cup games, small-time vendors of cheaper, unofficial T-shirts and baseball hats were moved on: 'They won't let the little people here sell anything with the words World Cup on it . . .' said one (Freedland 1994). Commodification even extended to the actual playing surface: within minutes of the conclusion of the last tie to be played in the Giants Stadium in New Jersey, chunks of the turf were being dug up for sale as souvenirs, at 20 dollars each (*Guardian*, 19 July).

The World Cup Final Championships of 1994 is indeed thought to have generated four billion dollars' worth of business and seems set to show a profit of 25 million dollars (Lacey 1994). Although the prospects for the US Major Soccer League, heralded for 1995, are not good – at the time of the tournament's conclusion in mid-July 1994, it had no big commercial backers – another award of the World Cup finals to the USA, early in the next century, is already being talked about (Williams 1994; Inglis 1994).

IN SEARCH OF THE BEAUTIFUL GAME: NARRATIVES OF FOOTBALL AND NATION AT WORLD CUP '94

I want now to turn from business to showbusiness and to discuss the tournament as a spectacle. In this section, and in the next, I consider USA '94 as a text – as a cluster of interweaving representations and narratives (Whannel 1992, 186). All modern international, media-driven sporting encounters such as World Cup Finals generate and regenerate ideas, most crucially, first, of particular countries and their people (Blain, Boyle and O'Donnell 1993) and, second, of the sports themselves. I want therefore to look at the representing of particular nations-in-their-football in World Cup '94 commentary: that is, the mingling of assumptions about particular countries, their national identity and the football they play, and the more transcendent question of what, ultimately, football 'is all about'. In this context, there is reference to various nations from Europe, Latin America and the Middle and Far East, but the main focus is on the eventual winners, Brazil. For evidence, I draw on the British media coverage of the tournament – not, however, the popular press, whose routine xenophobia in this area (Wagg 1991) may have offered few surprises – but the broadcast media (mostly television) and the liberal, broadsheet newspapers the *Guardian* and the *Independent on Sunday*. These organs, importantly, are institutionally committed to universalism and anti-racism and assume these values in their audience.

Since the 1970s, the World Cup Finals tournament has been an all-consuming media event. In most of the countries involved, a variety of printed and broadcast media outlets will expect to report regularly from the tournament, whether there is 'hard' news (e.g. games) available or not. Each national FA party now travels in tandem with its own home press corps. This corps sees its role, not as passive reportage, but as active participation in the *altho' Brazilians kept that away that global ??? doesn't affect local ???.*

campaign, and this participation is usually shaped by its interpretation of the popular will, either of individual national publics or of the global TV audience of football enthusiasts (Wagg 1986, 1991). In this context, the principal narrative (Hall 1992) throughout these World Cup finals, was of Brazil.

The name of Brazil is etched indelibly on the consciousness of the post-war international football world. In the pantheon of that world, no name surpasses that of Pelé, who played as a 17-year-old in the World Cup winning side of 1958. For several generations of football devotees, born either before or in the two decades after the Second World War, the names 'Pelé' and 'Brazil' signified a kind of football that was untutored and touched by genius. This football, it was assumed, grew organically out of the Brazilian working classes, who, careless of material deprivations, learned to play it in their shanty towns and on the Copacabana beach. But love of football ran across all class, ethnic and gender boundaries (Lever 1983). Brazil was, to borrow a phrase from one of its own writers, 'a nation in football boots' (quoted in a TV documentary shown in Britain at the end of the competition: *A Whole New Ball Game*, BBC2, 19 July 1994). This representation – assertions of it, desires to see it preserved, attempts to reinterpret it – informed much of the media discourse of USA '94.

The picture was sketched in outline in late spring. Sports writer Richard Williams reported on the 'burden of the beautiful noise' – the hopes of an expectant nation and a host of overseas admirers – borne by Brazil's team manager Carlos Alberto Parreira. 'Brazilian football', wrote Williams, 'is slowly emerging from a period of domestic turmoil – decaying fabric, chaotic and corrupt organisation, emigrating stars and disappearing crowds – that mirrors the condition of the country.' In 1970, when Brazil last won the World Cup, all their players played for Brazilian clubs; now through the growing globalization of the football labour market (Maguire 1994), most of them are with European clubs. This has created problems for Parreira, but, he assures Williams, 'we're playing the traditional Brazilian way, 4-4-2, which is the way they've played since they were kids, so when they come back they don't find anything they don't already know' (*Independent on Sunday*, 24 April 1994).

In mid-June, Williams' colleague, former Republic of Ireland international footballer Eamon Dunphy effectively declares Brazil to be at the head of a crusade to save world football from dark forces. These forces include cynicism, brutality and their own manager. The climate of the USA, he suggests, favours the leading Latin American sides: Brazil, Argentina and Colombia. Thus:

> . . . it follows that this World Cup will either be glorious, if Brazil prevail, or a nightmare of cynicism and mediocrity from which the Argentines will emerge with a sly grin on their macho faces. We should pray for Brazil. Brazilian football is suited to the climate in which it is played. Possession is coveted. The pace is leisurely . . . then the moment of explosive acceleration, a rapid exchange of passes which leaves opponents for dead, victims of the sublime combination of pace and technique associated with the Brazilian teams of legend. In recent World Cups we have but

glimpsed Brazilian football at its glorious best . . . the evidence of the last two World Cup finals suggests that international football is a brutal, worldly business no longer hospitable to football played the Brazilian way . . . When I spoke to Pelé in March about the blight coaches have cast upon the contemporary game, the great man passionately endorsed that view. Parreira was Pelé's reference point. Parreira is the problem Brazil must overcome. (*Independent on Sunday*, 19 June 1994)

Several weeks later, with Brazil having won two and drawn the other of their opening three games, Williams finds Parreira's burden is paradoxically getting heavier. 'Parreira bad', a Brazilian supporter tells him at Detroit airport, 'Parreira too much *retranca*. Too much defensive.' Some travelling Brazilian supporters are hostile to Parreira and yearn for Tele Santana, Brazil's coach in the World Cups of 1982 and 86. Others parade a decade and a half of disgruntlement that thus encompasses the Santana period. A banner raised by two of them reads: BRAZIL. YOU MADE ME CRY IN 82, 86, 90. THIS TIME, MAKE ME DANCE AND I CAN DIE IN PEACE. Parreira, for his part, will not accept that Brazil are playing defensively – ('I think you have seen another game', he shouts at a journalist who suggests Brazil have played cautiously against the USA). And besides, according to Williams,

Parreira knows all too well that, whatever the fans think, a blind faith in the careless rapture of beach football is no longer enough to win World Cups, if indeed it ever was. The 1970 side, which played perhaps the greatest football anyone will ever see, was founded on a shrewd tactical pattern . . . (*Independent on Sunday*, 3 July 1994).

A fortnight on, and Brazil are to face Italy in the final and Dunphy has developed his populist theme:

Football is, at its most beautiful, the game of the dispossessed . . . The powerful, greedy and stupid for whom the game remained a mystery worked their way in, to the point where they could influence and ultimately destroy football as we had known and loved it. The most menacing intruder was the coach . . . In Italy, Brazil, Africa, the Arab world, in South Korea, and most spectacularly, in Bulgaria and Romania, the little man still counts, harmony has been achieved between player and coach, football has evolved, grown up, moved on . . . If Brazil win, we can be certain that the renaissance is more than an illusion. (*Independent on Sunday*, 17 July 1994)

Brazil are similarly the main text for TV commentary on the tournament, although the approach here has a strong promotional element: Brazil are the chosen selling line for the competition and its coverage by a particular channel. There are frequent showings of the goals which won the World Cup for Brazil in 1958 and 1970, and regular invocations of Brazil-the-myth: everywhere they go, according to news briefings, they bring charisma, create excitement, and so on. In Britain, the commercial channel, ITV, runs a viewers' competition to choose the best Brazilian goal from a series of clips.

The embattled position of the Brazilian manager, however, also becomes a news story: on 4th July BBC reporter Hazel Irvine meets Parreira and congratulates him on the team's success so far; 'Thank-you', he replies. 'Congratulations. I never heard this word from the Brazilian media. Thank-you BBC.' And, certainly, there is enough evidence, acknowledged incidentally during match commentary or in studio reflections, that this Brazil is not the Brazil of the 1950s: when Brazil play Holland in Dallas on 9 July, BBC commentator Barry Davies remarks early on that a couple of Brazil players have clearly been trying to feign injury in order to get Dutch players booked ('Full marks to the referee for not falling for it') and he judges that Brazil's winning goal has been gained, indirectly, in this fashion: 'Well, the manner in which he won the free kick was highly questionable. But the way he took it you could only admire.' After the game, won 3–2 by Brazil, BBC pundits Alan Hansen and Jimmy Hill agree that all three Brazilian goals have been of doubtful legitimacy.

On the eve of the World Cup Final of 1994, in which Brazil, as in 1970, are to play Italy, David Lacey of the *Guardian* tempers his optimism ('Surely Brazil and Italy cannot let everybody down now . . .') by suggesting it is unreasonable to expect Brazil 'to repeat the sweep and verve of their 1970 triumph. The players are no longer there, that particular style is no longer there. Brazil have assembled an excellent team but this is a team of mortals' (16 July 1994). On BBC television the same day, Pelé and ex-England footballer Sir Bobby Charlton preview the final in conversation:

Pelé: 'In 1982, Brazil had best team but lost the World Cup . . . too open'. He supports Parreira therefore in curtailing this openness in the team's play.

Charlton: 'Discipline has been very important . . .'

Pelé: 'This team . . . midfield . . . Dunga [the captain and an aggressive midfield player, currently playing for a German club] . . . very tight . . .'

Charlton: 'Could you explain to people in Europe and around the rest of the world what it means to Brazil to win the World Cup . . .'

On the day of the Final, in preamble to the game itself there is more film of Parreira, who, reporter Ray Stubbs once again informs the audience, has been described as 'too defensive'. 'In Brazil', protests Parreira, 'there is such passion. It is difficult to explain.' But it is not true, he insists, that Brazil now play 'the European way': '. . . the flat four, zonal marking . . . is all Brazilian'.

In the final stages of the match, with no score, Trevor Brooking, another ex-England player commentating for BBC, concludes: 'People talk about the 1970 [Brazil] side . . . for me, this 1994 team, in midfield, they just don't get near the 1970 one, or even the 1982 side. There's just not the variation . . .'

On ITV, Premiership club manager Ron Atkinson concludes his commentary by expressing disappointment over the negative way he feels Brazil have played; you'd *expect* such an attitude, he says, from Italy.

Back on BBC ex-Liverpool and Scotland player Alan Hansen declares in summary: 'The second half was a non-event. Still high technical ability but, unfortunately, high technical ability doesn't guarantee entertainment . . . Brazil have been as bad [as Italy]. They've hardly committed men forward.'

The following day, a mid-day news report on ITV states that when the World Cup Final had ended: 'From the Amazon to the Atlantic, Brazil erupted into one giant party.'

On 19 July BBC shows the first of four documentaries (generically entitled *A Whole New Ball Game*) about nations apparently devoted to a particular sport. This one examines Brazil and her football. In an early scene, a young man on the beach cheerfully admits his own 'false consciousness': 'Brazilians are born to suffer. The country is no good but we still support it. Because when Brazil are playing I forget about our problems. I just watch the games on TV and forget about the corruption, the killing of street kids. I'm just glued to the box, supporting Brazil.'

'There's no Brazilian football', says a young woman on the same beach, 'Our players are abroad. Once they grow up and reach the top, they leave the country.' One such player, Romario who now plays in Spain for Barcelona, asserts: 'Football can't be taught. It's a natural gift . . . Most Brazilians are born with it.' He adds: 'That's why Europeans are fascinated by our football.' Like most Brazilian players, Romario's family lived in poverty. Sometimes he missed training so that his brother could go: the family could not afford two bus fares. A spectator outside the national stadium, the Maracana, is mindful of this poverty when he says to the camera: 'There are far more important things than qualifying for the World Cup. Like qualifying for the First World.'

Looking back through these disparate invocations of 'Brazil', two things are clear. One is that, in the ongoing rendition of Brazilian football, a number of different narratives interweave: spontaneity versus contrivance; art versus business; Latin passion versus European repression; tradition versus modernity; the little people versus the powerful; good versus evil, and so on. The other is that, within a certain framework of assumption, there are obviously conflicting accounts of Brazil. 'Brazil' works as a paradigm, with certain givens – the Brazilian masses, their material poverty and their passion for football, the carefree and intuitive skill of the national side, Pelé, and so on. Within this paradigm, only certain explanations of events are viable. In 1994, Brazil were rarely accepted as an approximation of the team of the earlier eras and of myth (a definition favoured mostly only by public relations and marketing personnel). But, if the visible reality of Brazil did not correspond to the pre-established myth of Brazil, then there must be some human failing to account for it: specifically and principally, a coach imparting the wrong instructions, or players who simply don't measure up to those of previous generations. If only Santana, and not Parreira, had been running the side . . . If only a new Pelé, a fresh Garrincha, a latter-day Rivelino could be found . . .

The first problem with these accounts is that they contain serious anomalies. For instance, Pelé is produced *both* as witness for the prosecution of Brazilian coach Parreira *and* as welcoming the pragmatism that Parreira has apparently brought to the side, previous Brazilian teams having been 'too open'; likewise, a studio pundit acknowledges 'high technical ability' shown in the World Cup Final, then concedes that it 'doesn't guarantee entertainment', but nevertheless judges that Brazil were 'as bad' as their opponents. These anomalies are not particular to Brazil. Indeed they are to be found in most national football cultures – for example, competing assertions that, on the one hand, there is 'too much coaching' and, on the other, that there is too little of it (or too little of the right sort), are recurrent features of ongoing debates in various countries – and they can be explained by social, political and economic developments in the international football world.

In the post-war period, FIFA, as we have seen, has expanded to the point where virtually every established nation-state has successfully sought membership. During this process, the game has been required to carry an ever-growing cultural, political and economic weight. In European countries, such as England and West Germany, national success at football could assuage – or, increasingly in the case of England after 1970, fail to assuage – a sense of uncertainty at the loss of empires. In the east of Europe, football, at the behest of governments, was to manifest the moral superiority of the communist system. Elsewhere football has variously expressed the longings of millions of economically expropriated people in the shanty towns of Latin America and, especially in a succession of newly independent African countries, spurred the cohering of a new national identity. Often, indeed, it has taken on a significance for a transnational 'black consciousness': in the spring of 1994, for instance, Cameroon team shirts were on sale on the Caribbean island of Barbados and, on the eve of the World Cup Final, the beleaguered people of Haiti, living under military dictatorship and pondering the prospect of an American invasion, were said meanwhile to be hoping for a Brazilian victory (BBC Radio Five Live, 16 July 1994).

The progressively greater intervention of television since the late 1950s has had huge consequences. First, a growing number of national publics have become concerned about the performance either of their own national side or of the national side with whom they most closely identify. Second, enormous revenue from advertising and sponsorship can now be generated for a national FA whose team qualifies for the World Cup: for example, following the qualification of the Republic of Ireland for USA '94 and with six months still to go to the tournament, the Football Association of Ireland could already announce the award of 34 sponsorship contracts (Winterbottom 1993). Third, World Cup success can bring important publicity to countries, which may boost other areas of economic activity like trade and tourism.

These factors have dictated two crucial developments. One is that *all* national FAs, to a greater or lesser extent, now participate in the international football technocracy: that's to say, they see football as an area of professional expertise, to a significant extent transcending national cultures, and they seek to appoint qualified coaches, often from other countries, to organize their teams. One irony here is that the African national sides, widely depicted in the British media as being untutored and thus unspoiled, are in most cases coached by Europeans – and, indeed, usually play their club football in Europe.

The other is that, among all the vocabularies that mingle in international football culture, the most important, and the most decisive, is now the vocabulary of efficiency. For most people, in most contemporary national football cultures – players, administrators, sponsors, public and public chroniclers alike – an inefficient team (that is, one that doesn't win) is unacceptable, regardless of its artistic merits. Efficiency is the primary pursuit of coaches and it is the main criterion by which they are judged. Within this pursuit they make what compromises they may with local football lore and notions of national identity: this formation or that is reconciled to, or reinterpreted as, the national way.

Indeed, so successful had the quest for efficiency become, by the 1980s and 90s FIFA were concerned that there was a serious threat to the World Cup as a spectacle. For USA '94, they moved to give greater reward for attacking play (three points for a win) and to penalize play that was defensive, negative or violent – by outlawing the 'tackle from behind' and instructing referees to be strict in booking and sending off offenders. Partly as a result of this latter injunction, the record for cautions and dismissals (165 yellow cards and 14 red, set in the previous tournament) was broken: 235 players were booked in the '94 finals and 15 sent off. Most of those commentators, therefore, who judged the football at World Cup '94 to have been good, acknowledged this shift in the rules of engagement, rather than the spontaneous contribution of any individual football culture, to have brought this about: 'The flat back four has worked much better than man-to-man plus sweeper, since FIFA banned the tackle from behind, because, in man-to-man, you have to thump him [your opponent] from behind . . .', said England manager Terry Venables to BBC viewers on the day of the final.

The quest for efficiency has affected all national football cultures. Most of these cultures carry within them notions of a golden past; older members of these cultures remember a time when the national team played in a manner that was more skilful, less inhibited and embodied what was for them the true national spirit.

All this applies as much to Brazilian football culture as to any other. Certainly, public disquiet at national football failure has long been a feature of Brazilian life. In 1950, for example, Brazil hosted the tournament and reached the final, where they played Uruguay. They led the match 1–0 until near the end, but lost it 1–2. Sections of Brazilian opinion have always regarded this defeat as a national catastrophe and, according to sportswriter Jose Trajano, the players, especially the goalkeeper Moacir Barbosa and the other two black players in the team, bore the brunt of national indignation thereafter – as Barbosa confirms (*A Whole Different Ball Game*, BBC2, 19 July 1994).

Second, Brazil won the trophy in 1958, 1962 and 1970, but in the 1970s and 80s coaching and tactical developments in the international football world – coming, principally, out of Europe – effectively neutralized the attacking style of play adopted by Brazil hitherto; this style was now inefficient or, in Pelé's words, 'too open'. Modern managers, like Parreira, know therefore that they have to balance the public expectation of victory, and the rationalized methods which that now demands, with the national and international longing for new Pelés. This, they realize, is squaring the cultural circle. They have to present the modern as traditional: thus Parreira defines the 4-4-2 formation, a term unknown in football before the 1970s, as 'the Brazilian way'.

Tomas Peterson reports a similar process in Sweden, who came third in 1994. Although hosts in 1958, Sweden did not qualify for any World Cup finals tournament on their own merits between 1950 and 1970. In the mid-1970s, the English, FA-trained coaches Bob Houghton and Roy Hodgson introduced rationalized coaching methods to Swedish club football; these principally involved breaking the game up into individual work tasks. Their approach was universally labelled 'English' and, although it was apparently successful at clubs like Malmo FF and Halmstad, it was derided as 'robot football' in the Swedish sports press. (This is essentially a cultural displacement, similar to the frequent styling of hooliganism as 'the English disease'.) Local coaches encouraged a less fragmented approach, which was perceived as the 'Swedish model' and, as such, received the endorsement of the Swedish FA in 1980. However, the following year, a Swedish manager, Sven-Goran Eriksson adopted the 'English model' at IFK Goteborg, who then won the UEFA Cup. Eriksson was soon appointed to coach the national team. The national press now pronounced him the originator of a hybrid – the 'Svenglish model' – which was approved: under Hodgson, Malmo FF won the Swedish championship in five consecutive years, 1985–9 (Peterson 1994).

The sort of football which Brazil, Sweden or any other country played in the 1950s and 1960s was not viable in the 1990s because it was inefficient. This was the strong implication of much British media discourse on USA '94. Teams from comparatively new football nations, like Cameroon – popularly styled as 'carefree' in the 1990 tournament (Blain, Boyle and O'Donnell 1993, 71–6) – Nigeria and Saudi Arabia, have in recent World Cups played attacking football which was reminiscent of, and certainly inspired by, the Brazil teams of earlier eras. But, when they have conceded goals, they have frequently been described as 'naive': BBC's Bob Wilson said this of the Nigerian defence on 25 June, sharing the adjective with Ray Wilkins on ITV. Two days later Trevor Brooking, again on BBC, delivered the same judgement on the South Korean defenders. Liberal commentators (like Alison Pearson in the *Independent on Sunday*, 26 June 1994) understandably read 'naive' as 'code for black', but this is only because emergent, comparatively powerless (and usually black) nations are conventionally perceived as inefficient: the defenders of the United States team – and, in football terms, the US is also perceived as emergent – were also agreed to be 'naive' by Alan Parry and Kevin Keegan on ITV on 4 July. The previous evening, on BBC, Alan Hansen put it succinctly: 'With the exception of Brazil, the South Americans and the Africans have played too freely.'

(This perceived lack of judgement extended to officials. During Bulgaria v. Mexico on BBC (5 July) BBC commentator John Motson became animated by the number of cautions and dismissals issued by the referee. Motson, while allowing that the referee was acting on a FIFA directive to penalize foul play harshly, stressed that the official was from Syria, 'one of a high representation of referees from the lesser developed football countries'. He added that 'a Tunisian' had been in charge during England's game against

Argentina in the finals of 1986, when Maradona's 'Hand of God' goal had been allowed. Similarly, Barry Davies, in his commentary on the final, cited some early decisions by one of the linesmen as evidence 'that some of the appointments are rather more political than [to do] with knowledge of the game.' 'One does have sympathy with this Hungarian referee.' [Pause.] 'The linesman on this side is from Paraguay.')

By the same token, societies of the communist bloc were held in the West to be *too* efficient and to have exalted organization at the expense of the human spirit: thus the BBC's John Motson reassured viewers on 3 July that Romania were 'no longer a dour, defensive East European outfit' and, 10 days later, Hazel Irvine told BBC viewers that, in Bulgaria, World Cup success has brought 'the biggest display of emotion since the collapse of communism in 1989'.

Likewise, eyebrows were raised at Saudi Arabia, whose inefficiency lay in failing to distinguish between ownership and control in the football sphere. BBC Radio Five Live (3 July) reported on the Saudi royal prince who 'because of his wealth and power seems to think he can tell the coach what to do'. Later that evening, despite the judgement of match commentator Alan Parry that the Saudi's football 'has surprised a lot of people . . . [and] totally justified their place here among football's elite', ITV's half-time studio discussion concentrates on the team's Argentine coach, who is leaving after only two months. 'They get rid of their coaches very quickly out there', says former England coach Don Howe. 'Two months is a long time. The king wants to pick the team really.' In a technocracy, you leave it to the expert.

However, the most garish political metaphors were bestowed on the Argentine. Argentina is a 'developed' football nation and won the World Cup, as hosts, in 1978. But in conventional Western football discourse their pursuit of modern football efficiency is flawed by duplicity and ill temper. When the Argentinian player Diego Maradona was withdrawn from the tournament after failing a test for banned drugs, a BBC documentary (1 July) depicted a man with 'a flawed makeup' from 'the working class slum' of Villa Fiorito in Buenos Aires, a man with a problem of 'temperament' who had proved, by illegally using his hand to deflect the ball into the net against England in the World Cup Finals of 1986, that he was a 'cheat' as well as a 'genius'. While more discursive commentators have tried to place Maradona in some kind of social context – drawing on the political and football cultures of Argentina and Italy, where Maradona played club football (Duncan 1994; Freeman 1994) – this documentary pathologizes Maradona as a cheating ex-slum kid, further disabled by a Latin temperament. Since the 1970s, however, cheating has been seen less as an individual phenomenon in international football culture and has become, as the concept 'professional foul' demonstrates, simply an option in the quest for efficiency: importantly, in this connection, the 'Hand of God' incident, arguably the chief remembrance of Maradona in the English football world, was rendered in the language of efficiency and professionalism by the England camp at the time. If an England player had done it, said England manager Bobby Robson, 'I do not suppose we would have argued with referee' (Robson and Harris 1986, 208). 'But' as Simon Freeman suggests, fans in Europe, especially England, have always loathed Maradona as a ridiculous show-off. When he slyly used his hand to sweep the ball past England's goalkeeper, Peter Shilton, in the World Cup in Mexico in 1986 . . . it confirmed what every English fan had always known; Maradona was a cheat like all the South Americans, Spaniards and Italians, with their immaculate hair-dos and gold chains. (Freeman 1994)

These discourses of football and nationality carried over into other areas of media coverage of the World Cup – notably reporting on the consumption of USA '94, of which there was much. In a final section I'd like now to discuss the growing interpenetration of the worlds of football, consumption and the media.

FOOTBALL CUBED: MEDIA, CONSUMPTION AND WORLD CUP '94

The Italian writer Umberto Eco in the late 1960s coined the phrase 'sport cubed' to refer, in effect, to the layers of discussion which sport generated in the media and elsewhere. Sport, he suggests, becomes 'sport squared' when it is made a spectacle for others; it is 'cubed' when people begin to discuss the sporting spectacle they have witnessed; when they start to discuss other renditions of the spectacle then 'sport [is] raised to the nth power' (Eco 1969, 162). In Britain, and in the United States, World Cup '94 offered football, if not to the nth power, at least to the fourth or fifth.

Since the mid-1980s, a much greater emphasis has been placed in the British football world upon consumption. This new emphasis has had various manifestations and origins.

A number of initiatives have come from supporters. The fanzine movement, for instance, expresses the affection of supporters for their club and for the game and enables them to report their own consumption of the game, pitting their version of events in the football world against those of the mainstream media (see Jary, Horne and Bucke 1991). The Football Supporters' Association, founded in 1985 after the Heysel stadium disaster, has led a national campaign for supporters to be consulted by the clubs they support in the determining of club policy, especially in areas directly concerned with spectating, and makes representations to national administrative bodies. There is *When Saturday Comes*, a national football fanzine produced in London, which began in 1986 and is, effectively, the organ of more articulate and socially concerned football supporters (Haynes 1993, 49), including many FSA members.

Other initiatives have come from the clubs, anxious, where possible, to translate the loyalty of their supporters into extra income. For example, all Premiership and Football League clubs now have club shops, selling videos, replica kits and other memorabilia; there are bars and restaurants; daily updated telephone information services provide news of club affairs, and so on.

These developments have had clear reverberations in the mass media. In British book publishing, one of the most conspicuous non-fiction successes of the early 1990s was Nick Hornby's *Fever Pitch* (Hornby 1992), the wry account of an Oxford-educated professional writer's life as an Arsenal supporter; it sold around 250,000 copies in under two years.

Disc jockeys and television presenters now compulsively identify themselves as supporters of this football club or that, and weave much mention of football into their general discourse. Programmes in the broadcast media are devoted solely to the business of consuming football: Radio Four's 6.06, for instance, a fans' phone-in, hosted initially by a populist disc jockey who later gave way to an ex-cabinet minister, and *Fantasy Football League*, an idea developed for both radio and television. *Fantasy Football League*, in its original formulation, involved showbusiness figures, mostly comedians, 'buying' famous footballers for a fantasy team, whose performance was then determined by the achievements of its members in the real football world. In its transfer to television it incorporated relaxed interviews with football people – players, TV commentators, celebrity-supporters, and so on – and lighthearted discussion of television clips. Thus it merges the production, consumption and mediation of football. And, since it often involves talking on television about watching talk about football on television to the people who talk about it on television, it goes, in Eco's terms, some way beyond 'football cubed'.

These trends in media, popular and football culture were manifest in the framing of World Cup '94, in the following ways.

First, the media extensively reported supporters' consumption of the event: the travelling Brazilian contingent, making their 'beautiful noise'; the Italian Americans filmed by BBC in a bar in New York's Little Italy cheering Italy's winning goal against Norway (25 June); the angry expatriate Colombians interviewed on a floating restaurant on the Thames after watching their team lose to the USA (*Guardian*, 28 June 1994); the devoted Argentine Americans who, although unable to afford tickets, journeyed from New York to the Argentine Greece game in Boston, just to stand outside the Foxboro Stadium, where it was being played (*Observer*, 3 July 1994); and, during the televising of the games, regular shots of the supporters of the two sides, always in celebratory mood and together making faces for the camera. The imagery here was of happy carefree people in permanent party mode, their faces painted in national colours, banging drums, dancing and waving flags or comic accoutrements of some kind: some of the Dutch supporters, for example, wore large clogs – official parodies of equally official national symbols – on their heads and there were many wigs in the colours of the various teams. These harmonious images were reinforced by commentators' casual reference to ongoing revelry: 'The Brazilians/Dutch/Germans . . . woke us up at seven this morning.'

These pictures and allusions are signifiers in an important framing of USA '94 – namely, that this is a Feelgood World Cup. This framing is backed throughout the tournament by mutual supportive assertions to this effect ('It's been a dream of a tournament. Great atmosphere. Better than Italy' said Kevin Keegan on ITV on 4 July; 'It's been a good World Cup so far, hasn't it Terry?' said Desmond Lynam, prompting the England team manager on BBC1 nine days later); by the celebration of a low number of arrests (Barry Davies reported only two at the Germany South Korea game – BBC1, 27 June); and by the amusement with which it was reported that the games had provoked football hooliganism *abroad*. During ITV's transmission of the Romania v. Sweden match, refereed by an Englishman and won by Sweden (10 July), linkperson Matthew Lorenzo could barely suppress a smirk as he informed viewers that angry mobs were now menacing the Swedish and British embassies in Bucharest, and that 300 Dutch supporters had gone on the rampage in the Hague in the wake of Holland's defeat by Brazil the previous day.

'Passion' is the concept for which the now huge corps of public relations and marketing personnel attending to football around the world most readily reach. Brazil, on and off the field, represent the acceptable face of this passion, and hooliganism the unacceptable. In this most marketed and merchandised of World Cups, it was important that the 'good' passion be brought to the fore and translated into T-shirt sales. If some 'bad' passion is to threaten an embassy or a shopping precinct, then better by far that it takes place abroad and becomes merely a quirky piece of driftwood in the torrent of good football news.

Second, there was the question of what the Americans would make of the World Cup. In late June, British radio and TV reports carried frequent interviews with bemused Americans-in-the-street. What did they think of the World Cup? 'I'm not big on soccer. I'm from Missouri.' American newspapers tested opinion with references to the tournament that were alternately dismissive and approving. For instance, the same edition of the *Boston Globe* (23 June 1994) carries the following comment on the front page: 'I am sorry to upset people who are going crazy today over international soccer, but watching these games is almost as bad as going to a Streisand concert.' And on the sports page is the headline: 'Come On, Admit It: You're Noticing.'

No, a wealthy American businessman told *Channel Four News* (21 June), he hadn't seen a soccer match before: 'It's good. But more goals would be nice.' This sort of reportage helped to construct a composite impression of the average crowd at World Cup '94 as consisting of football-ignorant plutocrats and painted party-goers. But, the recourse of British media to *vox pop* street interviews with Americans was never great. Instead, in seeking to report America's experience of the World Cup, they looked to US media for indicators. For instance, after the US defeat of Colombia, *Guardian* writer Matthew Engel assessed public reaction via a sports talk radio station in California, whose host beckoned his listeners with 'We're talking soccer, like it or not.' 'They liked it' recorded Engel, 'for the most part, not' (25 June). And on 4 July BBC reporter Hazel Irvine supported her contrary conclusion, that the USA's win over Colombia 'has caught the country's imagination', with film of a constructed media event: the US squad receiving a goodwill telephone message from President Clinton.

This points to a third important element in the 'cubed' representation of World Cup '94: the intertextuality of media discourse – that is, the framing of the competition in terms of other media references. This was a constant feature. For instance, on 23 June, at half-time in the Italy v. Norway match, the BBC invited Frank Skinner and David Baddiel, presenters of *Fantasy*

Football League and comedians with a big following among the under-30s, into the studio to make humorous observations on the tournament thus far. Skinner chose a picture of the Mexican team singing their national anthem, with one arm across their chests. He commented: 'They're singing their national song, which is called We're Not Scared of the South Koreans Because They Only Come Up to About Here.' Baddiel said he has derived some amusement from the Saudi Arabian dancers who took part in the tournament's opening ceremony. The regular presenters smiled indulgently.

Given the recent changes in popular, media and football cultures that I outlined earlier, Skinner and Baddiel are important signifiers here. In the continued absence of very much commentary by women, they represent the 'ordinary bloke', climbing briefly into the cockpit to chat, a little tongue-in-cheek, to the pilots of TV coverage, who thus, although experts, are seen as not stuffy but able to enjoy a joke; as such, Skinner and Baddiel bring the colloquial humour of the English, salvaging, in an intendedly cosmopolitan un-jingoistic account of the World Cup, the popular notion that foreigners are funny; they represent the self-referential world of television, in which one programme pays homage to, and publicizes, another; and they represent consumption – they are, after all, football fans, styled here as no more than lads who go to the match, enjoy a laugh, read the fanzines and cut through the crap. Here they give their implicit approval to the broadcasters. Given also that, as 'alternative' comedians, they are publicly known as professional sceptics, theirs is a powerful endorsement: such people are much in demand for TV adverts.

Similarly, since the Quarter Final tie between Brazil and Holland was to be played in Dallas, BBC opened their broadcast with the theme from the TV soap opera *Dallas* and had presenter Lynam jokily map the evening's broadcast on to the drama of South Fork: 'Well, no JR tonight', he smiles, 'but we have got JH [shot of pundit Jimmy Hill]', 'Alan Hansen [fellow pundit] plays Bobby Ewing.'

And later, when the final is to be played in California, which encompasses Hollywood, there is a predictable flurry of film references: the game, since it features the same countries as in 1970, is announced by Ray Stubbs (BBC, 17 July) as 'Brazil v. Italy II' and as 'a remake', while his colleague Barry Davies approaches kick-off with the words 'Well, if they'd scripted it down the road in Hollywood, they'd have been accused of exaggeration . . . it's Back to the Future.'

Elsewhere, especially in the printed media, there are profiles of the commentators and linkpersons themselves: Lynam in the *Independent on Sunday* (19 June) and Motson in the *Guardian* (4 July). In this regard, though, the case of the Univision football commentator Andres Cantor went furthest beyond 'football cubed': he was shown on British TV news (13 July) demonstrating to an American chat show host and his studio audience how he shouted 'Goal' when commentating to his Spanish-speaking viewers. The same morning BBC Radio Four's *Today* programme quizzed Cantor on how long he would stretch out the word 'Goal', depending on which TV audience he was addressing. Here the 'passion' and the Funny Foreigners enter the discourse once again, as a half-submerged joke.

But by far the most important marriage of cultural signs was the 'Three Tenors Concert' given by Luciano Pavarotti, Placido Domingo and Jose Carreras at the Dodgers Stadium in Los Angeles on 16 July and broadcast in Britain by the BBC immediately before the World Cup Final. This more than anything symbolized the recent cultural trajectory of the World Cup. The BBC used Pavarotti's 'Nessum Dorma' as the theme music to its coverage of the World Cup Finals of 1990; international football was thus bathed in an aura of European high culture – it was being played, after all, in the Land of Opera. These links between the World Cup, television and opera were forged originally because of the competition's specifically Italian context; now, in 1994, they are made again independently of it. The concert has been trailed on TV by shots of Pavarotti, Domingo and Carreras kicking footballs around. Now, as these three classically trained European tenors, wearing morning dress and reading from music sheets, sing 'My Way' to Frank Sinatra and 'Singin' in the Rain' to Gene Kelly, high culture pays homage to low and Mediterranean sophistication acknowledges North American banality.

Looking back on the World Cup tournament of 1994, a number of things seem clear. Football now fully reflects the trend toward a globalized capitalist economy, dominated by multi- and trans-national corporations. The president of the games international ruling body, as we saw, counts his organization among these corporations – indeed, he sees it as the biggest of them all. Its constituent work-forces and its working methods have been internationalized; at an objective, economic level of operations it pursues profit and efficiency. At the level of the subjective and the cultural, the diplomats of national FAs, public relations people and journalists (including a handful of salaried romantics) variously manage the transition from tradition to modernity – expressing impatience, for example, to see 'the old Brazil', or insisting that it is still here. So, national football cultures adapt and bend: the footballers from the newly dismantled communist state of Bulgaria mumble the words of their national anthem as the TV camera comes in close for the adidas motif on their chests; the Nigerian back four ponder the widespread judgement that they are 'naive' in their defending; Swedes discover a 'Svenglish' way of playing; and they all take their place alongside the ghosts of footballers past and three Italian tenors in a postmodern, transnational culture based on television.

Thus the concert seals a new tradition of the World-Cup-on-Television: 'See you in '98', says Domingo, as he departs the stage.

ACKNOWLEDGEMENTS

I'd like to thank Garry Whannel and Alec McAulay for discussions which helped me in the writing of this chapter. Alec also commented on an earlier draft. Thanks also to Frank Dell'Apa of *The Boston Globe* and to John Williams of the Sir Norman Chester Centre, both of whom provided me with valuable information.

REFERENCES

Allison, Lincoln (1976) 'The Soccer Boom in America', *New Society* 11 March
Bannister, Nicholas (1994) 'Silicon Valley turns World Cup hi-tech'. *Guardian*, 24 January
Blain, Neil, Boyle, Raymond and O'Donnell, Hugh (1993) *Sport and National Identity in the European Media*, Leicester, Leicester University Press
Davies, Pete (1993) 'Tomorrow the world', *Guardian Weekend*, 26 June
Duncan, John (1994) 'End of the road for Maradona', *Guardian*, 1 July
Eco, Umberto (1969) 'Sports chatter', reprinted in Umberto Eco *Travels in Hyper-reality*, London, Picador (1987)
Engel, Matthew (1994) 'Soccer? Who's a sucker?', *Guardian*, 17 June
Frankel, Mark and Margolis, Mac (1994) 'The wholly rolling emperor', *Newsweek*, 20 June
Freedland, Jonathan (1994) 'Money men left sick as parrots by World Cup's no-score draw', *Guardian*, 1 July
Freeman, Simon (1994) 'Maradona: the final own goal', *Guardian*, 9 February
Hall, Stuart (1992) 'The question of cultural identity', in Stuart Hall, David Held and Tony McGrew (eds) *Modernity and its Futures*, Cambridge, Polity Press
Haynes, Richard (1993) 'Vanguard or vagabond? A history of *When Saturday Comes*', in Steve Redhead (ed.) *The Fashion and the Passion*, Aldershot, Avebury Press, pp.45–53
Hayward, Paul (1993) 'The guys aren't here to be beaten', *Independent on Sunday*, 6 June
Hornby, Nick (1992) *Fever Pitch*, London, Victor Gollancz
Inglis, Simon (1994) 'Visions of the great indoors', *Independent on Sunday*, 24 July
Jary, David, Horne, John and Bucke, Tom (1991) 'Football "fanzines" and football culture: a case of successful "cultural contestation"', *The Sociological Review*, vol.39, no.3, August
Katz, Ian (1993) 'The slick sales pitch', *Guardian*, 29 April
Lacey, David (1994) 'Tournament with the gentle touch' *Guardian* 19 July
Lever, Janet (1983) *Soccer Madness*, Chicago, University of Chicago Press
Maguire, Joseph (1994) 'Preliminary observations on globalisation and the migration of sport labour', *The Sociological Review*, vol.4, no.3, August
McCarthy, Terry (1994) 'Asian World Cup hopefuls clash', *Independent on Sunday*, 24 July
McGinn, Daniel (1994) 'A cupful of cash', *Newsweek*, Special World Cup Issue
McGuire, Stryker (1994) 'Firing up a nation of futbol fans', *Newsweek*, 20 June
McIlvanney, Hugh (1991) 'Coup that lifted the World Cup', *Observer*, 20 January
Miller, Arthur (1988) *Timebends: A Life*, London, Methuen
Murphy, Patrick, Williams, John and Dunning, Eric (1990) *Football on Trial*, London, Routledge.
Peterson, Tomas (1994) 'Split visions: the introduction of the Svenglish model in Swedish football', unpublished paper, University of Lund
Robson, Bobby with Harris, Bob (1986) *So Near and Yet So Far: Bobby Robson's World Cup Diary 1982–86*, London, Willow Books
Wagg, Stephen (1986) 'Naming the guilty men: managers and the media', in Alan Tomlinson and Garry Whannel (eds) *Off the Ball*, London, Pluto Press
Wagg, Stephen (1991) 'Playing the past: the media and the England football team', in John Williams and Stephen Wagg (eds) *British Football and Social Change*, Leicester, Leicester University Press

Whannel, Garry (1992) *Fields in Vision: Television Sport and Cultural Transformation*, London, Routledge
Williams, John, Dunning, Eric and Murphy, Patrick (1984) *Hooligans Abroad*, London, Routledge (2nd edn 1989)
Williams, Richard (1994) 'Romario-ville rejoices as the carnival begins', *Independent on Sunday*, 24 July
Winterbottom, Sarah (1993) 'Win or lose, firms set to score in the World Cup', *Guardian*, 20 December

INDEX